# CAMBRIDGE LIBRARY COLLECTION

*Books of enduring scholarly value*

## Travel and Exploration

The history of travel writing dates back to the Bible, Caesar, the Vikings and the Crusaders, and its many themes include war, trade, science and recreation. Explorers from Columbus to Cook charted lands not previously visited by Western travellers, and were followed by merchants, missionaries, and colonists, who wrote accounts of their experiences. The development of steam power in the nineteenth century provided opportunities for increasing numbers of 'ordinary' people to travel further, more economically, and more safely, and resulted in great enthusiasm for travel writing among the reading public. Works included in this series range from first-hand descriptions of previously unrecorded places, to literary accounts of the strange habits of foreigners, to examples of the burgeoning numbers of guidebooks produced to satisfy the needs of a new kind of traveller - the tourist.

## Memorials of the Empire of Japon

The publications of the Hakluyt Society (founded in 1846) made available edited (and sometimes translated) early accounts of exploration. The first series, which ran from 1847 to 1899, consists of 100 books containing published or previously unpublished works by authors from Christopher Columbus to Sir Francis Drake, and covering voyages to the New World, to China and Japan, to Russia and to Africa and India. Volume 8, first published in 1850, consists of documents relating to the earliest European experience of Japan, including a description of the country, its rulers and political system, and some letters from William Adams (1564–1620), possibly the first Englishman to reach that country. Adams became an advisor to the shogun Tokugawa Ieyasu, and played a crucial role in the establishment of the first Western trading posts in Japan. The book contains an introduction and explanatory notes.

Cambridge University Press has long been a pioneer in the reissuing of out-of-print titles from its own backlist, producing digital reprints of books that are still sought after by scholars and students but could not be reprinted economically using traditional technology. The Cambridge Library Collection extends this activity to a wider range of books which are still of importance to researchers and professionals, either for the source material they contain, or as landmarks in the history of their academic discipline.

Drawing from the world-renowned collections in the Cambridge University Library, and guided by the advice of experts in each subject area, Cambridge University Press is using state-of-the-art scanning machines in its own Printing House to capture the content of each book selected for inclusion. The files are processed to give a consistently clear, crisp image, and the books finished to the high quality standard for which the Press is recognised around the world. The latest print-on-demand technology ensures that the books will remain available indefinitely, and that orders for single or multiple copies can quickly be supplied.

The Cambridge Library Collection will bring back to life books of enduring scholarly value (including out-of-copyright works originally issued by other publishers) across a wide range of disciplines in the humanities and social sciences and in science and technology.

# Memorials of the Empire of Japon

*In the XVI and XVII Centuries*

EDITED BY THOMAS RUNDALL

CAMBRIDGE
UNIVERSITY PRESS

CAMBRIDGE UNIVERSITY PRESS

Cambridge, New York, Melbourne, Madrid, Cape Town, Singapore,
São Paolo, Delhi, Dubai, Tokyo, Mexico City

Published in the United States of America by Cambridge University Press, New York

www.cambridge.org
Information on this title: www.cambridge.org/9781108008051

© in this compilation Cambridge University Press 2010

This edition first published 1850
This digitally printed version 2010

ISBN 978-1-108-00805-1 Paperback

WORKS ISSUED BY

# The Hakluyt Society.

MEMORIALS OF THE EMPIRE

OF JAPON.

M.DCCCL.

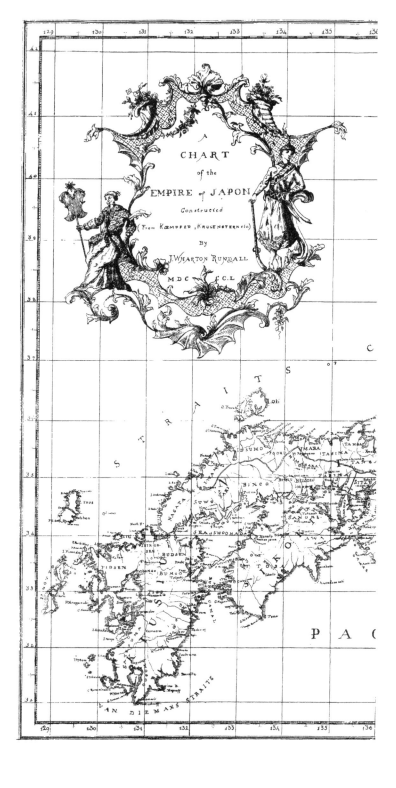

A
CHART
of the
EMPIRE of JAPON
Constructed
(From Kœmpfer, Krusenstern etc)
By
J. WHARTON RUNDALL
MDC CCL

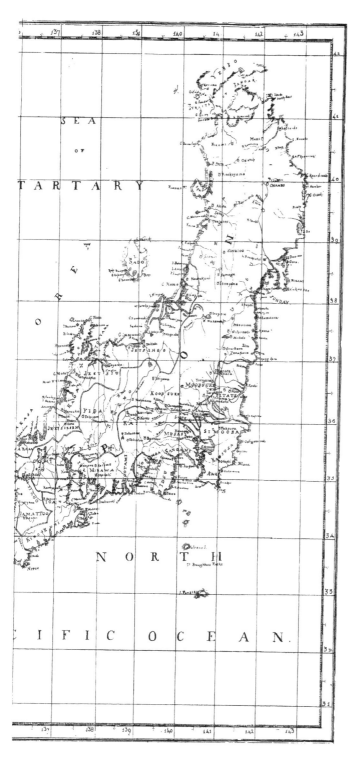

# MEMORIALS

OF THE

# EMPIRE OF JAPON:

IN THE XVI AND XVII CENTURIES.

EDITED, WITH NOTES, BY

## THOMAS RUNDALL.

LONDON:

PRINTED FOR THE HAKLUYT SOCIETY.

———

M.DCCC.L.

LONDON:
RICHARDS, 100, ST. MARTIN'S LANE.

# THE HAKLUYT SOCIETY.

## Council.

# MEMORIALS OF JAPON.

## PREFATORY REMARKS.

Mortalitatis incommoda, famem, sitim, aestum, algorem, vigilias, laboresque admirabili patientia tolerant . . . . . Multa insuper variis locis gymnasia, quas Academias dicimus . . . . In vniuersum, acuta, sagax, ac bene a natura informata gēs est: iudicio, docilitate, memoria. Paupertas dedecori aut probro est nulli. Maledicta, furta, impiam temere iurandi consuetudinem, aleae genus omne auersantur.

Ortelius, 1595. (Japon. Ins. Descript.)

United and peaceable, taught to give due worship to the Gods, due obedience to the Laws, due submission to their Superiors, due love and regard to their Neighbours, civil, obliging, virtuous; in art and industry excelling all other nations; possess'd of an excellent country, enrich'd by mutual trade and commerce among themselves; couragious, abundantly supplied with all the necessaries of life; and withal, enjoying the fruits of peace and tranquillity.

Kæmpfer, 1692. (Hist. of Japon.)

The gentlemen of Japon were most polite and courteous, conducting themselves with refined and polished urbanity; and exhibiting in their actions a dignified and respectful demeanour, that put to shame the ill-breeding of the seamen who ventured to laugh at them.

Voy. of H.M.S. Samarang, 1845.

# PREFATORY REMARKS.

----

COMPARING obvious circumstances with the facts adduced in this volume, the reader, who may not have had the means of investigating the subject, will become aware, probably with feelings of some surprise, that a remarkable change has taken place in the character of the relations which formerly subsisted, and in the character of the relations which now subsist, between the empire of Japon and the states of the Western-hemisphere.

In the early intercourse which existed between the empire and the states of the west, the government of Japon is exhibited in a most favourable light. It was distinguished, at that period, by high-bred courtesy: combined with refined liberality in principle, and generous hospitality in practice. Without any reservation in regard to circumstances, rank, calling, or nation, the hand of good-fellowship was, then, cordially extended to the stranger. In the instance of a Governor of the Phillipines, although ship-wrecked and destitute, the claims of rank were admitted. He was received with the honours due to a prince: while he sojourned in the land, similar honours were paid him; and to facilitate his departure, he was furnished with all the means generosity could dictate.[1] The lowly-born William Adams, when cast in wretchedness on the shores of Japon, was not, indeed, received as a prince: yet this man, commencing life in the capacity of "apprentice to Master Nicolas Diggines, of Limehouse", eventually attained rank, and acquired possessions in the empire equal to those of a prince. With no claims to consideration but talent and good conduct, he became the esteemed councillor of the sagacious and powerful monarch by whom the land that had afforded him shelter was ruled. In the course of his career, this man of humble origin appears as the negotiator between the sovereign of his native country and the foreign sovereign by whom he was patronized; and in that capacity securing for his countrymen important advantages and privileges. Merchants, for a century, found a free and open market for their wares. They realized enormous profits, if *cent. per cent.* may be so deemed; and, if reliance may be placed on the imperfect materials that exist for forming an estimate, they were enabled to enrich their native lands with stores of the precious metals to an incalculable amount of value.[2] Missionaries, from their advent, were allowed to commence a career of proselyteism; and they pursued it with zeal and success.

---

[1] See *Summary of the Narrative of Don Rodrigo de Vivero y Velasco* in the APPENDIX: also the *Letters of William Adams, passim.*

[2] A statement which, however, must be viewed as an approximation only, of the exports of the precious metals from the empire during certain periods, will be found appended to NOTE A A.

Assuming their statements to be correct, they made nearly two millions of converts in little more than a quarter of a century. With the unqualified concurrence of the authorities, they erected in several of the principal cities of the empire, edifices for the celebration of Divine-worship, according to the ritual of the Romish church: while, with the sanction of the authorities also, numerous institutions for the instruction of their neophytes were established. But this spirit of toleration has not been confined to the Romish faith. Some centuries since, the doctrines of *Boodh* were introduced into Japon. From the date of their introduction to the present time, they have been freely disseminated: so that now, the votaries of the sect far out-number the followers of the *Sinto*, or national creed. Besides the Boodhists, there are thirty-four sects, who, as regards the state, indulge their respective opinions without restraint; and who, in respect to each other, live in peace and love.[1] William Adams,

[1] In emoluments and dignity, all sects in Japon are on an equality. On these points, causes for dissension do not arise. Doctrinal differences have occasionally excited fierce disputes: which, on two occasions, have been summarily decided by the reigning emperors. In 1580, contention ran so high between the *Xodoxins* and the *Foquexus*, that despairing of being able to settle the difference without intervention, they appealed to Nobunanga. That emperor agreed to accept the office of arbitrator; but only on condition that the leaders of the vanquished party should submit to be put to death. The condition was accepted, and at the appointed time the disputants proceeded to discuss their differences. In the sequel, the *Foquexus* orators, with more candour than is usually displayed by controversialists, admitted they were unable to answer the arguments of their adversaries. They were immediately stripped and scourged, compelled

although a Christian, retained to the day of his death his influence with the emperor. Saris, too, was well received. Neither the members of the English or of the Dutch factory, nor the lay-members of the Romish church, were subjected to any inconvenience on account of their creed, even when the Romish ecclesiastics and the native converts were under the ban of the state. In regard to the people of different nations of Europe, the government of Japon, at that period, exhibited more liberality than the nations of Europe exhibited towards each other. How the Spaniards and Portuguese conducted themselves in respect to William Adams and his unfortunate comrades, is fully set forth in his correspondence, together with the remarkable contrast afforded by the proceedings of the Emperor, Ogosho Sama.[1] In the first instance, they also vigorously opposed the settlement of the Dutch in Japon. When that could not be prevented,

to sign an acknowledgment of their defeat with their blood ; and having done so, were decapitated. Heavy fines and banishment were inflicted on the residue of the defeated schismatics. A similar occurrence took place in 1609, on which occasion Ogosho Sama acted as arbitrator. The fact is, the Japonese government appears to have exhibited a stoical indifference to mere matters of doctrine, so long as they did not interfere with the tranquillity of the state. When the Bonzes were desirous that the Romish faith should be suppressed in Japon, the emperor, Nobunanga, is reported to have inquired, "How many sects may there be in Japon ?" The answer was, "Thirty-five." "Well," said the emperor, "where thirty-five sects can be tolerated, we can easily bear with thirty-six ; leave the strangers in peace." (Appendix, p. 184.)

[1] *Minna-Motto-no-yei-yeas;* or, *Iejas*; or, *Gongin Sama :* the emperor by whom the privileges were granted to the English, A.D. 1613. See NOTE Y.

no means were left untried by them to effect the expulsion of the new comers from the empire. The plea urged, was, that the Dutch were refractory subjects of Spain, and that it ill-became the emperor to treat with favour rebels to the authority of his Catholic majesty, with whom he professed to maintain relations of amity. These efforts invariably failed. The answer Ogosho Sama constantly gave, was: that he denied the right of any power to dictate the policy he should pursue in regard to strangers visiting his dominions: that he did not consider it was necessary to mix himself up, in any degree, with feuds existing among the states of Europe: that all he cared for was the tranquillity of the country and the welfare of his people; and that so long as strangers paid obedience to the laws, and by their fair and honourable dealings promoted the convenience and enjoyment of his subjects, it mattered not to him to what nation they belonged, or to what power in the west they were nominally subject. On the last occasion, when a joint memorial was presented on the subject by the Spaniards and Portuguese, the monarch seems to have lost all patience, and he drove the remonstrants ignominiously from his presence: vehemently declaring, that if "devils from hell" were to visit his realm, they should be treated like "angels from heaven", so long as they conducted themselves conformably with the principles he had laid down. This sovereign carried his sentiments, or rather his practice of justice, even further. The Spaniards, at one time requiring men for an expedition that was being fitted out in Nova Spania against the Dutch, preferred a request, that the subjects of his Catholic majesty might be sent out of the empire forthwith, as they had not the permission of their liege to reside there. " Nay," said the emperor peremptorily, "*Japon is an asylum for people of all nations.* No man who hath taken refuge in my dominions, and conducts himself peaceably, shall be compelled, against his will, to abandon the empire; but if his will be to quit, he is welcome to depart."[1]

Unhappily, this desirable state of affairs has ceased to exist. Since the middle of the seventeenth century, *exclusiveness* is an element in the polity of the empire that has been obtruded on observation. The government of Japon is now regarded as little, if in any degree, removed from barbarism. It is viewed as mean, selfish, and arbitrary: as acting ungenerously towards the foreigner, by depriving him of the just reward of commercial enterprize; and as inflicting injustice on the native, by depriving him of commodities with which the foreigner, if he were permitted, would willingly supply him. By one section of the public in the Western-hemisphere, it is thought that coercive measures may justifiably be applied against a government of the character ascribed to that of Japon. Another section, not advocating absolute hostilities, is of opinion, that "*Justice to them* [of Japon]

---

[1] See the account of the proceedings of the Spanish and Portuguese in relation to the Dutch in *Charlevoix* (*Hist. du Japon,* t. iii. ed. 1754). As this author derived his information from the works of the missionaries, his representations may be considered to be authentic. It is remarked the *English were too insignificant to excite apprehension,* and therefore were not meddled with.

*and the good of mankind, may imperiously demand
the interference of civilized nations";* or, that the
treatment experienced by strangers attempting to
visit the empire, *" may call for explanations which
may end in opening a door long and obstinately
closed to the Merchant and the Missionary."*[1] Adverting to the profession of the parties by whom these
opinions are promulgated, it must be presumed they
are dictated by feelings of the purest benevolence, and
with the best intentions; but doubts may be entertained, whether the means suggested are really calculated to promote the objects in view. The right of
*" interference"* may be denied: the character of the
*" explanations"* demanded, may be misunderstood :
feelings of exasperation may ensue on both sides; and
consequences may result as little calculated to exalt
the character of Christianity, as to promote the interests of commerce.[2]

---

[1] See *" Journal of an expedition from Sincapore to Japan,"* etc.
*" By P. Parker, M.D.,* medical missionary from the American mis-
sionary board" (page 72) ; and the preliminary *"Notice,"* by *"* the
*Rev. Andrew Reed, D.D."* London, 1838.

[2] The sentiments of the Jesuit author, *Charlevoix,* who confines
his views entirely to the religious part of the question, are as follow :
" Dieu seul, dont les secrets sont impénétrables, mais dont les
miséricordes sont infinies, sçait, si une Terre cultivée avec tant de
fatigues, qui a produit tant de Saints et tant de Héros, que tant
d'Hommes Apostoliques ont arrosée de leurs sueurs, et tant de
Martyrs de leur sang, ne recouvrera point un jour sa première
fécondité : Si la voix de ces généreux Confesseurs, qui demandent
à Dieu, non la vengeance, mais le fruit de leur précieuse mort, ne
touchera point le cœur du Souverain Pasteur des Ames ; et si les
vœux de tant de fervents Missionaires, qui ne souhaitent rien tant
au monde, que de se consacrer au salut d'un Peuple si propre au

The system of exclusion in respect to missionaries
and merchants, which has occasioned opprobrium to
be cast on the government of Japon, was evidently
not inherent in the constitution of the state, but must
be attributed to extrinsic circumstances. It remains
then to be ascertained: of what character were the proceedings of foreigners in connexion with the empire?
As brief a review of them as possible will therefore
be presented.

*The Portuguese* first visited in the empire about the
year 1542; and the arrival of *the Spaniards* may be
dated a little later. The first indication of any misun-
derstanding between the government and the Europeans resident in the empire appears in 1587. In that
year, Taico Sama, the reigning emperor, despatched two
imperial commissioners, in rapid succession, to *Father
Cuello*, the vice-provincial of the Portuguese, to demand: 1°. Why he and his associates forced their creed
on the subjects of the empire? 2°. Why they incited
their disciples to destroy the national temples? 3°.
Why they persecuted the bonzes [*native priests*]?
4°. Why they, and the rest of their nation, used for
food animals useful to man, such as oxen and

Royaume de Dieu, ne seront point enfin favorablement écoutés."
(Tentative de M. l'Abbé Sidotti, Ecclésiastique Sicilien, pour s'in-
troduire au Japon l'an 1702. *Hist. du Japon*, t. vi. p. 59,
edn. 1754.) It has been well observed : " The Christian dispen-
sation was given to the human race, when the whole world was
at peace, and when, consequently, all mankind were best fitted to
receive the laws ordained by the God of peace, of justice, and of
mercy." (*Academical Questions ; by the Right Hon. William
Drumond. Lond.* 1805.)

cows?[1] Finally, why they permitted the merchants of
their nation to traffic in his subjects, and carry them
away as slaves to the Indies? To these demands, the
vice-provincial replied, in substance : that no force was
used in the conversion of the people but the force of
reason : that if, under the influence of holy zeal,
their disciples destroyed the temples of the false gods
of the country, the missionaries were not accountable : that the bonzes were only persecuted by having
the absurdities they taught exposed : that the use,
for food, of the flesh of oxen and cows was not an
intentional offence, but an error committed in ignorance, which, being disapproved, would not be repeated.
On the last point it was observed : the traders acted
in opposition to the wishes of the missionaries; but his
majesty might prevent the traffic in human flesh by
issuing his commands prohibiting the system, and by
enforcing proper regulations at the different ports in
the empire.[2] It will be perceived, the vice-provincial
did not deny the fact of the destruction of the national
temples by the converts. He is content with denying
the complicity of the missionaries ; and how far, being
considered the effects of *holy zeal*, the excesses were
viewed with aversion by those who may be regarded
as having excited the ardent feeling, is not indicated. The denial of the charge relating to the
persecution of the bonzes cannot be characterized
in polite terms. In many parts of the empire, *the*

[1] See NOTE M : for the reasons which render the Japonese
averse to the use of the flesh of oxen and cows for food.

[2] *Charlevoix, Hist. du Japon*, t. iii. p. 249.

*bonzes had been persecuted :* their dwellings having
been razed to the ground; and the extent of the evil
may be comprehended, in connexion with the fact
of the bonzes living together in communities, and in
buildings similar in construction to the monasteries
of Catholic lands.¹ How ignorance, after so long a

¹ In an eulogy on *François Civan,* king of Bungo, who died
about 1587, it is remarked : " On peut juger de son zèle pour le
salut des âmes, par ce que disoient les missionaires, qui l'avoient
le plus pratiqué, à sçavoir. . . . *par le nombre des Temples et des
Maisons de Bonzes qu'il renversa, et que quelques-uns font monter à
trois mille.*" (*Charlevoix, Hist. du Japon,* t. iii. p. 234.) The subject is further elucidated by an address made by one of the
ministers of the state, to the emperor, Taico Sama ; and which is
interesting for the acuteness it displays in other respects. The
functionary in question is reported to have addressed his sovereign
in these terms:—" My Liege ! Be wary of these Christians.
Mistrust, my Liege, the union that exists among them, and the
blind obedience they render to their leaders. Are not the members
of this sect dispersed throughout the whole extent of the Empire ?
Do they not number among them kings and princes, with the
bravest and most skilful of our generals, and the most exalted of
our nobility ? If need be, cannot they bring into the field at least
an hundred thousand men at arms ? Bethink thee what destruction there hath been of our temples and holy establishments, so
that our provinces seem as if they had been laid waste by fire and
sword. Hath not Uncon Dono, that valiant leader, alone destroyed
more than the piety of our rulers created in the space of ages ? ...
These bonzes [*priests*] from Europe proclaim they have come from
a mighty distance to enlighten us in spiritual matters, and to save
us from perdition. A brave purpose, of a verity, if the pretence be
true ! But may not some dangerous project lurk beneath this fair
seeming ? Hath it escaped thy remembrance, my Liege, how that
arch-traitor the bonze of Osacca did comport himself ? He, as
these bonzes from Europe do, promulgated a new law. He drew
about him a multitude of the common sort, of whom he made stout
soldiers. He promised his followers they should become the inhe-

residence in the country, in regard to the prejudice, it may be, entertained by the people of the country against using the flesh of oxen and cows for food, could be sincerely urged, cannot be readily conceived. That it should have required a special enactment, as intimated by the vice-provincial, to prevent the traders from trafficking in their fellow-beings, does not exhibit the humanity of those parties in a favourable light: while, if really earnest in decrying the system, it demonstrates how inefficient the influence of the missionaries was, when directed to a good end, in opposition to mercenary propensities. As may be supposed, the answers submitted by the vice-provincial to these demands, did not prove satisfactory to the emperor. An imperial edict was issued. In this document, the European priests were commanded to quit the empire

ritors of a paradise, far exceeding in delights that promised by our holy Camis. He so inflamed their minds, that, as thou art aware, there was no peril they would not affront to secure the felicity with which he excited their imaginations. Did he not, when he had gained absolute power over their wills, proclaim himself king? Aye, and emperor, too, he would have been, but for the efforts of the mighty Nobounanga, aided by the prowess of thy arm. Yet, how difficult it was to quell this rebellious bonze thou dost well know. May it be, that these European bonzes are less ambitious than the traitorous bonze of our own land? Art thou ignorant how bold a front these people do maintain? At Nangasaki, do they not hold a strong fortress, well plenished with the engines and the munitions of war? Is not Nangasaki an harbourage to which succours of men and munitions may freely come from abroad? Possess they not the means of intelligence among themselves, from one extremity of the kingdom to the other? My Liege! would you consult the safety of the state, not a moment is to be lost." (*Hist. du Japon*, t. iii. pp. 243-4!.)

forthwith, and sentence of perpetual exclusion was pronounced against them; but this part of the edict remained a dead letter. All crosses and churches were, also, ordered to be razed; but there is no evidence of the order having been carried into effect: the presumption is to the contrary. It was further declared, that no distinctive marks of Christianity should in future be borne. All converts to the Christian faith were threatened with death and exile if they did not abandon the new creed: " ménace", it is observed by Charlevoix, " qu'il n'effectua pourtant jamais." The missionaries were allowed twenty days to enable them to retire to Firando, preparatory to their final departure from the empire, during which period, it was declared, their persons would be safe; but should they be found in the empire after that time, they would render themselves liable to decapitation. They did not depart, and were not subjected to the threatened penalty. In fact, terrible as this edict was in denunciations, no practical evils resulted from its promulgation. The only part of it to which effect was given, was a liberal and just discrimination relating to the traders. Those parties were informed, that not being implicated in the disorders charged against the ecclesiastics, they were at liberty to remain in the empire, and to pursue their usual avocations: being at the same time admonished not to converse with the people of the state on religious topics, and also to be on their guard against conniving at the introduction of priests.[1]

[1] *Hist. du Japon*, t. iii. p. 251.

To the excesses of the converts may be ascribed the first invasion of the system of tolerance, that had prevailed for nearly half a century. To their acts may be attributed the introduction of doubt and suspicion into the minds of the government, and the origin of those rancorous feelings that were subsequently displayed. Whether the result of *holy zeal*, or of fanatical intemperance, these excesses are to be reprehended; and there is no evidence to shew why the missionaries should be exempted from the censure. If the missionaries did not incite, there is no proof of their having endeavoured to restrain their disciples. If they did endeavour to restrain their disciples, it only shews, that though they possessed sufficient influence to lead parties out of the ways of religious error, they could not prevent them from, also, abandoning the paths of political rectitude.

The forbearance in deeds, though not in stern words, of Taico Sama, did not produce the beneficial effects that might have been contemplated. Fresh disorders of an aggravated character occurred, and some examples were made, against which the viceroy of Goa remonstrated. In reply to that functionary, in a letter addressed to him in the year 1592, Taico Sama observed: " Japon is the kingdom of the holy *Camis*, proceeding from *Dsin*, the first principle and prime source of all things. The law of the empire was promulgated by the Camis themselves. The end for which the law was promulgated was good government. Good government cannot be maintained unless the law be strictly observed. If the law be not strictly observed, those bonds of obedience will be rent asunder, that should be binding between sovereign and subject, husband and wife, parent and child, prince and vassal, master and servant. In a word, the strict observance of the law is essential, not only for the maintenance of tranquillity within the realm, but to secure respect from without. The law promulgated by the Camis is wisely framed : too wisely framed to be lightly cast aside. The adoption of a new law would only tend to produce confusion in the state. Now, the fathers, those denominated of the Company [*of Jesus*], have come into these parts to bring in a new law, and with it they have introduced confusion into the state. Therefore have I issued my imperial edict, commanding them to cease from teaching the new law; and my will is, they avoid the empire presently."[1] Active hostility to the state still marked the conduct of the converts to the "new law", and further examples were made. At length, in 1597, the governor of the Phillipines despatched an envoy to Taico Sama, to confer with him on the subject. In conversation with the envoy, the emperor justified the proceedings he had adopted with regard to the fathers, on these grounds: that the priests from Europe had traversed the country accompanied by large bands of disorderly persons, to the destruction of peace and good order, and in violation of the law: that they had endeavoured to seduce his subjects from their allegiance; and that they made no secret of their design to effect the conquest of the country, as had been the case

---

[1] *Hist. du Japon. Purchas.*

in the Phillipines. The emperor then made the following pertinent observations : " Conceive yourself
in my position, the ruler of a great empire; and suppose certain of my subjects should find their way into
your possessions, on the pretence of teaching the doctrines of Dsin. If you should discover their assumed
zeal in the cause of religion to be a mere mask for
ambitious projects : that their real object was to make
themselves masters of your dominions, would you not
treat them as traitors to the state? I hold the Fathers
to be traitors to my state; and as such I do treat them."
He concluded by expressing his willingness to afford
every facility in his power to the operations of the
merchants, and voluntarily conceded to the Spaniards
the right of punishing such of his subjects visiting
Nova Spania, as might bring themselves under the
censure of the law.[1]

Thus matters continued till the death of Taico
Sama, who, throughout his career as emperor, exhibited a degree of moderation that has been ill requited.[2]
Soon after Ogosho Sama, the successor of Taico Sama,
became emperor, it is said, " some Franciscan friars,
whom the governour of the Manillas in the Phillipine
islands had sent up as his ambassadors to the emperor,
did, during the whole time of their abode in the country,
preach openly in the public streets of Miaco, where
they resided; and where, of their own accord, and
contrary to the imperial commands, they did build a

[1] *Hist. du Japon*, t. iv. p. 104.
[2] See the conclusion of Note W, *career of Faxiba*, or *Taico
Sama*.

church."[1] This proceeding, justly characterized as "untimely and imprudent", led to fatal consequences. The priests were ordered to quit the empire without delay. The command was disobeyed. Assuming various disguises, the majority of the ecclesiastics spread themselves abroad in all directions, their professed object being "to gather up the fold of Christ". What measures the priests adopted to carry out their professed object, are not apparent; but, simultaneously with their dispersion, numerous and extensive revolts on the part of the Christian converts broke out. Then ensued a persecution, on the part of the state, of the direst description, which has not been surpassed in atrocity by any persecution in any age or clime. In this deplorable state, with occasional intermissions, affairs continued till the year 1637, and then the end arrived. At that period the Dutch laid before the Japonese authorities a correspondence, alleged to have been carried on with Portugal, purporting to invite the European power to send forces for the conquest of the empire, on pretence of aiding the native Christians : which was confirmed, it is alleged, by a subsequent discovery. The consequence was, all the European residents in the empire, with the exception of the Dutch, were expelled : a price was set on Christians generally, on priests particularly : the promulgation of the Christian doctrine was prohibited; and all natives were forbidden from proceeding beyond the limits of the country, or, if they quitted the country, they were prohibited from returning, on pain of death. To use

[1] *Kæmpfer*, vol. i. p. 316.

the homely but expressive phrase of Kæmpfer, "*Japon was shut up.*"[1]

In corroboration of the views entertained by the government of Japon, of the proceedings of the Portuguese and Spaniards, the representations of the residents of other European nations in the empire may be cited. In the correspondence of William Adams evidence is to be found of the insubordinate conduct of the native Christians, and traces are not wanting of the agency of the priests in the tumults he records. In his diary, Captain Cock constantly refers to the disorders arising in the state through the intriguing spirit, and the insolent disregard of the laws, evinced by the latter. He represents them, further, as being demoralized and avaricious: as men who did not scruple to make their holy calling subservient to their worldly interests, by the keen pursuit of traffic. Kæmpfer also distinctly alludes to the ambitious interference of the priests with the rights of the state; and, entering on the conduct of the European residents generally, he makes the following remarks: "Now as to the fall of the Portuguese, I heard it often affirmed by people of good credit among the Japonese themselves, that pride and covetousness (in the first place, pride among the great ones, and covetousness in people of less note) contributed very much to render the whole nation odious. Even the new-converted Christians were

---

[1] The details will be found in *Kœmpfer*, vol. i. p. 317-18. It may be observed that the expulsion of the Spaniards and Portuguese from Japon was preceded by the banishment of the Japonese from Nova Spania.

*d*

astonished, and grew impatient, when they saw that their spiritual fathers aimed not only at the salvation of their souls, but had an eye also to their money and lands; and that the merchants disposed of their goods in a most usurious and unreasonable manner.[1] The growing riches, and the unexpected success in the propagation of the Gospel, puffed up both laity and clergy. ¡Those who were at the head of the clergy thought it beneath their dignity to walk on foot any longer, in imitation of Christ and his apostles. Nothing would serve them but they must be carried about in stately chairs, mimicking the pomp of the pope and cardinals at Rome. They not only put themselves on an equal footing with the greatest men of the empire, but, swelled with ecclesiastical pride, they fancied that a superior rank was nothing but their due."[2]

The authors that have been cited were Protestants, and their testimony may be viewed with suspicion: it may be thought to have been given under the influence of religious prejudice. The representations of the sovereigns of Japon may be considered as *ex parte;* and, in that respect, liable to objection. No suspicion, however, can attach to the evidence of Charlevoix, the Jesuit historian of the empire, and of the Romish Church in the empire. His evidence does not tend to the exculpation of the Europeans.

[1] So early as 1587, *Charlevoix* notices the lively alarm that the scandalous life led by many of the Portuguese residents in Japon occasioned the Fathers. (*Hist. du Japon*, t. iii. p. 237.)

[2] *History of Japan*, vol. i. p. 314.

To the emperors, this writer awards the merit of being men "*naturellement pleins d'équité et de modération*": into whose minds, by the combination of powerful causes, mistrust and suspicion were introduced: by which was engendered an access of fury that excited astonishment throughout the world. These causes, he says, were: the commercial jealousy existing between the Portuguese and Spaniards, and the arts to which each had recourse to supplant the other: various scandalous proceedings, and gross indiscretions on the part of the Castilians; and the calumnies of the Dutch, which, to use his words, "*d'un même coup renversaient le commerce des Catholiques, et la Christianisme au Japon.*" The representations of Kæmpfer, Charlevoix affirms to be exaggerations: yet he admits the conduct of the missionaries was not invariably discreet or prudent, but occasionally liable to misconstruction. He acknowledges the Christian converts were prone to rebellion; but endeavours to palliate their conduct, on the plea, that the sovereigns against whom they revolted were usurpers. The correctness of this description of these emperors is open to doubt; but, admitting it to be correct, the author does not adduce any reasons to shew why the Christian converts should have felt themselves specially aggrieved by submission to an authority, that was willingly acknowledged and obeyed by the unconverted portion of the nation, including an overwhelming majority of the population. The genuineness of the correspondence that led to the expulsion of the Portuguese and Spaniards, the jesuit author indignantly denies. He emphatically declares the letters produced by the Dutch to have been gross forgeries, committed by them purposely to effect the ruin of their commercial rivals. There is no evidence by which the fact can be decided; and probability is not in favour of one allegation more than the other. Circumstances might have impelled the Portuguese party in Japon to seek aid from Europe; and nobody acquainted with the proceedings of the Dutch in the Eastern seas, at that period, will deem them incapable of having committed the crime laid to their charge.

*The Dutch* have maintained their position, if not their credit, in the empire. Their conduct in regard to the letters which caused the expulsion of their rivals from Japon, has been seen ; but how it was viewed by the people of the empire is not apparent. In regard to their "*submissive readiness*", on another occasion, when they assisted the state to suppress the Christians of Simabarra, the opinion entertained by the Japonese is recorded. It is very decided, and no less disparaging. This "*submissive readiness*" was not a solitary instance: it has been exhibited, generally; by the Dutch in their intercourse with the Japonese, by whom they have been treated with much contumely and no little scorn.[1] Eventually, unceremoniously extruded from Firando, they "were removed from

---

[1] For an account of this affair, see NOTE I, *martial character.* Adverting to the transaction, Kæmpfer remarks : " By *submissive readiness* to aid the emperor in the execution of his designs, with regard to the final destruction of Christianity in his dominions, 'tis true indeed that we stood our ground so far as to maintain ourselves in the country, and to be permitted to carry on our

the protection," as Kæmpfer observes, "of a kind and indulgent prince, to be placed under the control of a strict and severe government, that of Nangasaki ; thereafter to be treated as traitors and professed enemies of the empire." To preserve the shadow of a trade. But *many generous and noble persons, at court and in the empire, judg'd* quite otherwise of our proceeding, and *not too favorably of the credit we had thereby endeavoured to gain.* It seem'd to them inconsistent with reason, that the Dutch should ever be expected to be really faithful to a foreign monarch, and one too whom they look upon as a heathen prince, whilst they showed so much forwardness to assist him in the destruction of a people, with whom they otherwise agree in the most essential parts of their faith, and to sacrifice to their own worldly interests those who follow Christ the very same way, and enter the Kingdom of Heaven through the very same gates : expressions I have often heard the natives make use of, when the conversation happened to turn upon the subject." Two years after the affair of Simabarra, the Dutch were required to attend before a commissioner, who had been specially deputed by the emperor to Firando. After drawing an accurate parallel between the creeds professed, respectively, by the Dutch and Portuguese, which he pronounced to be identical in all essential points, the functionary proceeded to address the Dutch in the following terms : " In former times it was well known to us, you both served Christ, but on account of the bitter enmity you ever bore each other, we imagined there were two Christs. Now, however, the emperor is assured to the contrary. Now he knows, you both serve one and the same Christ. From any indication of serving him you must for the future forbear. Moreover, on certain buildings you have newly erected, there is a date carved : which is reckoned from the birth of Christ. These buildings you must raze to the ground, presently." The buildings in question were of hewn stone, and had been erected at considerable expense ; but without remonstrance, or hesitation, the work of demolition was instantly commenced, and so vigorously pursued, as to secure the approbation of the imperial commissioner, who did not quit Firando till the order was completely carried out. (*Charlevoix, Hist. du Japon.*)

once lucrative trade,[1] or for some other motive which is not avowed, the Dutch are content to remain at Nangasaki, subject to restrictions, physical and moral, which cannot render their position altogether agreeable.[2]

[1] The trade of the Dutch from the date of their removal from Firando up to the present time, has been limited to two ships yearly, the united cargos of which must not exceed in value £70,000. The profits of the trade are as limited as the extent is insignificant. From the cargos, on the arrival of the ships, valuable presents according to regulation are selected for the emperor. Other valuable commodities are selected as presents, but not subject to any regulation, or limitation, for official authorities of various grades and of various denominations. The Japonese merchant sets his own price on the merchandize, and of course studies his own interests rather than those of the seller. The Japonese merchant also pays in coin to which an arbitrary value is affixed : of course to his own advantage. The exports from Japon are very trifling; and the native trader again takes care of himself.

[2] The island of Desima, to which the Dutch are restricted, is about a fathom and a half above high water mark, less than six hundred feet in length, and scarcely so broad. It is strongly barricadoed by the water side, so that escape is impossible ; and it is connected with the main by a bridge well protected and guarded. One of the ordinances to which they have to submit is " No Hollander shall come out but for weighty reasons." Accordingly (except on the occasion of the periodical visits they are compelled to make to the court) the Dutch do not " come out" without the special authority of the governor of Nangasaki, which must be humbly solicited, in writing, twenty-four hours beforehand. The period of relaxation is limited to a few hours; and the extent of the excursion is also circumscribed : being generally confined to the tea and sacki houses, mostly brothels, in the vicinity of the city. Even on these occasions, the Dutchmen are not entirely free from restraint. They are attended by a numerous escort of police agents, and subordinate officials, all of whom are to be *treated*, which renders the indulgence of a walk beyond the confines of Desima somewhat too costly to be often enjoyed. "... *only, and no*

Of *the English*, it is simply to be observed, that in their commercial project they failed, and that they retired with honour, and regretted, from the scene of their misadventure.[1] The English retired from Japon in 1623, and a subsequent attempt was made (in 1673) to renew the intercourse; but it proved unsuccessful. The mission, despatched under the authority of Charles the Second, was courteously received, and hospitably entertained. The Japonese, however, had been informed, apparently by the Dutch, that the king of England was wedded to the " daughter of Portugal", and that circumstance proved an insurmountable barrier to the success of the negotiation.

*other females, shall be allowed to enter Desima,*" is an imperial order affixed to the posts of the bridge, by which the island is connected with the main : for the instruction, if not the edification, of the natives. *The observance of the Sabbath is prohibited ;* and the residents in Desima carefully abstain from any manifestation of their faith ; but there does not appear to be any foundation for the statement, that in common with the natives, the Dutch are required at certain periods to trample on the sign of the cross, and the effigy of the Virgin Mary. If the practice were ever enforced, which is doubtful, it has certainly fallen into disuetude. The Dutch are required to be the *intelligencers* of the government of Japon. " *Whatever comes to your knowledge in all countries you trade to, we expect you should notify to our governor of Nangasaki,*" is the concluding sentence of the " strict imperial commands" issued to the Dutch at Yedo, on the occasion of each periodical visit to the court ; and evidence might be adduced, to shew that the order is not regarded by either party in the light of a mere formality. It is but justice, however, to the Dutch, to observe, that on the visit of Captain Belcher, their conduct was most friendly and courteous ; though, as required by the state, they had given notice of his coming to the Japonese authorities.

[1] See NOTE A A. *Fate of the English Factory.*

It now remains to be seen what has been the conduct of the Europeans, in connexion with Japon, during casual intercourse, and at a later period.  In 1805, at the instigation of Count Resanoff, *a Russian diplomatist*, who had taken umbrage at the treatment he experienced while engaged in negotiations with the authorities at Nangasaki, two officers of the Russian imperial navy, named Chowstoff and Davidoff, made a descent on one of the Kuriles.  They landed within territories dependent on the government of Japon, inhabited by Japonese subjects, and governed by Japonese authorities.  Pillage, slaughter, rape, and incendiarism, marked their track.  They seized many persons, carrying them away into captivity; and left behind them numerous placards, printed in various languages, in which the occasion of the incursion was stated; and which teemed with threats of further vengeance.  It is to be regretted, that the conduct of the *British* has not been altogether irreproachable.  In 1808, a most impolitic proceeding, though no doubt prompted by honest zeal in the performance of his duty, was adopted by Captain Pellew, of H.M.S. Phaeton.  This officer entered the bay of Nangasaki with the view of seizing any Dutch vessels that might happen to be in the port.  On the appearance of the vessel, a boat was despatched by the Japonese, having on board two Dutchmen, members of the factory.  Before the messengers reached their destination, they were met by a boat from the Phaeton, unceremoniously transferred from one craft to the other, and taken, as prisoners, on board the British

ship. This occurred on the 4th of October. On
the 5th, the Dutchmen were liberated, and set on
shore. The Phaeton then made sail, without any
prize, having previously received supplies from the
Japonese, which were furnished gratuitously; but
whether voluntarily, or under the influence of fear, is
not apparent.

The indignation of the Japonese was excited by
the ignominious treatment of persons they considered
themselves bound in honour to protect from injury
or insult, and an attack on the Phaeton was contemplated. The intention, however, was frustrated by
the rapid movement of the vessel, combined with
other circumstances. But the matter did not end
here. In regard to several of the Japonese function-
aries, the proceeding was followed by tragical effects.
In the first instance, the governor of Nangasaki
summoned the troops appointed to guard the coast,
to his aid; but discipline, through the long continuance of peace, had become relaxed, and neither officers
nor men were at their posts to obey the summons.
The governor, though not formally invested with the
command of the troops, was responsible for their effi-
ciency when their services were required. He was
conscious he would be deemed to have neglected his
duty: that he had rendered himself amenable to the
severest punishment; and he considered, also, he
was disgraced by not having made any attempt to
avenge the insult that had been offered to the national
honour. There was but one course for him to pursue,
and that he promptly adopted. Within an hour from

*e*

the sailing of the British vessel, he assembled his household, and having delivered a farewell address, ripped himself up. This example was followed by the several commanders of the neglected posts.[1]

The *Americans* must be placed in the same category with ourselves. In the year 1837, the *Morrison*, a vessel belonging to citizens of the United States, sailed from Singapore, on an expedition to Japon. The object of the expedition is not very clear.[2] Whatever it may have been, it failed. In the first instance, the Morrison was anchored in the bay of Yedo, *not many miles distant from the imperial residence;* and from thence she was driven the next morning, by the guns of a battery that had been thrown up during the night. Expelled from the bay of Yedo, a southerly course was shaped, to the bay of Kago-Sima (Kiusiu), in the territories of the Prince of Satzuma : where the reception was similar to that experienced in the previous instance.[3] Thereon, all sail was made direct

[1] *Siebold.* For an account of this national custom, see NOTE L; *Additional Traits of Manners and Customs.* The visit of the Phaeton and its tragical consequences, were commented on with regret by the Japonese in 1813, when Dr. Ainslie visited Nangasaki, though the conduct of the British, generally, was favourably contrasted with that of the Russians.

[2] The missionary attached to the vessel, in one page of his published journal, intimates some *commercial views* were entertained. In another page, he represents the undertaking to have been *"purely benevolent"*, to restore to their native country some shipwrecked Japonese. In the title-page it is announced to have been *" an attempt, with the aid of natives educated in England, to create an opening for missionary labours in Japon."* (Journal, etc., by P. Parker, ut sup.)

[3] What is termed *" the expulsion of the Morrison from the shores*

for Singapore. The peculiarity of this proceeding is: that with the full knowledge of only one port, the port of Nangasaki, being open to foreigners, no attempt was made to enter that port; but attempts were made

of *Japon,*" gave rise to the suggestions, which have been the subject of comment, respecting "*interference*" and "*explanations.*" The authors of these suggestions, the American missionary and his reverend friend, the editor of the journal, may derive information on international law from the following case. In *Carolina,* and in *Louisiana* also, a law exists by which free men of colour, of whatever country they may be, whether citizens of some other state of the American Union, or foreigners, are subject, on their arrival in either of those states, to imprisonment, with a view to their ultimate removal from the territories of those states. *The law of Carolina and of Louisiana* also prescribes, that persons of colour arriving in ships, shall be taken from such vessels, and kept in prison till the departure of the vessels by which they may have been brought within the authority of the states. By this law, the captain of the ship is held responsible not only for the removal of such coloured persons when he himself may leave the port, but for the expenses of their maintenance while they are kept in durance. He also loses their services, and may have to incur the expense of hiring other persons to perform their work. He is further responsible, according to a recent decision in a British Court of Justice, to the coloured persons in question, for the amount of the wages accruing during the period of their incarceration. Against this local regulation, opposed to the polity of the paramount government, inconsistent with the established polity of nations, and in direct violation of a portion of the articles of the treaty of 1815, between Great Britain and the United States, under which all citizens of the two countries are to be permitted freely to enter, freely to reside in, and freely to quit, the territories of the government of the United States, the British government remonstrated in 1847. To a note presented by the British minister at Washington, Mr. Buchanan, the Secretary of State for Foreign Affairs of the United States, verbally replied, that the federal government had no power to induce the legislature of the state of Carolina to revoke the law ; and, that if the British government insisted on its right, and pressed the government of the to enter two other ports, with the full knowledge of their being closed by the laws of the empire against foreigners. The manner in which this proceeding was conducted, seems to have been eminently calculated to provoke the result that actually occurred: while the United States on the ground of that right, so based on the treaty of 1815, the government of the United States would find the question not merely so difficult, but so impossible to deal with, that they would be obliged, however reluctantly, and at whatever inconvenience to themselves, or to the British government, to take advantage of the stipulation contained in the treaty of 1827, by which either of the contracting parties was to be at liberty, at any time it pleased, subsequent to 1828, to put an end to the treaty of 1815, upon giving twelve months' notice. On this representation being made, the British government refrained from pressing the matter. In the British House of Commons, on the 30th of April 1850, Her Britannic Majesty's Secretary of State for Foreign Affairs made the following declaration with reference to this case, namely : "Whatever may be thought of the principle of the law, it is matter of public notoriety ; so that free persons of colour, subjects of Her Majesty, or otherwise, who voluntarily go within the operation of the law, know beforehand the inconvenience to which they expose themselves." These are material points of difference between the law of the two American states, and the law of the empire of Japon. The law of the empire is no mere local regulation, opposed to the polity of the paramount authority, and which the paramount authority *dare* not attempt to annul, or even modify, though, by its maintenance, the hazard attending a rupture with a powerful ally may be imminent. The law of the empire, on the contrary, extends over the entire state; while, such is the habit of obedience, or such is the power of the government to enforce obedience, that it is obeyed by the most independent princes, such as the prince of Satzuma, and in the uttermost parts of the realm, where the island of Kiusiu is to be found. The law of the empire is also to be contrasted with the law of the American states, insomuch as it does not contravene the provisions of any treaty with any other state. The principle of the law depends on the right of a perfectly independent state to make such laws for its own peace and well-being as may be best adapted to its own wilful violation of the law of the state is utterly inde-fensible.[1]

Calmly reviewing these circumstances, it must be confessed, that the nature of the intercourse between the Europeans and the Japonese cannot have tended either to elevate the character of the former in the estimation of the people of the empire, or to have pro-duced such feelings as can lead to a desire for the formation of intimate relations. By the intercourse that has hitherto subsisted between the Europeans and the Japonese, all the worst features of the Euro-pean character have been paraded before the people of the empire, and few of their good qualities have been displayed. In fact, the character of the former has been abused by unworthy representatives, and the perception of the latter has been grossly deceived. The Japonese have had intercourse with governments

peculiar circumstances ; and the term *perfectly independent state,* is intended to convey the idea of a state which is supreme throughout its territories, with the power of enforcing its supremacy : which may not be conversant with the conventional laws and regulations regarding inter-communication, prevailing among states, differing from it in political views, and situated in a distant quarter of the globe : or, which, if cognizant of such conventional laws and regu-lations, has not bound itself by any compact to observe them. However, so far like the law of Carolina and Louisiana, *the law of the empire is matter of public notoriety ; so that subjects of her Majesty, or otherwise, who may voluntarily go within the operation of the law, know beforehand the inconvenience to which they expose themselves.*

[1] There is a report, not involving the government of Japon, however, and which cannot be traced to an authentic source, that Commander Biddle, of the U. S. navy, being with his ship in the bay of Yedo, some short time since, was violently assaulted by one of the mariners of a native junk that he had been invited to visit : but why, or wherefore, is not apparent.

animated by a wild spirit of aggression, to which every principle of right, humanity, justice, and honour, was sacrificed. They have seen some wrong, real or imaginary, for which the state was alone responsible, vindictively and barbarously avenged on a peaceable and defenceless part of the population. They have been exposed to annoyance, if they have not been irritated, by want of discretion in other quarters. They have had intercourse with degenerate ecclesiastics, no less crafty than arrogant and ambitious. They have had intercourse with traders, abjectly submissive, or over-reaching: or, blood-thirsty, piratical, and treacherous. Hence has arisen strong prejudice against the character of Europeans, and others, with suspicion and distrust, if not apprehension. Yet, of disinterestedness, probity, justice, honour, true devotion, and magnanimity, there is no deficiency among the Western nations; and when the Japonese become practically acquainted with the fact, sound friendship, based on esteem and confidence, may be expected to prevail.

Notwithstanding, however, such an accumulation of untoward circumstances, some facts may be adduced, which seem to indicate the Japonese are not so rigidly indisposed to friendly intercourse with foreign nations as they are popularly supposed to be. In 1803, *an American vessel*, named the Eliza, appeared on two occasions, under very suspicious circumstances, at Nangasaki; yet on both occasions, the commander, at his request, was furnished with abundant supplies. In 1804, *a Russian mission*, under Count Resanoff, arrived in the same port. Intercourse between the

Russians and the Japonese authorities commenced auspiciously. Negotiations were opened, and for some time proceeded favourably. At length, a difference arose on some point of etiquette; and of this circumstance the Dutch adroitly took advantage. By the intrigues of the Dutch, a complete breach was effected. The negotiations were abruptly broken off, and Count Resanoff departed, denouncing vengeance against the Japonese. His threats were eventually carried into effect by the Russian captains Chowstoff and Davidoff, in the manner already narrated. Aid and supplies were afforded to a second *American vessel*, in 1807. A most courteous and hospitable reception was given to *Dr. Ainslie*, in 1813.[1] In 1845, *Captain Sir Edward Belcher*, of H.M.S. Samarang, visited Nangasaki. Probably, this officer arrived with somewhat of prejudice on his mind; for, he states, he had been "*warned by Mr. Gutzlaff, the interpreter at the visit of the Morrison, to expect treachery, and be prepared to punish it.*"[2] Nothing, however, could exceed the friendly feelings with which Captain Belcher was received. He was allowed to land on an island for the purpose of making observations. He was earnestly requested to prolong his stay, which was short. When it was found he could not comply with the request, he was urgently, and with every appearance of sincerity, solicited to renew his visit: the nobles and the leading men of the government expressing a hope they might

[1] This gentleman had been deputed by Sir Stamford Raffles to negotiate with the Dutch factors for the surrender of Desima to the English. He was not successful.

[2] *Voyage of the Samarang*, vol. ii. p. 1.

have the gratification, on some future occasion, of shewing him their houses, and of introducing him to their households. Finally, he was furnished with all the supplies he required, and that *gratuitously;* it being represented, the Japonese were not in the habit of taking money from their visitors.

The force of the allegation, that injustice is inflicted on a people by depriving them of the use of foreign productions, depends on the fact of such commodities being necessary to them. One, at the close of the seventeenth century, who had resided some time in Japon, who had conversed freely with the best informed and most intelligent in the empire, and who had associated freely with the population, arrived at the following conclusion on the subject. He remarks: " The Japonese confined within the limits of their empire enjoy the blessings of peace and contentedness, and do not care for any commerce, or communication with foreign parts; because, such is the happy state of their country, that they can subsist without it."[1]

A native writer, at the commencement of the eighteenth century, states his views of the subject in the following terms, viz.: " The ancients compared the metals to the bones in the human body; and taxes[2] to the blood, hair, and skin, that incessantly undergo the process of renewal; which is not the case with metals. I compute the annual exportation of gold at about one hundred and fifty thousand kobans; so that in ten years this empire is drained of fifteen hundred

[1] *Kæmpfer,* vol. ii. p. 54.

[2] *i. e.* RENT, *the only description of tax known in Japon,* and which is invariably paid in kind. See *Revenues,* NOTE A.

thousand kobans.[1]  With the exception of medicines,
we can dispense with every thing that is brought us
from abroad.  The stuffs and other foreign commodities are of no real benefit to us.  All the gold, silver,
and copper, extracted from the mines during the
reign of Gongin [*Ogosho Sama*], and since his time,
is gone, and, what is still more to be regretted, for
things we could do well without."[2]  In fact, the infinite variety in the productions of the empire, and the
astonishing abundance in which each variety is produced, render the inhabitants of Japon completely
independent of foreigners for all the necessaries of
life; and, as yet, they are unacquainted with, and
consequently have no desire for, the elegancies and
luxuries that lend a charm to European life.  It
must be considered, moreover, the people of the empire
are not destitute of the advantages of commerce; but,
on the contrary, that an extensive and lucrative traffic
exists within the empire.  This results from the physical peculiarities of the country.  Extensive tracts of
land, each with its own climate and its peculiar productions, separated from each other by ranges of rug-
ged mountains, by impervious forests, or by broad
arms of the sea, promote an immense coasting trade,
by which the various productions are disseminated
and circulated, to the great comfort of the population,
and the no small gain of the trader.[3]  But still, though

[1]  Equivalent to about £2,500,000 sterling.

[2]  From *a treatise composed in* 1708 *by the Prime Minister of the
Emperor Tsouna-Yosi :* quoted by Titsingh in the *Illustrations of
.Japan,* pp. 28, 29, 4to. Lond. 1822.

[3]  TRACTS, or PRIMARY DIVISIONS of the EMPIRE, designated in
the MAP by double lines, viz.: THE IMPERIAL DOMAINS (*Gokinai-*
*f*

foreign commerce be not essential, may not intercourse with foreigners be beneficial to a nation? It has been remarked: "it must be very much to the advantage of a country, that its inhabitants, so long as they can subsist without the produce and manufactures of foreign countries, should be kept also from their vices: from covetousness, deceits, wars, treachery, and the like."[1] It is a sad and undeniable fact, that the evils above enumerated have too frequently accompanied intercourse with foreigners in many parts of the world: but if it be meant such evils must necessarily follow from such a cause, the conclusion is unsound and unjust. By a well regulated intercourse between nations, intelligence may be promoted: intellect im-

goka-kohf) about Meaco: including the PROVINCES of: 1, Jamasijro: 2, Jamattoo: 3, Kawatzii: 4, Idsumi: 5, Sitzu.—I. SOUTH EASTERN TRACT (Tookaido). PROVINCES: 1, Iga: 2, Isie: 3, Ssima: 4, Owari: 5, Mikawa: 6, Tootomi: 7, Surunga: 8, Kai: 9, Idsu: 10, Sangami: 11, Musasi: 12, Awa: 13, Kadsusa: 14, Simoosa: 15, Fitats.—II. EASTERN MOUNTAINOUS TRACT (Toosando). PROVINCES: 1, Oomi: 2, Mino: 3, Fida: 4, Sinano: 5, Koodsuke: 6, Mood-suke: 7, Mutsu: 8, Dewa.—III. NORTHERN TRACT (Foku Rokhudo). PROVINCES: 1, Wackasa: 2, Jetsissen: 3, Kaga: 4, Noto: 5, Jeetsju: 6, Jetsingo: 7, Sado.—IV. NORTHERN MOUNTAINOUS, or, COLD TRACT (Sanindo). PROVINCES: 1, Tanba: 2, Tanga: 3, Tasima: 4, Imaba: 5, Fooki: 6, Idsumo: 7, Iwami: 8, Oki.—V. SOUTHERN MOUNTAINOUS, or, WARM TRACT (Sanjodo). PROVINCES: 1, Farima: 2, Mimasaka: 3, Bidsden: 4, Bitsju: 5, Bingo: 6, Aki: 7, Suwo: 8, Nagata.—VI. WESTERN COAST TRACT (Saikado). PROVINCES: 1, Tsikudsen: 2, Tsikungo: 3, Budsen: 4, Bungo: 5, Fidsen: 6, Figo: 7, Fingo: 8, Oosumi: 9, Satzsuma.—VII. SOUTHERN COAST TRACT (Nankaido). PROVINCES: 1, Kijnokuni: 2, Awadsi: 3, Awa: 4, Sanuki: 5, Ijo: 6, Tosa.—VIII. THE ISLANDS of TSUS and IKI, between Nipon and Corea.—See also NOTE A: Trade and Commerce.

[1] Kæmpfer, vol. ii. p. 55.

proved : science advanced : the fine and mechanical arts
perfected; and the germs of noble qualities so cultivated as to be made to flourish, and to produce good
fruits.   In science, the Japonese have made some ad-
vances; and they are represented to be desirous of
making further progress.   In some of the mechanical
arts they exhibit great skill, and are said to possess
great aptitude for improvement.   The knowledge of
the fine arts is limited in extent, but in those branches
to which their knowledge extends, their performances
are admirable.   To poetry and the drama they are
enthusiastically devoted; and in their compositions
they are represented to show talents of no mean order.
To music they are greatly addicted, though sadly
deficient in skill.   If daring crime may be imputed to
this people, they are not disgraced by any mean vices.
They exhibit the elements of some noble impulses,
which only require full development to elevate them
in the rank of nations : an effect, which might, probably, be produced by means of well regulated intercourse with foreigners.

With the disposal of the general charges, the subject might be dismissed, did not some specific points
appear to demand notice.   With regard to the Japonese, it has been publicly asserted, that, recently,
" *many of the crew of an American vessel wrecked
on the coast, were literally starved to death by order
of the government.*"   This charge rests on the authority of the party, by whom Captain Sir Edward
Belcher was misinformed as to the reception he might
expect in the empire; and it is the reverse of the
treatment experienced by the Russian Captain Golow-

nin, who, in opposition to the warning that had been given him, landed in Yesso, and was seized, whilst the minds of the Japonese were in a state of irritation on account of the outrages committed a short time previously by his countrymen.[1] As regards the Europeans, it has been stated, that *descents have been made on the coast, and that atrocities have been perpetrated on the inhabitants of the empire, by the crews both of British and American whalers.* This rests on rumour. Without corroboration, it would be inconsistent with justice to admit the truth of either representation. If true, however, the germ of a widespreading evil is in existence, which, unless checked in the growth, may lead to the most disastrous results. In this case, the interests of humanity, and the honour of the European and Japonese governments, equally, appear to be involved, and seem to demand the adoption of some mutual arrangement, by which the contingent evils may be averted. Coercion, if politic, or desirable, might. be resorted to, most probably, with success; but whether justifiably under such circumstances, may be doubtful. The clear enunciation of principles: expostulations earnestly but cautiously urged: offers of good-will made with frankness and sincerity: with dignified forbearance when requisite, seem calculated to win cheerful cooperation, which is to be desired rather than the churlish obedience of enforced submission. The experiment may be made, and it may fail. Yet the attempt would not be ignoble.

---

[1] See the Narrative of Golownin's Captivity. London, 1818.

# MEMORIALS OF JAPON.

## PART I.

A

## DESCRIPTION OF THE EMPIRE

IN THE 16TH CENTURY.

[From "THE FIRSTE BOOKE OF RELATIONS OF MODERNE STATES".— *Harleian Mss.* 6249. The date of the Ms. is not given; but in the "*Relation of England*", the following passage occurs: "The *Princesse* or *Queene* hereof at this day is *Elizabeth by name.*" Some illustrative passages, included between asterisks, are incorporated from the narrative of ARTHUR HATCH, *Minister.—Purchas*, vol. ii, pp. 1696, 1702.]

B

# THE KINGDOME OF JAPONIA.

## The Description.

JAPONIA may be said to be, as it were, a bodye of many and sundry Ilandes, of all sorts of bignesse; which Iles, as they are separated in situation from the rest of the whole worlde, so are they, in like maner, inhabited of people, most different from all others, both for maners and customes. They are devyded asunder, with the armes of the sea; and for most parte with little channels, as the Iles Maldiuae are in the Indian sea, or, as the Iles Hebrides and Orcades, which lye in the Northern seas, are. They contain 66 kyngdomes, which are distributed and devided into three principall members of Japonia. Of which members, one conteyneth nyne realmes, the seconde fowre; and the third fiftie-three. Fyve of these kyngdomes are more noble and famous then the rest: COQUINAI, where the famous cytie of MEACUM is seene; and it happeneth for the most parte, that he that obteyneth the dominion of these fyve kyngdomes getteth the whole Empire of Japonia.[1]

This countrey is distant from Nouva Hispania about 150 leukes, from China 60. ✳ Yt is mountainous and craggie, full of rockes and stonie places, so that the third part of this

---

[1] NOTE A. *Situation : extent : division : finances : population.*

Empire is not inhabited or manured: neither indeed doth it afford that accommodation for inhabitants which is needful, or that fatnesse and convenience for the growthe of corne, fruit, and small grayne, as is requisite. Yet is the countrey barreine, not so much through nature, as through the slouthfulness and negligence of the inhabitants.[1]*

In these Isles the sommer is very hote and burnynge, and the winter extreme coulde. Yet is the climate temperate and healthie, not much pestred with infectious or obnoxious ayres; but very subject to fierce windes, tempestuous stormes,[2] and terrible earthquakes,[3] insomuch that both ships in the harbour have been oversete, and driven ashore by the furie of the one, and houses on the land disjoynted and shaken to pieces by the fearful trembling of the other. Of gold and silver mynes, there be many.[4]

The inhabitantes shewe a notable witte, and an incredible pacience in sufferinge, labour, and sorowes. They take greate and diligent care lest, either in worde or deede, they shoulde shewe either feare, or dulnesse of mynde, and lest they should make any man (whosoever he be) partaker of their trowbles and wantes. They covet exceedinglye honour and prayse; and povertie with them bringeth no dammage to the nobilitie of bloude. They suffer not the least iniurie in the worlde to passe vnrevenged. For gravitie and curtesie they gyve not place to the Spainardes. They are generally affable and full of compliments. They are very punctuall in the entertayning of strangers,[5] of whom they will curiously inquyre even tryfles of forreyne people, as of their maners, and such like thinges. They will as soone lose a limbe as omit one ceremonie in welcoming a friend. *They use to

[1] Note B.   *The industrious character of the Japanese.*
[2] Note C.   *Tempestuous storms.*
[3] Note D.   *Earthquakes and volcanic phenomena.*
[4] Note E.   *Mineral productions.*
[5] Note F.   *Punctuality in entertaining strangers.*

give and receive the cup at one the other hands, and before the master of the house begins to drinke, hee will proffer the cup to every one of his guests, making shew to have them to begin. Fish, rootes, and rice, are their common junkets, and if they chance to kill a hen,[1] ducke, or pigge, which is but seldome, they will not like churles eat it alone; but their friendes shall be surely partakers of it. * The most parte of them that dwell in cyties can write and reade.[2] They only studie martiall feates and are delighted in armes.[3] They are far from all avarice, and for that cause detest both dice and all other playe which is for gayne.

The people be fayre and verye comely of shape. The marchantes, althoughe very riche and wealthye, yet nothing accompted of there; those that are of nobilitie are greatly esteemed althoughe they be never so poore. Both men and women goe bareheaded without any difference, bothe in the sunne and rayne. They washe theyre yonge children in rivers as sone as they are borne, and when they are weaned they are taken out of their mothers sight, and are exercised in huntinge and armes. When theyre children once come to fourteene yeares oulde, they wear sword and dagger, and as they be taught, do revenge the least iniurye that is offred them.[6]

*They are very neate and fyne, (4) and vse forkes when they eate for cleanlinesse, as they doe in Italy.—Ms.*

*They chastice their children with wordes onlye, and the admonishe theire children when they are fiue yeares oulde as yf the' weare oulde men.(5)—Ms.*

They have the same kyndes of beastes[7] that we have, both tame and wilde, but they seldome eat anye flesh, but that which is taken with huntinge. Indeed they delighte not much in fleshe, but they lyve for the most parte with hearbes, fyshe,[8] barley and ryce; which thinges are their chieffe nowrishments. Their ordinarye drinke is water, and that is made most times hot in the same pot where they seeth their ryce,

*These nowrishments are very holesome, for they that eate these thinges liue very longe.(9)—Ms.*

---

[1] NOTE G. *Birds.*
[2] NOTE H. *Education.*
[3] NOTE I. *Martial character.*
[4] NOTE J. *Neat and fine habits.*
[5] NOTE K. *Family intercourse.*
[6] NOTE L. *Additional traits of character and manners.*
[7] NOTE M. *Beasts.*
[8] NOTE N. *Fish.*
[9] NOTE O. *Produce of the fields.*

that so it may receive some thicknesse and substance from
the ryce. They have strong wine and rack distill'd of ryce,
of which they will sometimes drinke largely, especially at
their feasts and meetings, and being moved to anger, or
wrath, in the heate of their drinke, you may as soone per-
swade tygres to patience and quietnesse as them, so obstinate
and willfull they are in the furie of their impatience. As
concernynge another drinke, they take great delighte in
water mingled with a certeine powder which is very pretiouse,
which they call CHIA.[1]

They eate<br>moderately,<br>and drinke<br>lustilie.<br>—Ms.

Theire buyldinges are for the most parte of tymber, for
the mediterranean countreys hath almost no stonne, and it
aboundeth with trees very fytte for buyldinges, amongst
which there are cedars that growe to a marvelous height and
bignesse.[2] At Falcata there is a wood of pine trees neere
about three mile square, which is all the summer time swept
and kept so cleane, that you shall hardly see any small twig,
boughe, or leafe, under the trees, and the trees stand so close
together, that you may solace and recreate yourselfe there at
all houres of the day without any hurt or heate of the sunne.
In the midst of it there is a great pagod, or church, very
richly adorned with gilded images, and all sortes of curious
carved workes. Yet be they cunninge workers in stone.
∗ Ozechya, the most famous castle that the emperour hath, or
that is within the empire, is of an extraordinarie bignesse,
and compassed round with three severall walls. The castle
of Edo is likewise walled and moated, having some few
ordnance on it. At Crates and Falcata there are likewise
castles, both walled and moated; the circumference of each
of them beinge neere about two miles. The chiefe noblemen of those kyngdomes have houses within the castle walls
to come and live there, either at the king's or their own
pleasures. Within each of those castles there is a storehouse

---

[1] NOTE P. *Chia, or tea.*          [2] NOTE Q. *Trees.*

kept ordinarily full of ryce, which may serve for their provision at all occasions and needs. *

Every one may change his name three times :[1] when he is a childe ; when he is a young man ; and when he is ould. Some change their names more often. Every one as he pleaseth may make choyce of his owne name ; and they are commonly named either by the king, or else by some noble or great-man with whom they are chiefly in favour. They have the use of writing and printing, and have had, the space of many years : no man knowes certeinely how long. They have seven sorts of letters, each single letter serving for a word, and many of them in their placing serve for six or seven, and each alphabet hath eight and fortie letters ; and yet with all these letters they have not the true pronunciation of H, B, T, and some other letters.

They observe no Sabbath, but certaine Faste Dayes, according to the moone,—as the first of the moone, the 15, or 28. On these dayes they goe to the church, and visit the sepulchres of the dead. The ninth daye of the moone throughout the year they hold for accursed ; and therefore on that daye they will not begin, or undertake, any worke of consequence or importance. They strictly observe a faste on that daye of the moneth on which their father or mother died ; which they doe so precisely keepe, that they will not touch or eate any thing that hath blood.

* The lawes are very strict and full of severitie, affordinge no other kinde of punishment, but either death, or banishment. Murther, theft, treason, or the violation of any of the emperour's proclamations or edicts, are punished with death; so is adulterie also, if it be knowne, and the parties pursued; but the devill, their master in those actions, hath taught them such cleanly conveyances, that seldom, or never, are they apprehended. They proceed both in controversies and

[1] NOTE R. *Change of names.*

criminal cáuses according to the verdict of the produced witnesses, and the sentence being once past, they will not revoke
or mittigate the severitie of it; but if the parties attached
have deserved death, they shall surely have it.  And for the
maner.  They are eyther beheaded, or crucified.  He kneels
down on his knees, and then comes the executioner behinde
him and cuts off his head with a catan, or theyre countrie
sworde; and, his head beinge off, the young cavalliers trie
their weapons on his limbes, and prove whether they can cut
off an arme or lege at a blowe.  The other have their armes
and leges spread abroad on a crosse; which done, they set
the crosse upright in the ground, and then comes one either
with a lance, or speare, and runnes the partie through the
bodie.  There he hangs untill he rots off: no man being suffred to take him downe.[1]*

There lieth an ample region about 300 leukes from Meacum,
on the northe syde of Japonia [Yedzo], inhabited with men
that weare the skynnes of beastes; theire bodies are full of
hayre; they have long beardes; and are great wyne drinkers;
and stoute warriors; and a terror to the Japonians.  They
have a certeyne kind of trafficke with the Yquitaynes, which
are a people of Japonia; but these seldom enter into the
countrey of those barbarous people, lest they should evill
entreate them.

## The Hystorie.

In tyme past, all Japonia acknowledged the Government
of a certeyne Prince, whose name was Dairis, whom it obeyed
in all thynges with great reverence; whoe also governed all
these dominions with greate estimation and maiestie; and
this continued about 1700 yeares; but since som 500 yeares
agone, hitherto, twoe of his principall servauntes exalted

[1] NOTE S.  *Laws and administration of justice.*

themselues, and have disturbed the whole empire : for either of them invaded as greate a parte of the dominions as he coulde by force of armies, and took it from Dairis. In tyme encreased ambition, and they advancynge and exalting themselves, one while the one, and another while the other, became lordes, he of one parte, and the other of another parte of the empire ; taking vppon them the title of Jacatai, that is, of Kynges. Notwithstandinge, they lefte to Dairis the name of Universall Lorde of Japonia, but without either iurisdiction or seignorie. These princes, whoe have gotten the dominions that are neere to Meacum, scarcelye aforde him meate and aparell, insomuch that there remayneth to him, of the auncyent greatnesse and monarchy of Japonia, nothing almost, but, as it were, a shadowe thereof.[2]

For these 500 hundred yeares past, he is called Emperour, or Kynge of Japonia, in the place of Dairis, that obteyneth the dominion of Coquinai (he is also called Lorde of Tenza), where those fyve kyngedomes are seene about the citye of Meacum : of which sort, Nabunanga hath beene in our tyme, and at this present Fassiba is, whoe for greatnes of dominions and power hath far excelled all his predecessors ; for Nabunanga, whoe exceeded others in power, obteyned no more but 36 kyngedomes ; but Fassiba hath subdued no lesse then fyftye.

*Marginal note: Bungos is a kyngdome of Japonia ; the kynges brother that now raygneth there was of late yeares at Rome with others accompanyinge hym. Ms. [A.D. 1582-86]. 1*

## The Regiment.

The regiment of Japonia dyfereth very far from all other formes of government which are vsed in Europe ; for the power and greatnesse of this prince consisteth not in ordinarye revenues and love of his people, but in authoritye and empire, for he having gotten one or many dominions, devideth his realmes and provinces amonge his frendes ; whom he

1 NOTE T. *Embassy from Japan to Rome.*
2 NOTE U. *Reverses of the Daïri, or Mikado.*

C

bindeth to serve him as well in peace as in war, with a certeine number of men, which they must maynteyne at theire
owne costes and charges.   These also distribute, moreover,
theire seigneiories to theire frendes, to whome they truste,
that they maye in like maner have them readye to serve
them, reservinge somewhat for themselves and theire families.   So that all the wealthe and substance of Japonia, as
well private as publicke, dependeth of a fewe, and those fewe
of one who is lorde of Tenza, whoe without any stay or lette,
gyveth and taketh away whatsoever he will : exalteth and
humbleth ; and maketh princes either mightie or miserable.[1]
Also, when one hath his state or dignitie taken from him,
all the noblemen of that province, with their soldiers, are
changed, leavyne onlye the husbandmen and artyficers.   This
forme of regiment causeth continuall revolutions and changes
of the states : fyrste, because that Dairis (whoe, although
hee neither hath power nor empire, yet is had in great estimation and honour with the people) is the cause that the
lordes of the Tenza and the other princes are accounted
tyrantes, vsurpers, destroyers of the monarchye, and enemyes
of the greatnes of Japonia : which thinge taketh away their
estimation, and hindreth them of the good will of the people.
Hereof it cometh that they are easily moved to take armes,
and the rather, for that one hopeth that he may be exalted
through another's fall.   Moreover, the people cannot love
these princes as their naturall lordes, which are daylye
changed ; and they, because they are vncerteyne howe longe
a tyme they shalbe lordes, take no more care for one state
then for another ; yea, they hopinge that they maye with as
much facilitie gette a better as they gotte one before, like
carders and disers, doe hasarde the one to winne the other ;
and sometymes alone, and sometymes beinge a number ioyned
together, thē attempt divers thinges ; by reason whereof those
iles are continually exercysed with warres.

In time past
all Japonia
obeyed this
man, nowe
only the
title is lefte
him, but not
without
great ho-
nour, for
the Japo-
nians do
thinke yet
that he
ought to
have the
empire.—
Ms.

[1] Note V.   *Government and policy.*

But FASSIBA, to the ende that he may become lorde, or
rather absolute tyrant, is wonte to remove the princes out
of one province into another : not ignorant, that lordes
beinge taken out of theire dominions and placed over strange
subiectes, become weake, and unable either to vse, or to take
armes against him; and that they may the lesse practise and
devise any revoulte, he devideth their realmes and dominions.
So those that are lordes, have not theire state so ioyned,
or knytte together ; and that they never want cause of war
and debate, and the streitenes of the limites is the cause.
Besides all this, in all these mutations of states, he will
have theym, as well those that are made thereby better, as
those that become worse, to come and yelde him reverence
and obedience, and to offer vnto him everye year precyouse
gyftes; by which meanes he draweth to himself a greate
parte of the wealthe and riches of Japonia. ✱ For though all
rivers doe in a kinde of thankfull remuneration returne their
waters to the sea, because they drawe them from hence,
yet the princes of Japonia doe cleane contrarie. They
receive nothing from the emperour, and yet give all to the
emperour. They doe impoverish themselves by enriching
him by presents at his comaunde. Nay they even strive and
contend whoe may give the greatest and chiefest present.
And the emperour doth ordinarily requite his princes in this
sorte. He doth geve them a feather for a goose : some few
kerrimones, or coates, for gold, silver, or other precious
comodities ; and that they may not growe riche, and of suffi-
tient abilitie to make head against him, he suffers not their
fleeces to growe, but sheares them cleane off : by raising taxes
on them for the buyldinge of castles, and the repearinge of
fortifications, and yet they are not suffred to repeare theire
owne, or any waye to fortifie themselves. ✱

Moreover he exercyseth the people in buyldinge, as of
mervelous pallaces, greate temples, castles, and incomparable
cyties. Aboute which buyldinges he kepeth above an hun-

*For this
cause
kynges and
monarckes
doe often
change their
viceroys and
lieutenants.
—Ms.*

dred thousande workemen occupied, which are maintained as his subiectes. Among other thinges at this tyme he is in of buyldinge of a temple, in the buyldinge whereof he purposseth to consume all the iron in Japonia : for he hath commanded that all handicraftes men and common people shall bring all theire armour and weapons to a place appointed for that purposse, which must serve to the foresayd buyldinge. By which facte he vnarmeth the people, and maketh magnificent and sumptuouse workes. Insomuche that he hath in twoe places onlye an 100,000 workmen and above, who are all kept at his subiectes charges. Besides the kinges and princes which are bounde to gyve him gyftes, and to serve him as well in tyme of peace as of war, he receaveth yearelye twoe millions of goulde of the rentes of ryce which is gathered in these possessions which are reserved to himself. He purposseth when the Japponian warres are ended to attempt China, for which purpose he hath appoynted tymber to be fallen for the buyldinge of 2000 sayle, wherewith he may convey over his armye. He trusteth through these greate buyldinges, famous expeditions, and through such amplenesse of dominions, and ioyninge together of kingedomes vnder one crowne, that he shall obtayne an immortall name, and be accounted for a god : which thinge all they have done, that have obteyned the opinion of gods amonge the Japonians : for Amida, Xaca, Camis, and Fatoques, to whom they attribute divine honour, were nothing els but lordes of Japonia, whoe by the glory of war, or skill in tyme of peace, obtained the opinion of divinitie among the Japonians : no otherwise then did Hercules and Bacchus in Grece, Saturnus and Janus in Italie, and there be no lesse fabulous and tryffelynge tales spreade abroade of those then of these. Therefore Fassiba, perceavinge that the lawe of Christ permitteth not any other god besydes him that created heaven and earthe of nothinge, and therefore that all gods fayned foolishlie of men, are to be detested as thinges accursed, hath decreed to sende the

He doth these thinges that he may gette immortal fame and be honored as a god after his death.— Ms.

Such a one was Combendaxis, of whom they tell many vaine and foolyshe fables.—Ms.

fathers of the socyetie into banishment which have preached that lawe; and to plucke vp by the rootes that yonge vine, which hath begonne to take deepe roote in those countreys. An acte of pride worthye to be had in remembrance: for the Romaine emperours withstode the preachinge of the Crosse and Gospell whereby they might defende their idols, which the lawe of God declared to be but devils and vayne thinges; but this man for his owne private commoditie, maketh warre against the Christian fayth, the same war being founded vpon a certeyne extreme ambition, or rather foolishnes, wherewith he being pricked forwarde wolde be estemed as a god, and maketh war against the Christian fayth. But in the middest of these his greate and immoderate cogitations, God hath styrred vp against him a newe enemye (as we vnderstande by letters sent this laste yeare) in the easte parte of Japonia whoe oppugneth him.[1]

*They had a care of theire gods, although they were false gods, but this man hath a care of himselfe. —Ms.*

Theire Highe Preist hathe his pallace or courte at Meacum, whome thē honour as God. In the howses 366 idolles, of which there standeth one euerye nyght by him, like, as it were, a certein watcheman. The commone people esteeme him to be so holye, that he ought not so muche as once to touche the grounde, which thinge yf he happen by chance to doe, he looseth his dignitie. He is served not with any greate pompe, for he is maintayned with almes. His servantes, whose authoritie is greate throughout all Japonia, goe in embassage for the Cubucana [Cubo Sama], that is, the Emperour. These they call Cangues.

There is also another magistrate to whom they also almost yelde devine honour, named in the Japonicall tonge Vo. This man, for maiestie sake, never goeth forth of the doores, and nowe and then he will not be seene. At whom [? home] he is eyther caried aboute in his seate, or goeth vpon wodden soales lyfted vp from the groūde. Oftentimes he sytteth in a chayre, havinge a sworde placed on the one syde of hym,

---

[1] NOTE W. *Career of Fassiba, or Taico Sama.*

and a bowe and arrowes on his other syde. His garment is blacke on the inner syde, and redde on the other syde. His hat is not far vnlike a bisshop's myther. His forehead is paynted with redde and white. All the dishes and vessells wherein meate is brought to his table are of earth. This man determineth all tytles of honour. And for because that nation doth thirst myserably after prayse and honour, everye nobleman hath his sollicitor with the Vo, and they offer vnto him gyftes as it were by stryffe. By these meanes that heraulde becometh so ryche, that althoughe he neyther hath landes nor rentes, yet he may be thought to be the richest man in all Japonia. There are three thinges which may depryve him of this his office and dignitie. The first is, yf he touche the grounde with his foote; the seconde is, yf he kill anye man; and the thirde is, yf he be founde to be an enemye to peace and tranquyllitie.[1]

For the good orderinge of his state, the Emperour hath a Privie Councell of five,[2] whoe commonly are such that for wisdome, policie, and careful vigilancie in managing the State affairs, in preventing of treasons and rebellions, in executing of justice, and continuing of peace and quietnesse, may be compared with many, nay with most in Christendome. Moreover, they have iudges, which doe decyde matters in controversie in the temporall courte; and also others, called Tundi, which doe decyde matters in controuersie in the spirituall consistorye.

*There are great store of these in that great Iland, everye one being knowen by theire ensignes or armes, which appeare in the sealinge of their letters.—Ms.*

*These Tundi are as it were bysshops, and are greatlye honored of all men.—Ms.*

---

[1] Regarding the "High Priest" and the "Vo", see NOTE U : *The Reverses of the Daïri.*

[2] NOTE X. *The Privy Council and State Officers.*

# MEMORIALS OF JAPON.

## PART II.

———————————

THE

## LETTERS OF WILLIAM ADAMS.

### 1611 TO 1617.

# LETTERS OF WILLIAM ADAMS.

## Introduction.

THE first letter sent by William Adams for England, he thus addresses: "*TO MY VNKNOWNE FRINDS AND COUNTRI-MEN: dessiring this letter by your good meanes, or the newes or copie of this letter, may come into the hands of one, or manny of my acquayntance in LIMEHOVSE or else wheare, or in KENT in GILLINGHAM, by ROCHES-TER.*"

Probably through the agency of their Factors recently settled at Bantam, two copies of the letter were transmitted to the "Worshipfull Felowship of the Merchants of London trading into the East Indies"; and in the sequel it will be perceived the communication led to the opening of commercial intercourse between England and Japon.

Purchas has given a version of this letter (*Pilgrims,* vol. i, page 125, etc.); but it is to be viewed as a loose paraphrase only. In the variations he has adopted, erroneously or capriciously, the sense is not unfrequently destroyed; and the unaffected earnestness which characterizes the original, is rarely preserved. The version now given is founded on two manuscript copies, preserved among the records of the East India Company. Many of the variations between the printed and manuscript copies are noted; but to exhibit the whole, it would be necessary to print the two versions in juxtaposition, which would occupy more space than seems adviseable.

D

## Letter No. I.

Hauing so good occasion, by hearing that certaine English marchants lye in the island of *Iaua*, although by name vnknowen, I haue ymboldened my selfe to wryte these few lines, desiring the Worshipfull Companie being vnknowen to me, to pardon my stowtnes. My reason that I doe wryte, is first as conscience doth binde me with loue to my countrymen, and country. Your Worships, to whom this present wryting shall come, is to geve you to vnderstand that I am a Kentish man, borne in a towne called *Gillingam*, two English miles from *Rochester*, one mile from *Chattam*, where the Kings ships doe lye: and that from the age of twelue yeares olde, I was brought vp in *Limehouse* neere *London*, being Apprentice twelue yeares to Master *Nicholas Diggines;* and my selfe haue serued for Master and Pilott in her Maiesties ships; and about eleuen or twelue yeares haue serued the Worshipfull Companie of the Barbarie Marchants, vntill the Indish traffick from *Holland* [began], in which Indish traffick I was desirous to make a littel experience of the small knowledg which God had geven me. So, in the yeare of our Lord 1598, I was hired for Pilot Maior of a fleete of five sayle, which was made readie by the Indish Companie: *Peeter Vander Hay* and *Hance Vander Veek*. The Generall of this fleet, was a marchatt called *Iaques Maihore,* in which ship, being Admirall, I was Pilott. So being the three and twentieth or foure and twentieth of Iune ere we sett sayle, it was too late ere we came to the line, to passe it without contrarie windes. So it was about the middest of September, at which time we fownde much southerly windes, and our men were many sick, so that we were forsed to goe to the coast of *Guinney* to Cape *Gonsalves*, where wee set our sicke men a lande, of which many dyed: and of the sicknesse few bettered, hauing little or no refreshing, beinge an vnhealthfull place.

So that to fulfill our voyage, wee set our course for the coast of *Brasill*, beinge determined to passe the Streightes of *Magilanus*; and by the way cam to an Iland called *Annabona*,[1] which island we landed at, and tooke the towne, in which was about eightie houses. In which Iland we refreshed our-selues, hauing oxen, oranges, and diuers fruites, etc. But the vnwholesomenesse of the aire was very bad, that as one bettered, an other fell sicke: spending vpon the coast vp the cape *Gonsalues*, and vp *Annabona*, a two moneths tyme, till the twelfth or thirteenth Nouember. At which time, wee set sayle from *Annabona*, finding the windes still at the south and south by east, and south south-east, till wee got into foure degrees to the southwards of the line: at which time the winde did fauour vs comming to the south-east, and east south-east, and so that we were vp betweene the Iland of *Annabona*, and the Streightes of *Magilano*, about a fiue monethes. One of our fiue sayle hir maine mast fell over bord, by which we were much hindred; for in the sea with much troubell we set a new mast. So that the nine and twentieth of March, we saw the lande in lattetude of fiftie degrees, hauing the winde a two or three daies contrarie: so, in the ende, hauinge the windes good, came to the Streightes of *Magilano*, the sixt of Aprill, 1599, at which time, the winter came, so that there was much snowe: and with colde on the one side, and hunger on the other, our men grew weake. Hauing at that time the wind at the north-east, six or seven dayes, in which time wee might haue past through the Streightes. But, for refreshing of our men we waited, water-ing and taking in of wood, and setting vp of a pynnas of fif-teene or twentie tonnes in burthen. So at length, wee would haue passed through, but could not by reason of the southerly windes: the weather[2] being very cold, with aboundance of snowe and yce. Wherefore, we were forced to winter and to stay in the Streightes from the sixt of Aprill, till the foure and

---

[1] *Illha da Nobon.* [P.]          [2] *with wet.* [P.]

twentieth of September, in which time our victualles was for
the most part of spent, and for lacke of the same, many of
our men dyed of hunger. So, hauinge passed through the
Streightes, and comming in the South Sea, wee found many
hard stormes,[1] being driuen to the southward in fiftie foure
degrees, being very cold. At length we found reasonable
windes and weather, with which wee followed our pretended
voyage towards the coast of *Perow :* but in long traves[2] we
lost our whole fleet, being separated the one from the other.
Yet wee had appointed before the dispersing of our fleet by
stormes and foule weather, that if wee lost one another, that
in *Chili* in the lattetude of fortie sixe degrees, wee should
stay the one for the other the space of thirtie dayes. In
which height according to agreement, I went in sixe and
fortie degrees, and stayed eight and twentie dayes where we
refreshed our selues, findinge the people of the countrey of a
good nature : but by reason of the Spaniardes, the people
would not trade with vs. At first, they brought vs sheepe[3]
and potatoes, for which we gaue them bills[4] and kniues, whereof
they were very glad : but in the end, the people went vp
from their houses into the countrey, and came no more to
vs. Wee stayed there eight and twentie dayes, and set vp a
pynnas which we had in our ship in foure partes, and in the
end departed and came to the mouth of *Baldiuia,* yet by
reason of the much wind it was at that present, we entred not,
but directed our course out of the bay, for the iland of *Much*
[*Mocha*], vnto the which the next day wee came ; and finding
none of our fleet there, directed our course for *St. Maria,* and
the next day cam by the Cape, which is but a league and an
halfe from the Iland, and seeing many people luffed[5] about
the cape, and finding good grownde, anchored in a faire sandy

---

[1] *streames.* [P.]

[2] *i. e. :* but in long *traverses*, or " in making long stretches in working
up against the wind, we lost them." *Purchas* reads, *trauels.*

[3] *they would not trade with vs at first. They brought vs sheepe.* [P.]

[4] *bels.* [P.]                    [5] *tossed.* [P.]

baÿ in fifteene fathom; and went with our boats hard by the
water side, to parle with the people of the lande, but they
would not suffer vs to come a lande, shooting great store of
arrowes at vs. Neuerthelesse, hauing no victualls in our
ship, and hoping to find refreshing by force, wee landed some
seuen and twentie or thirtie of our men, and droue the wilde
people from the water side, most of our men being hurt with
their arrowes. And¹ being on land, we made signes of friendship, and in the end came to parle with signes and tokens of
friendship, the which the people in the end did vnderstand.
So wee made signes, that our desire was for victualls, shewing them iron, siluer, and cloth, which we would give them
in exchange for the same. Wherefore they gaue our folke
wine, with potatoes² to eate, and drinke with other fruits, and
bid our men by signes and tokens to goe aboord, and the
next day to come againe, and then they would bring vs good
store of refreshing : so, being late, our men came aboord,³
very glad that we had come to a parle with them, hoping that
we should get refreshing. The next day, being the ninth of
Nouember 1599, our capten, with all our officers, prepared
to goe a lande, hauing taken counsell to goe to the water
side, but not to lande more then two or three at the
most ; for there were people in aboundance vnknowen to
us : wilde, therefore not to be trusted ;⁴ which counsell
being concluded vpon, the capten himselfe did goe in one
of our boats, with all the force that we could make ; and
being by´ the shore side, the people of the countrie made
signes that they should come a lande ; but that did not well
like our capten. In the end, the people not comming neere
vnto our boats, our capten, with the rest, resolved to land,
contrary to that which was concluded abord our shipp, before
their going a lande. At length, three and twentie men landed

---

¹ *They.* [P.]                           ² *batatas.* [P.]
³ *the most part of them being hurt more or less.* . . . [P.]
⁴ *our men therefore were willed not to trust them.* [P.]

with muskets, and marched vpwardes towardes foure or fiue houses, and when they were about a musket shot from the boates, more then a thousand Indians, which lay in ambush, immediately fell vpon our men with such weapons as they had, and slewe them all to our knowledge. So our boats did long wait to see if any of them did come agen; but being all slaine, our boates returned : which sorrowfull newes of all our mens deaths was very much lamented of vs all; for we had scarce so many men left as could winde vp our anker. The next day wee weighed,[1] and went ouer to the Iland of *St. Maria*, where we found our Admiral, who had ariued there foure daies before vs, and departed from the Iland of *Much* the day before we came from thence, hauing the Generall, Master, and all his Officers, murthered a lande;[2] so that all our officers were slaine, the one bemoning the other : neuerthelesse, both glad to see the one the other, and that we were so well met together. My good friend *Timothy Shotten* was Pilott in that ship.

Being at the island of *St. Maria*, which lieth in the lattetude to the s° ward of the line of thirtie seuen degrees twelue minutes on the cost of *Chili*, wee tooke counsell to take all things out of one ship,[3] and to burne the other; but that the captens that were made newe, the one nor the other, would not, so that we could not agree to leave the one or the other; and having much cloth in our ships, it was agreed that wee should leaue the coast of *Perow*, and direct our course for *Iapon*, having understood that cloth was good marchandiz there; and also how vpon that coast of *Perow*, the king's ships were out seeking vs, hauing knowledge of our being there, vnderstanding that wee were weake of men, which was certaine; for one of our fleet,[4] for hunger, was forced to seeke

---

[1] *waited*. [P.]   [2] *and God had so plagued vs*. . . [P.]

[3] *our shipps*. [original] *one ship*. [P.]

[4] *as we vnderstood afterward was forced to yeeld themselves into the enemies hand in*. . . [P.]

reliefe at the enemies hand in Saint *Ago*. For which reason, hauing refreshed ourselues in this Iland of *St. Maria*, more by policie then by force, we departed the twentie seuen of Nouember, from the Iland of *St. Maria*, with our two ships; and for the rest of our fleete we had no newes of them.  So we stood away directly for *Iapan*, and passed the equinoctiall line together, vntill we came in twentie-eight degrees to the northward of the line: in which lattetude we were about the twentie third of February[1] 1600.  Wee had a wonderous storme of wind, as euer I was in, with much raine, in which storme wee lost our consort,[2] whereof we were very sorry: neverthe-less,[3] with hope that in *Iapon* we should meet the one the other,[4] we proceeded on our former intention for *Iapon*, and in the height of thirtie degrees, sought the northermost [?] Cape of the forenamed Iland; but found it not, by reason that it lieth faulce in all cardes, and maps, and globes; for the Cape lieth in thirtie-fiue degrees $\frac{1}{2}$, which is a great difference. In the end, in thirtie-two degrees $\frac{1}{2}$, wee cam in sight of the lande, being the nineteenth day of April.  So that betweene the Cape of *St. Maria* and *Iapon*, we were foure moneths and twentie-two daies; at which time there were no more then sixe besides my selfe that could stand vpon his feet.  So we in safetie let fall our anchor about a league from a place called *Bungo*.  At which time cam to vs many boats, and we suffred them to come abord, being not able to resist them, which people did vs no harme; neither of vs vnderstanding the one the other.[5]    Within a 2 or 3 daies after our arivall, ther cam a Iesuit from a place called *Langasacke*, to which place the Carake of *Amakau*[6] is yeerely wont to come, which

---

[1] *the twenty second and twenty third.* [P.]

[2] *greatest ship.* [P.]

[3] *being left alone.* [P.]

[4] *Then according to wind and weather we followed our.* . . [P.]

[5] *but by signes and tokens.* [P.]

[6] AMACAU. " The *Portugals* of those times [about the middle of the 16th century] were very desirous of trade with the *Chinois*, who on the other hand were very suspitious of them. . . . yet desire of gaine pre-

with other Iaponers that were Christians, were our inter-
preters, which was not to our good, our mortal ennemies
being our Truchmen.[1] Neuerthelesse, the King of *Bungo*,
the place where we arriued, shewed vs great friendship. For
he gaue vs an house a lande, where we landed our sicke men,
and had all refreshing that was needfull. We had when we
cam to anker in *Bungo*, sicke and whole, foure and twentie
men, of which number the next day three dyed. The rest
for the most part recouered, sauing three, which lay a long
time sicke, and in the end also died. In the which time of
our being here, the Emperour hearing of vs, sent presently
fiue gallies, or friggates, to vs, to bring mee to the Court,
where his Highnes was, which was distant from *Bungo* about
an eightie English leagues. Soe that as soon as I came
before him, he demanded of me, of what countrey we were;
so I answered him in all points; for there was nothing that
he demanded not, both conserning warre and peace betweene
countrey and countrey: so that the particulars here to wryte
would be too tedious. And for that time I was commanded
to prisson, being well vsed, with one of our mariners that
cam with me to serue me.

A two dayes after, the Emperour called me agein, de-
maunding the reason of our comming so farre. I aunswered:
We were a people that sought all friendship with all nations,
and to haue trade in all countries, bringing such merchandiz as our countrey did afford into strange landes, in the way
of traffick.[2] He demaunded also as conserning the warres

vayled, that they were admitted to trade; till the *Chinois* growing less
fearfull, granted them in the greater Iland a littel *Peninsula* to dwell in.
In which place was an *Idoll* called AMA, whence the Peninsula was called
AMA CAO: that is *Amas Bay*." Such is the derivation of the modern
MACAO, given by Purchas on the authority of the Jesuit Fathers. [*Pil-
grims*, vol. iii, p. 319.]

[1] *which was ill for vs, they being our mortal enemies.* [P.]

[2] *bringing such merchandizes as our countrye had, and buying such merchandizes in strange countryes as our country desired; through which our
countryes on both side were inriched.* [P.]

betweene the Spaniard or Portingall and our countrey, and
the reasons; the which I gaue him to vnderstand of all
things, which he was glad to heare, as it seemed to me.   In
the end, I was commaunded to prisson agein, but my lodging
was bettered in an other place.   So that 39 dayes I was in
prisson, hearing no more newes, neither of our ship, nor capten, whether he were recouered of his sickenesse or not, nor
of the rest of the company : in which time, I looked euery
day to die : to be *crossed*, as the custome of iustice is in *Iapon*,
as hanging is in our land.   In which long time of imprissonment, the Iesuites and the Portingalls gaue many euidences
against me and the rest to the Emperour, that wee were
theeues and robbers of all nations, and were we suffered to
liue, it should be ageinst the profit of his Highnes, and the
land : for no nation should come there without robbing : his
Highnes iustice being executed, the rest of our nation without doubt should feare and not come here any more : thus
dayly making axcess to the Emperour, and procuring friendes
to hasten my death.   But God that is always merciful at
need, shewed mercy vnto vs, and would not suffer them to
haue their willes of vs.   In the end, the Emperour gave them
aunswer that we as yet had not doen to him nor to none of
his lande any harme or dammage : therfore against Reason
and Iustice to put vs to death.   If our countreys had warres
the one with the other, that was no cause that he should put
vs to death :  with which they were out of hart, that their
cruell pretence failed them.   For which God be for evermore
praised.[1]   Now in this time that I was in prisson, the ship

[1] *And to this intent they sued to his maiestie daily to cut vs off, making
all the friends they could to this purpose.   But God was mercifull vnto vs,
and would not suffer them to haue their wills of vs.   At length, the Emperour gaue them this answer, that as yet wee had done no hurt or damage to
him, nor to any of his land ; and therefore that it was against reason and
iustice to put vs to death : and if our countreys and theirs had warres one
with the other, that was no cause that he should put vs to death.   The emperour answering them in this manner, they were quite out of heart, that their
cruell pretence failed : for the which, God be praised for euer and euer.* [P.]

E

was commaunded to be brought so neere to the citie where the Emperour was, as she might be (for grownding hir); the which was done. 41 daies being expired, the Emperour caused me to be brought before him agein, demanding of mee many questions more, which were too long to write. In conclusion, he asked me whether I were desirous to goe to the ship to see my countreymen. I answered very gladly: the which he bade me doe. So I departed, and was freed from imprissonment. And this was the first newes that I had, that the ship and company were come to the citie. So that, with a reioicing hart I tooke a boat, and went to our ship, where I found the capten and the rest, recouered of their sickenesse; and when I cam abord with weeping eyes was received :[1] for it was given them to vnderstand that I was executed long since. Thus, God be praised, all we that were left aliue, came together againe. From the ship all things were taken out: so that the clothes which I took with me on my back I only had. All my instruments and books were taken. Not only I lost what I had in the ship, but from the capten and the company, generally, what was good or worth the taking, was carried away. All which was doen unknowen to the Emperour. So in process of time hauing knowledg of it, he commaunded that they which had taken our goods, should restore it to vs back again; but it was here and there so taken, that we could not get it again : sauinge 50000 R$^s$ in reddy money was commaunded to be geven vs; and in his presence brought, and delivered in[2] the hands of one that was made

---

[1] *But at our meeting aboord, we saluted one another with mourning and sheadding of teares.* [P.]

[2] *All things were taken out of the ship, together with all my instruments, etc., and I had nothing left me, but my clothes on my backe : likewise whatsoeuer the rest of the company had, was also taken away, vnknowne to the Emperour : which when he vnderstood, he gaue order that they should be restored to vs againe. But being so dispersed abroad, they could not be had : yet fiftie thousand rials in ready money, were commanded to be giuen us, the Emperour himselfe seeing the deliuery thereof to . . .* [P.]

our gouernour, who kept them in his hands to distribute
them vnto vs as wee had neede, for the buying of victualls
for our men, with other particular charges. So in the end of
thirtie dayes, our ship lying before the city called *Sakay*,
two leagues ½ or three leagues, from *Ozaca*, where the Emperour at that time did lye, commaundement cam from the
Emperour, that our ship should be carried to the eastermost
part of the land, called *Quanto*, whither according to his
commaundement we were carried, the distance being about
an hundred and twenty leagues. Our passage thither was
long, by reason of contrarie windes, so that the Emperour was
there long before vs. Comming to the land of *Quanto*, and
neere to the citie *Eddo*, where the Emperour was : being
arriued, I sought all meanes by supplications, to get our ship
cleare, and to seeke our best meanes[1] to come where the
Hollanders had their trade : in which suit we spent much of
the mony geven vs. Also, in this time, three or foure of our
men rebelled against the capten, and my selfe, and made a
mutinie with the rest of our men, so that we had much
trouble with them. For they would not abide noe longer in
the ship, but euery one would be a commander : and perforce
would haue euery one part of the money that was geven by
the Emperour. It would bee too long to wryte the particulars. In the end, the money was devided according to euery
man's place ; but this was about two yeeres that we had been
in *Iapon ;* and when we had a deniall that we should not
haue our ship, but to abyde in *Iapon*. So that the part of
every one being devided, every one tooke his way[2] where he
thought best. In the end, the Emperour gaue euery man,
to liue vpon, two pounds of rice a day, daily, and yeerely so
much as was worth eleuen or twelue ducats a yeare, yearely :
my selfe, the capten, and mariners all alike.

[1] *profit.* [P.]

[2] *our companie having their parts of the money dispersed themselves
euerie one* . . . [P.]

So in processe of four or fiue yeeres the Emperour called me, as diuers times he had done before. So one time aboue the rest he would haue me to make him a small ship. I aunswered that I was no carpenter, and had no knowledg thereof. Well, doe your endeavour, saith he: if it be not good, it is no matter. Wherefore at his commaund I buylt him a ship of the burthen of eightie tunnes, or there about : which ship being made in all respects as our manner is, he comming aboord to see it, liked it very well; by which meanes I came in more fauour with him, so that I came often in his presence, who from time to time gaue me presents, and at length a yearely stypend to liue vpon, much about seuentie ducats by the yeare, with two pounds of rice a day, daily. Now beeing in such grace and fauour, by reason I learned him some points of *jeometry,* and vnderstanding of the art of *mathematickes,* with other things : I pleased him so, that what I said he would not contrarie. At which my former ennemies did wonder; and at this time must intreat me to do them a friendship, which to both Spaniards and Portingals have I doen :[1] recompencing them good for euill. So, to passe my time to get my liuing, it hath cost mee great labour and trouble at the first; but God hath blessed my labour.

In the ende of fiue yeeres, I made supplication to the king to goe out of this land, desiring to see my poore wife and children according to conscience and nature. With the which request, the emperour was not well pleased, and would not let me goe any more for my countrey, but to byde in his land. Yet in processe of time, being in great fauour with the Emperour, I made supplication agein, by reason we had newes that the Hollanders were in *Shian*[2] and *Patania* ; which reioyced vs much, with hope that God should bring us to our

---

[1] ...*Jesuites and Portugals did greatly wonder, and intreated me to befriend them to the Emperour in their businesse : and so by my meanes both Spaniards and Portugals have receiued friendship from the Emperour; I recompencing their euill vnto me with good.* [P.]

[2] *Achen.* [P.]

countrey againe, by one meanes or other.   So I made supplication agein, and boldly spake my selfe with him, at which
he gaue me no aunswer.   I told him, if he would permit me
to depart, I would bee a meanes, that both the English and
Hollanders should come and traffick there.   But by no means
he would let mee goe.   I asked him leave for the capten, the
which he presently granted mee.   So by that meanes my
capten got leave; and in a *Iapon* iunk sailed to *Pattan;* and
in a yeares space cam no *Hollanders.*   In the end,[1] he went
from *Patane* to *Ior,* where he found a fleet of nine saile: of
which fleet *Matleef* was General, and in this fleet he was made
Master againe, which fleet sailed to *Malacca,* and fought with
an armado of Portingalls: in which battel he was shot, and
presently died: so that as yet, I think, no certain newes is
knownen, whether I be liuing or dead.   Therefore I do pray
and intreate you in the name of Jesus Christ to doe so much
as to make my being[2] here in *Iapon,* knowen to my poor
wife: in a manner a widdow, and my two children father-
lesse: which thing only is my greatest griefe of heart, and
conscience.   I am a man not vnknowen in *Ratcliffe* and
*Limehouse,* by name to my good Master *Nicholas Diggines,*
and M. *Thomas Best,* and M. *Nicholas Isaac,* and *William
Isaac,* brothers, with many others; also to M. *William Iones,*
and M. *Becket.*   Therefore may this letter come to any of
their hands, or the copy: I doe know that compassion and
mercy is so,[3] that my friends and kindred shall haue newes,
that I doe as yet liue in this vale of my sorrowfull[4] pil-

---

[1] *He answered, that he was desirous of both those nations company for
trafficque, but would not part with me by any meanes: but bade me write
to that purpose.   Seeing therefore I could not preuaile for my selfe, I sued
that my captaine might depart, which suit hee presently graunted me.   So
hauing gotten his libertie, he imbarqued in a Iapans iunck, and sayled to
Patane: but he tarried there a yeers space, waiting for Holland ships.
And seeing none came....* [P.]

[2] ... *my desire is that my wife and two children may heare that I
am...* [P.]

[3] ... *that companies mercy is such...* [P.]          [4] *sinfull.* [P.]

grimage: the which thing agein and agein I do desire for Iesus Christ his sake.

You shall vnderstand, that the first ship that I did make, I did make a voyage or two in, and then the King commaunded me to make an other, the which I did, being of the burthen of an hundred and twentie tunnes. In this ship I have made a voyage from *Meaco* to *Eddo*, being as far as from *London* to the *Lizarde* or the *Lands end* of *England*: which in the yeere of our Lord 1609, the King lent to the Gouernour of *Manilla*, to goe with eightie of his men, to saile to *Acapulca*. In the yeere 1609 was cast away a great ship called the *S. Francisco*, beeing about a thousand tunnes, vpon the coast of *Iapon*, in the lattetude of thirty fiue degrees and fiftie minutes. By distresse of weather she cut ouer-boord her maine mast, and bore vp for *Iapon*, and in the night vnawares, the ship ranne vpon the shore and was cast away: in the which thirtie and sixe[1] men were drowned, and three hundred fortie, or three hundred fiftie saued: in which ship the Gouernour of *Manilla* as a passenger, was to returne to *Noua Spania*. But this Gouernour was sent in the bigger ship which I made, in *ann*. 1610, to *Acapulca*. And in *ann*. 1611, this Gouernour returned another ship in her roome, with a great present, and with an Embassadour to the Emperour, giuing him thankes for his great friendship: and also sent the worth of the Emperours ship in goods and money: which shippe the Spaniards haue now in the *Philippinas*.

Now for my seruice which I haue doen and daily doe, being employed in the Emperours seruice, he hath given me a liuing, like vnto a lordship in *England*, with eightie or ninetie husbandmen, that be as my slaues or seruants: which, or the like president, was neuer here before geven to any stranger. Thus God hath prouided for mee after my great miserie; and to him only be all honnor and praise, power and glory, both now and for euer, worlde without ende.[2]

---

[1] ONE HUNDRED *thirtie and six*. [P.]

[2] *his name hath and haue the prayse for ever.  Amen.* [P.]

Now, whether I shall come out of this land, I know not. Vntill this present there hath been no meanes; but now, through the trade of the Hollanders, there is meanes. In the yeere of our Lord 1609, two Holland ships came to *Iapon*. Their intention was to take the Caracke, that yeerly cam from *Macao*, being a fiue or six dayes too late. Neuerthelesse, they cam to *Firando*, and cam to the Court to the Emperour, where they were in great friendship receiued, making condition with the Emperour yearely to send a ship or two; and so with the Emperour's passe they departed. Now, this yeare 1611, there is a small ship arriued, with cloth, lead, elephants teeth, dammaske, and blacke taffities, raw silke, pepper, and other commodities; and they haue shewed cause why they cam not in the former yeare 1610, according to promise yearely to come. This ship was wonderously well receiued.[1] You shall vnderstand that the *Hollanders* haue here an Indies of money; for out of *Holland* there is no need of siluer to come into the East *Indies*. For in *Iapan*, there is much siluer and gold to serue for the *Hollanders* to handell wher they will in the *Est Indies*. But the merchandiz, which is here vendible for readie money, is raw silke, damaske, blacke taffities, blacke and red cloth of the best, lead, and such like goods. So, now vnderstanding by this *Holland* ship lately arriued here, that there is a settled trade by my countrey-men in the *Est Indies*, I presume that amongst them, some, either merchants, masters, or mariners, must needs know mee. Therefore I haue ymboldened my selfe to write these few lines in breife; being desirous not to be ouertedious to the reader.

This Iland of *Iapon* is a great land, and lyeth to the northwards, in the lattetude of eight and fortie degrees, and the souther-most part of it in fiue and thirtie degrees, and it lyeth east by north, and west by south or west south west,

---

[1] *This ship is well receiued and with great kindness intertained.* [P.]

two hundred and twentie English leagues.[1]  The people of
this Iland of *Iapon* are good of nature, curteous aboue
measure, and valiant in warre : their iustice is seuerely
excecuted without any partialitie vpon transgressors of the
law.  They are gouerned in great ciuilitie.  I meane, not a land
better gouerned in the world by ciuill policie.  The people
be verie superstitious in their religion, and are of diuers
opinions.  There be many Iesuites and Franciscan friars in
this land, and they haue conuerted many to be Christians,
and haue many churches in the Iland.

Thus, in breife, I am constrained to write, hoping that by
one meanes or other, in processe of time, I shall heare of my
wife and children : and so with pacience I wait the good will
and pleasure of Allmighty God.  Therfor I do pray all
them, or euery one of them, that if this my letter shall com
to their hands to doe the best, that my wife and children, and
my good acquaintance may heere of mee; by whose good
meanes I may in processe of time, before my death heare
newes, or see som of my freindes agein.  The which thinge
God turn it to his glory.  *Amen.*[2]

Dated in *Iapan* the two and twentieth of October 1611.

By your vnworthy friend and seruant, to
command in what I can,

WILLIAM ADAMS.

---

[1] *The breadth south and north of it thirteene degrees, twenty leagues to
the degree, is two hundred sixty leagues, and is almost square.* [P.]

[2] *. . . God Almightie, desiring all those to whom this my letter shall come,
to vse the meanes to acquaint my good friends with it, that so my wife and
children may heare of me : by which meanes there may be hope that I may
heare of my wife and children before my death : The which the Lord grant
to his glorie, and my comfort.  Amen.* [P.]

## Letter No. II.

CONCURRENTLY with the preceding, William Adams addressed
a letter to his wife, of which a fragment has been preserved
by *Purchas*. It contains some interesting additional touches
that contribute to the completion of the picture already
given.

### WILLIAM ADAMS TO HIS WIFE.

Louing wife, you shall vnderstand how all things haue
passed with mee from the time of mine absence from you. We
set saile with fiue ships from the *Texel*, in *Holland*, the foure
and twentieth of Iune 1598. And departed from the coast of
*England* the fift of Iuly. And the one and twentieth of
*August*, we came to one of the isles of *Capo Verde*, called
*Sant' Iago*, where we abode foure and twentie dayes. In
which time many of our men fell sicke, through the vnwhol-
somenesse of the aire, and our generall among the rest. Now
the reason that we abode so long at these ilands was, that
one of the captaines of our fleet made our generall beleeue
that at these ilands we should find great store of refreshing,
as goats and other things, which was vntrue.

Here I and all the pilots of the fleet were called to a
councell; in which wee all shewed our iudgements of dislik-
ing the place; which were by all the captaines taken so ill,
that afterward it was agreed by them all, that the pilots
should be no more in the councell, the which was executed.
The fifteenth day of September we departed from the isle of
*Sant' Iago*, and passed the equinoctiall line. And in the
latitude of three degrees to the south, our generall dyed :
where, with many contrarie windes and raine, the season of
the yeare being very much past, wee were forced vpon the

F

coast of *Guiney*, falling vpon an head-land called *Cabo de Spirito Sancto*. The new generall commanded to bear vp with *Cape de Lopo Consalues*, there to seeke refreshing for our men, the which we did. In which place we landed all our sicke men, where they did not much better, for wee could find no store of victuals. The nine and twentieth of December, wee set saile to goe on our voyage, and in our way we fell with an island called *Illha da Nobon*, where we landed all our sicke men, taking the iland by force. Their towne contayned some eightie houses. Hauing refreshed our men, we set saile againe. At which time our generall commanded, that a man for foure dayes should haue but one pound of bread, that was a quarter of a pound a day; with a like proportion of wine and water. Which scarcitie of victuals brought such feeblenesse, that our men fell into so great weaknesse and sicknesse for hunger, that they did eate the calves' skinnes wherewith our ropes were couered. The third of Aprill 1599, we fell in with the Port of Saint *Iulian*. And the sixt of Aprill we came into the *Straight of Magellan* to the first narrow. And the eighth day we passed the second narrow with a good wind, where we came to an anchor, and landed on *Penguin* Island, where we laded our boate ful of penguins, which are fowles greater then a ducke, wherewith we were greatly refreshed. The tenth, we weighed anchor, hauing much wind, which was good for vs to goe thorow. But our generall would water, and take in prouision of wood for all our fleet. In which straight there is enough in euery place, with anchor ground in all places, three or foure leagues one from another.

In the meane time, the wind changed, and came southerly, so we sought a good harbour for our ship on the north-side, foure leagues off *Elizabeth's* Bay. All Aprill being out, wee had wonderfull much snow and ice, with great winds. For in April, May, Iune, Iuly, and August, is the winter there, being in fiftie-two degrees ½ by south the equinoctiall. Many times in the winter we had the wind good to goe through the straights, but our generall would not. We abode in the straight till the foure and twentieth of August 1599. On the which day wee came into the South Sea; where sixe or seuen dayes after, in a greater storme, we lost the whole fleet one from another. The storme being long, we were driuen into the latitude of fiftie-foure degrees ½, by south the equinoctiall. The weather breaking vp, and hauing good wind againe, the ninth of October we saw the admirall, of which we were glad; eight or ten dayes after, in the night, hauing very much wind, our fore-sayle flew away, and wee lost companie of the admirall. Then, according to wind and weather, we directed our course for the Coast of *Chili*, where the nine and twentieth of October we came to the place appointed of our generall in fortie-sixe degrees, where wee set vp a pinnesse, and stayed eight and twentie dayes: In this place we found people, with whom wee had friendship fiue or sixe dayes, who brought vs sheep; for which we gaue them bels [? bills] and kniues, and it seemed to vs they were contented. But shortly after they went all away from the place where our ship was, and we saw them no more. Eight and twentie dayes being expired, we set sayle, minding to goe for *Baldivia*. So wee came to the mouth of the bay of *Baldivia*. And being very much wind, our captaines minde changed, so that we directed our course for the isle of *Mocha*.

The first of Nouember, we came to the ile of *Mocha*, lying in the latitude of eight and thirtie degrees. Hauing much wind, we durst not anchor, but directed our course for Cape *Sancta Maria*, two leagues by south the iland of *Sancta Maria;* where, hauing no knowledge of the people, the second of Nouember our men went on land, and the people of the land fought with our men, and hurt eight or nine; but in the end, they made a false composition of friendship, which our men did beleeue.

The next day, our captaine, and three and twentie of our

chiefe men, went on land, meaning for marchandize to get victualls, hauing wonderfull hunger. Two or three of the people came straight to our boat in friendly manner, with a kind of wine and rootes, with making tokens to come on land, making signes that there were sheep and oxen. Our captaine with our men, hauing great desire to get refreshing for our men, went on land. The people of the countrey lay intrenched a thousand and aboue, and straight-way fell vpon our men, and slew them all; among which was my brother *Thomas Adams.* By this losse, we had scarse so many men whole as could weigh our anchor. So the third day, in great distresse, we set our course for the Island of *Santa Maria,* where we found our admirall; whom when we saw, our hearts were some-what comforted : we went aboord them, and found them in as great distresse as we, hauing lost their Generall, with seuen and twentie of their men, slaine at the Island of *Mocha,* from whence they departed the day before we came by. Here we tooke counsell what we should doe to get victualls. To goe on land by force we had no men, for the most part were sicke. There came a Spaniard by composition to see our shippe. And so the next day he came againe, and we let him depart quietly. The third day came two Spaniards aboord vs without pawne, to see if they could betray vs. When they had seene our shippe, they would haue gone on land againe, but we would not let them, shewing that they came without leaue, and we would not let them goe on land againe without our leaue; whereat they were greatly offended. We shewed them that we had extreame neede of victualls, and that if they would giue vs so many sheepe, and so many beeues, they should goe on land. So, against their wils, they made composition with vs, which, within the time appointed, they did accomplish. Hauing so much refreshing as we could get, we made all things well againe, our men beeing for the most part recouered of their sicknesse. There was a young man, one *Hudcopee,* which knew nothing, but had serued the admirall, who was made generall : and the master of our shippe was made vice-admirall, whose name was *Iacob Quaternak* of *Roterdam*. So the generall and vice-admirall called me and the other pilote, beeing an Englishman, called *Timothy Shotten* (which had been with M. *Thomas Candish*, in his voyage about the world), to take counsell what we should doe to make our voyage for the best profit of our marchants.[1] At last, it was resolued to goe for *Iapon*. For by report of one *Dirrick Gerritson*, which had been there with the Portugals, woollen cloth was in great estimation in that Iland. And we gathered by reason, that the *Malucos*, and the most part of the East Indies, were hot countreyes, where woolen cloth would not be much accepted : wherefore, we all agreed to goe for *Iapon*. So, leauing the coast of *Chili* from thirtie-sixe degrees of south-latitude, the seuen and twentieth of Nouember 1599, we tooke our course directly for *Iapon*, and passed the line equinoctiall with a faire wind, which continued good for diuerse moneths. In our way, we fell with certain islands in sixeteene degrees of north latitude, the inhabitants whereof are men-eaters. Comming neere these islands, and hauing a great pinnesse with vs, eight of our men beeing in the pinnesse, ranne from vs with the pinnesse, and (as we suppose) were eaten of the wild men, of which people we tooke one : which afterward the generall sent for to come into his shippe. When wee came into the latitude of seuen and twentie and eight and twentie degrees, we found very variable winds and stormy weather. The foure and twentieth of February, we lost sight of our admirall, which afterward we saw no more : Neuerthelesse, we still did our best, directing our course for *Iapon*. The foure and twentieth of March, we saw an island called *Vna Colonna :* at which time many of our men were

[1] A summary of this eventful and disastrous voyage will be found in the Appendix, Note B, to *Narratives of Voyages towards the North-West, etc.*, 1496 to 1631.—Hakluyt Society, 1849.

sicke againe, and diuers dead. Great was the miserie we were in, hauing no more but nine or tenne able men to goe or creepe vpon their knees : our captaine, and all the rest, looking euery houre to die. The eleuenth of Aprill 1600, we saw the land of *Iapon*, neere vnto *Bungo :* at which time there were no more but fiue men of vs able to goe. The twelfth of Aprill, we came hard to *Bungo*, where many barkes came aboord vs, the people whereof wee willingly let come, hauing no force to resist them ; at which place we came to an anchor. The people offered vs no hurt, but stole all things they could steale ; for which some paid deare afterward. The next day, the king of that land sent souldiers aboord to see that none of the marchants goods were stolen. Two or three dayes after, our shippe was brought into a good harbour, there to abide till the principall king of the whole island had newes of vs, and vntill it was knowne what his will was to doe with vs. In the meane time we got fauour of the king of that place, to get our captaine and sicke men on land, which was granted. And wee had an house appointed vs, in which all our men were laid, and had refreshing giuen them. After wee had beene there fiue or sixe dayes, came a Portugall Iesuite, with other Portugals, who reported of vs, that we were pirats, and were not in the way of marchandizing. Which report caused the gouernours and common-peeple to thinke euill of vs: In such manner, that we looked alwayes when we should be set vpon crosses ; which is the execution in this land for theeuery and some other crimes. Thus daily more and more the Portugalls incensed the justices and people against vs. And two of our men, as traytors, gaue themselues in seruice to the king, beeing all in all with the Portugals, hauing by them their liues warranted. The one was called *Gilbert de Conning*, whose mother dwelleth at *Middleborough*, who gaue himselfe out to be marchant of all the goods in the shippe. The other was called *Iohn Abelson Van Owater*. These traitours sought all manner of wayes to

get the goods into their hands, and made knowne vnto them
all things that had passed in our voyage.  Nine dayes after
our arriuall, the great king of the land sent for me to come
vnto him.  So, taking one man with me, I went to him,
taking my leaue of our captaine, and all the others that were
sicke, commending my selfe into His hands that had pre-
serued me from so many perils on the sea.  I was carried in
one of the king's gallies to the court at *Osaca*, where the king
lay, about eightie leagues from the place where the shippe
was.  The twelfth of May 1600, I came to the great king's
citie, who caused me to be brought into the court, beeing a
wonderfull costly house guilded with gold in abundance.
Comming before the king, he viewed me well, and seemed to
be wonderfull fauourable.  He made many signes vnto me,
some of which I vnderstood, and some I did not.  In the
end, there came one that could speake Portuges.  By him,
the king demanded of me, of what land I was, and what
mooued vs to come to his land, beeing so farre off.  I shewed
vnto him the name of our countrey, and that our land had
long sought out the East Indies, and desired friendship with
all kings and potentates in way of marchandize, hauing in
our land diuerse commodities, which these lands had not :
and also to buy such marchandizes in this land, which our
countrey had not.  Then he asked whether our countrey had
warres?  I answered him yea, with the Spaniards and Portugals, beeing in peace with all other nations.  Further, he
asked me, in what I did beleeue?  I said, in God, that made
heauen and earth.  He asked me diverse other questions of
things of religion, and many other things :  As what way we
came to the country.  Hauing a chart of the whole world, I
shewed him, through the *Straight of Magellan*.  At which he
wondred, and thought me to lie.  Thus, from one thing to
another, I abode with him till mid-night.  And hauing asked
mee, what marchandize we had in our shippe, I shewed him
all.  In the end, he beeing ready to depart, I desired that

we might haue trade of marchandize, as the Portugals and
Spanyards had.   To which he made me an answer : but
what it was, I did not vnderstand.   So he commanded me
to be carried to prison.   But two dayes after, he sent for me
againe, and enquired of the qualities and conditions of our
countreys, of warres and peace, of beasts and cattell of all
sorts; and of the heauens.   It seemed that he was well content with all mine answers vnto his demands.   Neuerthelesse, I was commanded to prison againe : but my lodging
was bettered in another place. . . . . . .

## Letter No. III.

To my assured good frind *Augustin Spalding,* in Bantam,
    deliuer this, per a good frind *Thomas Hill,* whom God
    presserue.

*Lavs dei : written in Japan in ye Iland of Ferrando, the
                        12 of Jeneuari 1613.*

My good and louing frind : I do imbolden my self to wrytt
theess feaw lines vnto you in which I do hartylly sallute me
vnto you with all the rest of my good country men with
you, with hope of your good health, which God long continew : as I prayss God I am at this pressent, etc.

Your ffrindly and christian letter I hau receued by the
Hollanders which be heer arriued this yeer 1612, by which
I do vnderstand that you have receued my letter which I sent
by Peetter Johnssoon, of which I am veri glad, hoping yt my
poor wyf and frindes shall heer I am alyve.   For vnto this
pressent ther hath not coum to ye hands of my frinds anny
letter of myne : being by the Hollanders intercepted alwayes :
for by the company of thees ship I haue sertain newes of

trewth yt it is exprsressley forbid by the Winthabers so called, or Indish Company, yt they shall carri nor bring anny letters in no maner of wayes : for by both thees shipes I have had diuers letteers sent me by my wyf and other good frinds out of Ingland and Holland, but feaw coum to my hand and thooss yt I hau receued the most part were 2 lettrs which cam from London by the convayance of the Gloob of London, which arriued at Pattania [. . . . . .] which is heer arriued : which 2 lettrs, the on is from [*? the honour-able Sir*] Thomass Smith, and on from my good frind John Stokle, soum tym on of the [. . . . . .]. Thees 2 lettrs hau not bin oppened, but a 40 or 50 dayes detayned from mee, etc.

Some words obliterated by a crease in the paper.

You shall [*? understand*] by the letter of Sr Thomass Smith, he hath written that he will send a ship heer in Japan to establish a facktori, of which, yf yt may be profitt I shalbe most glad : of which newes I told the Emperour thearof, and told him yt in ye next yeer the kinges ma$^{ti.}$ of Ingland would send his imbashador with mony and marchandiz to trad in his country ; and of the certenti theerof I had receued newes. At which hee wass veery glad, and rejoyced that strange nacions had such good oppinion : with many other good speeches. Now, my good frind, if it so fall out that on of our country shipes do coum heer to traffick thear [. . . . . .] not lee [. . . . . .] welcoum. And this I do inseur you of, for it is in my power to do it. I doo prayss God for it : who hath geuen me fauor with the Emperour, and good will to me, so farr as that I may boldly say our country men shalbe so welcoum and free in coumparisson as in the riuer of London.

And now to the purpose. I feear yt theer wilbe no profitt, which is principall : for ye coumodeties of our countri are heer good cheep, yt is clloth ; for by reason of the ship that comes from Novo Spaynia of the on party and the Hollanders on the other party, hath made the priss of cloth so good chep as in Ingland. An 8 or 9 years ago cloth was very deer, but

now verry chep. Now the coumodities yt yē bring from Holland are theess: cloth, leed, still [*steel*], louking glasses, drinking glasses, dans-klass-glasses, amber, dieeper and holland,
with other things of small importance. First of ther cloth
no profitt; leed at [. . . . . .] the l., or lees, 3d the which is
no profitt; steel 6d the l. and other things of small profitt.
By ye way [. . . . .] them bring peper, the priss thearof 40s.
the 100l.; clouess 5l. starlinge the 100l. and thees [. . . . .]
and the priss thay sell them for. The ship that coums from
Pattania [. . . . . .] of all prisses, damas, taffety, velvett,
satten, Brassill to dye with. All other china coumodities yt
[. . . . . .] is not sartain becass soum yeers good cheep, and
soum yeer deer [. . . . . .] of chinas goods they mad great
proffit at first. As the shipes coum lade, so thay go away
much deeper lade, for heer [? *they*] lad thear shipes with
rise, fish, bisket, with diuers other prouisions, monicion
[? *munition*], marriners, sojoures, and svch lyk, so that in
respeckt of the warres in the Mollowcouss [*Moluccas*] Jappan
is verry profittable vnto them; and yf the warres do continew
in ye Mollucous with ye traffick thay haue heer wilbe a greate
scourge vnto ye Spaynnards, etc.

Now my good frind: can our Inglish marchants get the
handelling or trad with the Chinas, then shall our countri
mak great profitt, and the worshippful Indiss Coumpany of
London shall not hau need to send monny out of Ingland,
for in Japan is gold and siluer in aboundance, for with the
traffick heer they shall hau monny to serue theer need; I
mean in the Indiss, etc.

The Hollandes be now settled, and I hau got them that
priuilledg as the Spaynnards and Portingalles could neuer
gett in this 50 or 60 yeers in Japan, etc.

This yeer 1612 the Spaynnards and Portingalles hau
evssed me as an instrument to gett there liberty in the
maner of the Hollandes, but vppon consideration of farther
inconvenience I hau not sought it for them.

It hath plessed God to bring things to pass, so as in ye eyes of ye world [? *must seem*] strange: for the Spaynnard and Portingall hath bin my bitter ennemis, to death; and now theay must seek to me an vnworth wr[*et*]ch: for the Spaynard as well as the Portingall must haue all their negosshes [? *negociations*] go thorough my hand. God hau ye prayse for it, etc.

The charges in Japan are not great: onlly a pressent for ye Emperour and a pressent for ye Kinge, and 2 or 3 other pressents for the Secretaris. Other coustoumes here be nonn. Now, once, yf a ship do coum, lett her coum for the esterly part of Japan, lying in 35d. 10m. whear the Kinge and ye Emperour court is: for coum our ships to Ferando whear the Hollanders bee, it is farr to ye court, about 230L., a wery soum way and foul. The citti of Edo lyeth in 36, and about this esterly part of the land thear be the best harbors and a cost so cleer as theayr is no sholdes nor rokes ½ a myll from the mayn land. It is good also for sale of marchandis and security for ships, forr which cass I haue sent a pattron [? *pattern, card, or chart*] of Japan, for which my self I hau been all about the cost in the shipping that I haue made for ye Emperour, that I hau experyence of all yt part of ye cost that lyeth in 36d., etc.

Now my good frind: I thank you for your good writting and frindly token of a byble and 3 other boukes. By your letter I vnderstand of ye death of many of my good frinds in the barbarous country of Barbary: for which death, and los of goods I am heartelie sorry. Nevertheles it is ye lot of all flesh: in this lyf manny trobelles and afflixcions, and in the end death. Thearfor it is a blessed thing to dy in the Lord, with a faithfull trust in God: for theay rest from theer labores, etc.

In this land is no strange newes to sertify you of: the whool being in peace: the peopell veri subiect to thear gouvernours and superiores: allso in thear relligion veri zellous, or svpersticious, hauing diuers secttes, but praying all them secttes, or the most part, to one saynt which they call AMEEDA : which they esteem to bee their mediator between God and them : all theess sectes liuing in frindship on with an other, not [. . . . .] on an other, but everi on as his conscience teacheth. In this land are many Christians according to ye romishe order. In the yeer 1612 is put downe all the sects of the Franciscannes. The Jesouets hau what priuiledge [. . . . . .] theare beinge in Nangasaki, in which place only may be so manny as will of all sectes : in other places not manny permitted. In justis very seuer, hauing no respecte of persons. Theer cittis gouerned with greatt ciuility and in lou : for ye most part nonn going to lawe on with an other; but yf questiones be bettween naybour and naybour, it is by justiss coummanded to be pressently taken vp, and frindship to be mad with out dellay. No theef for ye most part put in prisson, but pressently executed. No murther for ye most part can escap : for yf so bee yt yt murtherer cannot be found, ye Emperour coumands a proclimacion with a wryting, and by ye wrytting so mvch gold as is of vallew 300l. starlinge; and yf anny do know whear ye murtherer is, he cooms and receueth the gold, and goeth his way with out anny further troubell. Thus for the lukar of so moch monny it coumes to light. And their citties you may go all ower in ye night with out any trobell or perrill, being a peepell [? *well affected*] to strangers : ye lawe much lyk the Jud [. . . . . . .] truth. Thus by the way, in hast I hau imboldned [? *myself*] to writ somewhat of ye coustome and manners, etc.

If it bee yt thear coum a ship neer vnto the estermost part, let them inquir for me. I am called in the Japann tonge AUGIU SAMMA. By that nam am I knowen all the sea cost allonge, and feear not to coom neer the mayn, for you shall hau barkes with pillotts yt shall carry you wheer you will; and coumes thear a ship hcer, I hop the wourshippfull coumpani shall find me to bee a saruant of yr saruants to seru them in such a maner as they shalbe satisfied of my serues. Thus yf occasion semeth, I pray wryt my hombell sallutacion to ye wourshippfull Sr Thomass Smyth; and consserning his Christian charity and greate lou in lending my wyf 20l. starlling, God I hop will reward him; and I am, and shalbe allwayes reddy to make paiment to whoum he shall apoynt me. I pray yt capptain Stippon, capptain of the Gllobe [. . . . .] I pray him to mak known in Ingland to my frinds, that I am in good health, and I trust in God errlong to gett leeaue from the Emperour to get out of this country to my frinds agayne. Thus with this my poor request do I imbold my seelf to troubell you. Had I known our Inglish shipes hade trade with the Indiss, I had long a[go] troubled you with wrytting; but the Hollanders hau kept it most seccreet from me tell the yeere 1611, which wass the first newes yt I heerd of the trading of our shipes in the Indiss. I would gladdly a sent soum small token in signe of good will vnto you, but at this pressent no conuenient messadg [? *message, or opportunity of sending*]. For thes ships ass theay saye go no far [*ther*] as the Mollocouss in his coummand. Thus with my coummendacion only, and to all my countrimen, I beque[*ath*] you and your affares to the tuicion of God, who blless and keep you in body and soull from all your ennemys for euer and euer.

Your vnwourthe frind yet assured to coumand,

WILLIAM ADDAMES.[1]

I hau writt 2 letters all in on maner, so yt yf on coumes to your hand I shall be glad.

---

[1] E. I. Mss. *Japan Series.*

## 𝔏𝔢𝔱𝔱𝔢𝔯 𝔑𝔬. 𝔌𝔚.

---

INTRODUCTION.

In conformity with the intimation communicated by Sir Thomas Smith to William Adams, of the intention of the East India Fellowship to seek trade with Japon, CAPTAIN JOHN SARIS, in command of the CLOVE, was despatched on a mission to the EMPEROR: being accredited with a letter, and charged with presents, from the Sovereign of England, JAMES THE FIRST.

The Clove came to anchor in the vicinity of *Firando*, one of the Japonese islands, on the 11th of June, 1613. The arrival of the vessel was marked by many circumstances of highly interesting character; and the commander was greeted with no less cordiality than courtesy. These matters are fully set forth in his narrative, which is as follows:

CAPTAIN SARIS: HIS ARRIVAL AT FIRANDO, AND HIS INTER-
TAYNMENT.

The ninth [of June, 1613] in the morning wee had sight of land, bearing north north-east, and sixe great islands on a ranke. From the island we descried yesternight north-east and south-west, and at the northermost end of them all, many small rockes and hummockes, and in the bay to the eastward of the hummockes we saw an high land bearing east, east by south, and east south-east, which is the island called *Xima* in the Plats, but called by the naturals *Mashma*, and the island aforesaid, north north-east, is called *Segue* or *Amaxay*: it lyeth east by north, and west by south, with many small islands and rockes on the southerne side of them, and is distant from the island with the steepe point, (which wee did see the eight day) south south-west twelue leagues,

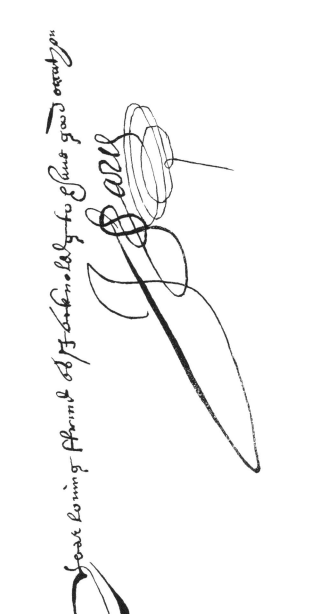

Your loving Friend & fellow labourer to serve you & yours
Barw

the winde calme all night, yet we got to the northward, as wee supposed, by the helpe of a current or tide.

The tenth, by breake of day the outward-most land to the westward did beare north by east ten leagues off, the wind at north-east by north: at nine, a gale at south, wee steered north by west, and had sight of two hummockes without the point. Then wee steered north north-west, and soone after came foure great fisher-boats aboord, about fiue tunnes apeece in burthen, they sailed with one saile, which stood like a skiffe saile, and skuld with foure oares on a side, their oares resting vpon a pinne fastned on the toppe of the boats side, the head of which pinne was so let into the middle part of the oare, that the oare did hang in his iust poize, so that the labour of the rower is much lesse, then otherwise it must be; yet doe they make farre greater speed then our people with rowing, and performe their worke standing, as ours doe sitting, so that they take the lesse roome. They told vs that we were before the entrance of *Nangasaque*, bearing north north-east, and the straights of *Arima*, north-east by north, and the high hill, which we did see yesterday, is vpon the island called *Vszideke*, which maketh the straights of *Arima*, where at the norther-most end is good riding, and at the south end is the going into *Cachinoch*. To this noone we haue made a north-way sixe leagues. Wee agreed with two of the masters of the fisher-boats (for thirtie rialls of eight a piece in money, and rice for their food) to pilot vs into *Firando*; which agreement made, their people entred our shippe, and performed voluntarily their labour, as readily as any of our mariners. We steered north by west, the pilots making account to be thirtie leagues off *Firando*. One of the foure boats which came aboord vs, did belong to the *Portugals*, living at *Langasaque*, and were new *Christians*, and thought that our ship had been the *Macau* ship; but finding the contrary, would vpon no intreatie stay, but made hast backe againe to aduise them.

The eleuenth, about three of the clocke in the afternoone, we cam to an anchor halfe a league short of *Firando,* the tide so spent that we could not get further in: soone after I was visited by the old king *Foyne Sama,* and his nephew *Tone Sama,* gouernour then of the iland vnder the old king. They were attended with fortie boats or gallyes, rowed some with ten, some with fifteene oares on a side: when they drew neare to the ship, the king commanded all, but the two wherein himselfe and his nephew were, to fall a sterne, and they only entred the ship, both of them in silk gownes, girt to them with a shirt, and a paire of breeches of flaxen cloath next their bodies. Either of them had two cattans or swords of that countrey by his side, the one of halfe a yard long, the other about a quarter. They wore no bands, the fore-parts of their heads were shauen to the crowne, and the rest of their haire, which was very long, was gathered together and bound vp on a knot behind, wearing neither hat nor turbant, but bare-headed. The king was aged about seuentie two yeeres, his nephew or grand-child, that gouerned under him, was about two and twentie yeeres old, and either of them had his gouernour with him, who had command ouer their slaues, as they appointed him.

Their manner and curtesie in saluting was after their manner, which is this. First, in presence of him whom they are to salute, they put off their shooes (stockings they weare none) and then clapping their right hand within their left, they put them downe towards their knees, and so wagging or mouing of their hands a little to and fro, they stooping, steppe with small steps sideling from the partie saluted, aud crie *Augh, Augh.* I led them into my cabbin, where I had prepared a banquet for them, and a good consort of musicke, which much delighted them. They bade me welcome, and promised me kind entertainment. I deliuered our kings letters to the king of *Firando,* which he receiued with great ioy, saying hee would not open it till *Auge* came, who could interpret the same vnto him; this *Auge* is, in their language, a pilot, being one *William Adams*, an *English* man, who, passing with a *Flemming* through the South Sea, by mutiny and disorder of the marriners shee remained in that countrey, and was seised vpon by the emperour about twelue years before. The king hauing stayed aboord about an houre and a halfe, tooke his leaue: he was no sooner ashoare, but all his nobilitie, attended with a multitude of souldiers, entered the ship, euery man of worth brought his present with him, some venison, some wild-fowle, some wild-boare, the largest and fattest that euer any of vs had seene, some fruits, fish, etc. They did much admire our shippe, and made as if they had neuer seene it sufficiently. We being pestered with the number of these visiters, I sent to the king, requesting him that order might bee taken to remoue them, and to preuent all inconueniences that might happen. Whereupon hee sent a guardian, (being a principall man of his owne guard) with charge to remain and lye aboord, that no injury might be offered vnto vs; and caused a proclamation to be made in the towne to the same effect. The same night *Henrick Brower*, captain of the *Dutch* factory there, came aboord to visite me, or rather to see what passed betwixt the king and vs. I did write the same day to master *Adams* (being then at *Edoo*, which is very neare three hundred leagues from *Firando*) to let him vnderstand of our arriual. King *Foyne* sent it away the next day by his Admirail to *Osackay*, the first port of note vpon the chiefe island, and then by post vp into the land to *Edoo*: giuing the emperour likewise to vnderstand of our being there, and cause thereof.

The twelfth in the morning, there was brought aboord such abundance of fish, and so cheape as we could desire. We weighed and set sail for the road. The king sent at the least threscore great boats or gallyes very well mand, to bring vs into the harbor. I doubted what the cause of their cōming might be, and was sending off the skiffe to cōmand them

H

not to come neare the ship, but the king being the head-most,
weaued with his handkercher, and willed the rest to attend,
and himselfe comming aboord, told me that he had commanded them to come to tow our ship in about a point, somewhat dangerous, by reason of the force of the tide, which
was such, that hauing a stiffe gale of wind, yet we could not
stemme it, and comming into the eddie, we should haue been
set vpon the rockes. So we sent hawsers aboord them,
and they fell to worke. In the meane while the king did
breake his fast with me. Being at an anchor, I would haue
requited the people for their paines, but the king would not
suffer them to take any thing. Wee anchored before the
towne in fiue fathome, so near the shoare, that we might
talke to the people in their houses. We saluted the towne
with nine peeces of ordnance, but were not answered, for
they haue no ordnance heere, nor any fort, but barricados
only for small shot. Our ground heere was ozie. Diuers
noblemen came to bid me welcome, whereof two were of extraordinary account, called *Nobusane* and *Simmadone*, who
were very well entertained, and at parting held very great
state, one staying aboord whilest the other was landed ;
their children and chiefe followers in the like manner. There
came continually such a world of people aboord, both men
and women, as that we were not able to go vpon the decks :
round about the ship was furnished with boats full of people,
admiring much the head and sterne of the ship. I gaue
leaue to diuers women of the better sort to come into my
Cabbin, where the picture of *Venus*, with her sonne *Cupid*,
did hang somewhat wantonly set out in a large frame. They
thinking it to bee our ladie and her sonne, fell downe and
worshipped it, with shewes of great deuotion, telling me in a
whispering manner (that some of their own companions which
were not so, might not heare) that they were *Christianos* :
whereby we perceiued them to be *Christians*, conuerted by
the *Portugall* Iesuits.

The king came aboord againe, and brought foure chiefe women with him. They were attired in gownes of silke, clapt the one skirt ouer the other ,and so girt to them, bare-legged, only a paire of halfe buskins bound with silke riband about their instep ; their haire very blacke, and very long, tyed vp in a knot vpon the crowne in a comely manner : their heads no where shauen as the mens were. They were well faced, handed, and footed ; cleare skind and white, but wanting colour, which they amend by arte. Of stature low, but very fat ; very curteous in behauiour, not ignorant of the respect to be giuen vnto persons according to their fashion. The king requested that none might stay in the cabbin, saue myself and my Linguist, who was borne in *Iapan,* and was brought from *Bantam* in our ship thither, being well skild in the *Mallayan* tongue, wherein he deliuered to mee what the king spoke vnto him in the *Iapan* language. The kings women seemed to be somewhat bashfull, but he willed them to bee frolicke. They sung diuers songs, and played vpon certain instruments (whereof one did much resemble our lute) being bellyed like it, but longer in the necke, and fretted like ours, but had only foure gut strings. Their fingring with the left hand like ours, very nimbly, but the right hand striketh with an iuory bone, as we vse to playe vpon a citterne with a quill. They delighted themselues much with their musicke, keeping time with their hands, and playing and singing by booke, pricked on line and space, resembling much ours heere. I feasted them, and presented them with diuers *English* comodities : and after some two houres stay they returned. I moued the king for a house, which hee readily granted, and tooke two of the merchants along with him, and shewed them three or foure houses, willing them to take their choice, paying the owners as they could agree.

The thirteenth, I went ashoare, attended vpon by the merchants and principal officers, and deliuered the presents to the king, amounting to the value of one hundred and fortie

pounds, or thereabouts, which he receiued with very great
kindnesse, feasting me and my whole companie with diuers
sorts of powdered wild fowles and fruits : and calling for a
standing cup (which was one of the presents then deliuered
him) he caused it to be filled with his country wine, which
is distilled out of rice, and is as strong as our *Aquauitæ* : and
albeit the cuppe held vpward of a pint and half, notwithstanding taking the cup in his hand, he told me hee would drinke
it all off, for health to the king of *England,* and so did myself, and all his nobles doing the like.   And whereas in the
roome where the king was, there was onely my self and the
cape merchant, (the rest of our company being in an other
roome) the king commanded his secretarie to goe out vnto
them, and see that euerie one of them did pledge the health.
The king and his nobles did sit at meat crosse-legged vpon
mats after the *Turkie* fashion, the mats richly edged, some
with cloath of gold, some with veluet, satten, and damask.

The fourteenth and fifteenth, we spent with giuing of presents.   The sixteenth, I concluded with captain *Andassee,*
captain of the *China* quarter here, for his house, to pay ninetie fiue ryals of eight for the monson of six moneths, he to
repair it at present, and wee to repair it hereafter, and alter
what we pleased : he to furnish all conuenient roomes with
mats according to the fashion of the Countrey.

This day our ship was so pestered with people, as that I
was enforced to send to the king for a guardian to clear them
out, many things been stolne, but I more doubted our owne
people, than the naturals.   There came in a *Flemming* in one
of the Countrey boates, which had been at the Island *Mashma,* where he had sold good store of Pepper, broad Cloth,
and Elephants teeth, but would not be aknowne vnto vs to
haue sold any thing, yet brought nothing backe in the boat
with him.   But the *Iapons* his waterman told vs the truth,
*viz.* that he had sold good quantitie of goods at a Mart
there, and returned with barres of siluer, which they kept
very secret.

The one and twentieth, the old King came aboord againe, and brought with him diuers women to be frolicke. These women were actors of comedies, which passe there from iland to iland to play, as our players doe here from towne to towne, hauing seuerall shifts of apparrell for the better grace of the matter acted ; which for the most part are of Warre, Loue, and such like.     These women are as the slaues of one man, who putteth a price what euery man shall pay that hath to doe with any of them ; more than which he is not to take vpon paine of death, in case the partie iniured shall complaine. It is left to his owne discretion to prize her at the first, but rise he cannot afterwards, fall he may.     Neither doth the partie bargaine with the wench, but with her master, whose command she is to obey.     The greatest of their nobilitie trauelling hold it no disgrace to send for these Panders to their Inne, and do compound with them for the wenches, either to fill their drinke at table (for all men of any rank haue their drinke filled to thē by women)or otherwise to haue the vse of them.     When any of these panders die (though in their life time they were receiued into company of the best, yet now as vnworthy to rest among the worst) they are bridled with a bridle made of straw, as you would bridle an horse, and in the cloathes they died in, are dragged through the streetes into the fields, and there cast vpon a dunghill, for dogges and fowles to deuoure.

The twentie ninth, a Soma or Iunke of the *Flemmings* arriued at *Langasaque,* from *Syam,* laden with Brasill wood and skins of all sorts, wherein it was said that there were *Englishmen,* but proued to be *Flemmings.*     For that before our comming, thē passed generally by the name of *Englishmen;* for our *English* Nation hath been long known by report among them, but much scandalled by the *Portugals* Iesuites, as pyrats and rovers upon the seas ; so that the naturals haue a song which they call the *English Crofonia,* shewing how the *English* doe take the *Spanish* ships, which they (singing) doe act likewise in gesture with their *Cattans* by their sides, with which song and acting, they terrifie and skare their children, as the *French* sometimes did theirs with the name of the Lord *Talbot*.

The first of Iuly, two of our Company happened to quarrell the one with the other, and were very likely to haue gone into the field, to the endangering of vs all. For it is a custome here, that whosoeuer drawes a weapon in anger, although he doe no harme therewith, hee is presently cut in peeces : and doing but small hurt, not only themselues are so executed, but their whole generation.

The seuenth, the King of the Iland *Goto*, not farre from *Firando* came to visit King *Foyne*, saying, that he had heard of an excellent *English* ship arriued in his dominions, which he greatly desired to see, and goe aboord of. King *Foyne* intreated me that he might be permitted, for that hee was an especial friend of his. So he was well entertained aboord, banqueted, and had diuers peeces shot off at his departure, which he very kindly accepted, and told me, that hee should bee right glad to liue to see some of our nation to come to his Iland, whither they should be heartily welcome.

The eighth, three *Iaponians* were executed, *viz.* two men and one woman : the cause this ; the woman none of the honestest (her husband being trauelled from home) had appointed these two their seuerall houres to repair vnto her. The latter man not knowing of the former, and thinking the time too long, comming in before the houre appointed, found the first man with her already, and enraged thereat, he whipt out his cattan, and wounded both of them very sorely, hauing very neere hewne the chine of the mans back in two. But as well as he might hee cleared himselfe of the woman, and recouering his cattan, wounded the other. The street taking notice of the fray, forthwith seased vpon them, led them aside, and acquainted King *Foyne* therewith, and sent to know his pleasure, (for according to his will, the partie is executed) who presently gaue order that they should cut off their heads: which done, euery man that listed (as very many did) came to trie the sharpenesse of their cattans vpon the corps, so that before they left off, they had hewne them all three into peeces as small as a mans hand, and yet notwithstanding did not then giue ouer, but placing the peeces one vpon another, would try how many of them they could strike through at a blow; and the peeces are left to the fowles to deuoure.

The tenth, three more were executed as the former, for stealing of a woman from *Firando*, and selling her at *Langasacque* long since, two of them were brethren, and the other a sharer with them. When any are to be executed, they are led out of the towne in this manner: there goeth first one with a pick-axe, next followeth an other with a shouell for to make his graue (if that bee permitted him), the third man beareth a small table whereon is written the parties offence, which table is afterwards set vp vpon a post on the graue where he is buried. The fourth is the partie to be executed, his hands bound behind him with a silken cord, hauing a litle banner of paper (much resembling our wind-vanes) whereon is likewise written his offence. The executioner followeth next, with his cattan by his side, holding in his hand the cord wherewith the offender is bound. On either side of the executioner goeth a souldiour with his pike, the head thereof resting on the shoulder of the partie appointed to suffer, to skare him from attempting to escape. In this very manner I saw one led to execution, who went so resolutely and without all appearance of feare of death, that I could not but much admire him, neuer hauing seene the like in Christendome. The offence for which he suffered was for stealing of a sacke of rice (of the value of two shillings six pence) from his neighbour, whose house was then on fire.

The nineteenth, the old King *Foyne* entreated me for a peece of Poldauis,[1] which I sent him; hee caused it presently

[1] POLDAUIS. Coarse linen, resembling *canvas* in texture.

to be made into coates, which he (notwithstanding that hee was a King, and of that great age, and famed to be the worthiest soldiour of all *Iapan*, for his valour and seruice in the *Corean* warres) did wear next his skinne, and some part thereof was made into handkerchiefes, which he daily vsed.

The nine and twentieth, M. *Adams* arriued at *Firando*, hauing been seuenteene dayes on the way comming from *Sorongo*, we hauing staied here for his comming fortie eight dayes. After I had friendly entertained him, I conferred with him in the presence of the merchants, touching the incouragement hee could giue of trade in these parts. He answered, that it was not alwaies alike, but sometime better, sometimes worse, yet doubted not but we should doe as well as others ; giuing admirable commendations of the Countrey, as much affected thereunto.

The third of August 1613, king *Foyne* sent to know of what bulk our kings present to the Emperour was, also what number of people I would take with me, for that he would prouide accordingly for my going vp in good fashion both for barke, horses, and pallanchins.

This day, I caused the presents to be sorted that were to be giuen to the emperour. and to those of office and esteeme about him. *viz* :

|  | £ | s. | d. |
|---|---|---|---|
| To *Ogoshosama*, the emperour, to the value of | 87 | 7 | 6 |
| To *Shongosama*, the emperours sonne . . . | 43 | 15 | 0 |
| To *Codskedona*, the emperours secretarie . . | 15 | 17 | 6 |
| To *Saddadona*, the emperours sonnes secretarie | 14 | 03 | 4 |
| To *Icocora Inga*, Iudge of *Meaco* . . . . | 04 | 10 | 6 |
| To *Fongo dona*, admirall of *Orango* . . . . | 03 | 10 | 0 |
| To *Goto Shozauero*, the mintmaster . . . . | 11 | 00 | 0 |
| Totall . . | 180 | 03 | 10[1] |

[1] *Purchas*, vol. i, page 366, etc.

The Almighti god by whome all enterprises and honours han hear full effect be blessed for ever amen

By your honourd servant and unknowne frinde faythfull to Commaunde

william Adames.

# WILLIAM ADAMS: HIS LETTER.

[*Endorsed*: " A vearey Larg Letter wrot from Japan by William
Adams, and sent home in the Cloue, 1614, touching of his assistance
rendred vnto ye Generall and of entertanem[t] into the Companies
Seruice. Decem. 1613."]

The Allmightye God by whoum all enterprisses and pur-
poosses hau thear full effect be bllessed for euer. Amen.

Right Woorshipfulls, hauing ssoo just occacion, I haue
imboldned my self although unwourth to writt thees feau
vnwourthy lines vnto you: in which first of all I crau your
woorships pardon in whatt I shall fayll in.

Hauing thorough the prouidenc of God ariued on of your
shipes called the Cloue, being Gennerall or Captain John
Sarris, who at his first ariuall in the Iland of Ferando sent a
letter vnto me, in all hast to haue me coum to him: vntill
svch tym he would tarri for me. Ye which so sooun as I had
receued his letter, I made no dellai, being at that tym at the
courte, being distant from the place of the ships ariuall 250
llegs. So coomming to the place of the ships ariual, I wass
gladly receued of the Gennerall and Master and all the wholl
covmpani. At which tym we did enter in to consultacon
what courss was to be taken: the Gennerall making knowen
vnto me that he had brought his Majesti [a] letter with a prees-
sent for him. Vppon which for the honner of his Mti. and
our covntri, both, I with him thought it good to mak all
speed and to go to the courte for the delliueranc thearof, etc.

I allso entred into speech with him what covmodites he
had brought with him: of which he made all thinges to mee
known. So finding that svch thinges as he had brought wass
not veri vendibel; I told him, for his arivall I was veri glad
theerof, but in respecte of the ventur by the wourshipfull

I

covmpani being so great, I did not see anny wayss in this land to requit the great charges therof. My reesson wass, for theer cloth at this pressent was very cheep, becass both from Nova Spania, Manilia, and ovt of Holland, which in thees 4 yeers there caem very mvch : soum sold and verry mvch vnsold. For *olliphant teeth* the Hollanders had brought aboundanc, that the priss theroff was fallen very mvch : vppon which occassion the Hollanders hau transported manny therof to Siam. *Stylle* [*steel*] in long barres still holding his old prise at 20 crownes the picoll, which is 125l. Inglish wayt, and sovmtymes being coum worth 3l. 15s. starling. *Leed,* [*lead*] holding his priss a llittell mor or less at 25s. and sovmtymes 30s. the picoll. *Tin* so good cheep heer as in Ingland, and *ordinance* not in any great request : not the picoll abou 30s. and sovmtym vnder. For *callecovs* and fine *Cambaya goods;* not in any request, becass this countri hath abovndanc of cotten. Thus for thoos thinges. Now for *peeper* and *cloues.* This covntri doth not evs [*use*] verri mvch therof, nor of any other spice : for which case senc [*since*] the trad of the Hollanders which hau brought mvch peper and cloues, that peper the pownd is noe more worth then 5d. a pownd, and soumtymes less, and at the deerest 6d. and cloues at 12d., which is of no proffit to bring hether. Affoor tym, when the Spaynard had the trad with the Jappanners, onlly, the peper was at 12d. the L. and cloues at 2s. 6d. and 3s. the L. : now being ouerlayd is verry chep, etc.

Thus hauing confferred heer vppon, the gennerall mad him self redy to go with me to the court : of which with all hast prosseeded theerof, etc.

### THE JOURNEY VP TO THE COURTE.[1]

THE seuenth of August, King *Foyne* furnished me with a proper galley of his owne rowed with twentie fiue oares on a side,

---

[1] The following account of the journey is given from the Narrative of Captain Saris (*Purchas*, vol. i, p. 370, etc.) ; Adams having omitted the particulars.

and sixtie men, which I did fit vp in a verie comely manner,
with waste cloathes, ensignes, and all other necessaries, and
hauing taken my leaue of the King, I went and remained
aboord the ship, to set all things in order before my departure.—Which done, and remembrances left with the master
and Cāpe merchant, for the well gouerning of the ship and
house ashoare during my absence, taking with mee tenne
*English*, and nine others, besides the former sixtie, which
were only to attend the gallie, I departed from *Firando* towards the Emperours court.  Wee were rowed through, and
amongst diuers Ilands, all of which, or the most part of them,
were well inhabited, and diuers proper townes builded vpon
them; whereof one called *Faccate*, hath a very strong castle,
built of free-stone, but no ordnance nor souldiers therein.
It hath a ditch about fiue fathome deepe, and twice as broad
round about it, with a draw bridge, kept all in very good re-
paire.  I did land and dine there in the towne, the tyde and
wind so strong against vs, as that we could not passe.  The towne
seemed to be as great as *London* is within the wals, very wel
built, and euen, so as you may see from the one end of the
street to the other.  The place exceedingly peopled, very
ciuil and curteous, only that at our landing, and being here
in *Faccate*, and so through the whole country, withersoeuer
we came, the boyes, children, and worser sort of idle people,
would gather about and follow along after vs, crying, *Coré,
Coré, Cocoré, Waré,* that is to say, *You Coréans with false
hearts:*[1] wondering, hooping, hollowing, and making such a
noise about vs, that we could scarcely heare one an other
speake, sometimes throwing stones at vs (but that not in
many townes) yet the clamour and crying after vs was euery
where alike, none reproouing them for it.  The best aduice
that I can giue those who hereafter shall arriue there, is

---

[1] In the recent wars between the Japonese and the Coreans, the latter
had practised many acts of the basest treachery, and were inveterately
hated by the people of the Empire.

that they passe on without regarding those *idle rablements,* and in so doing, they shall find theer eares only troubled with the noise. All alongst this coast, and so vp to *Ozaca* we found women diuers, that liued with their household and family in boats vpon the water, as in *Holland* they do the like. These women would catch fish by diuing, which by net and lines they missed, and that in eight fathome depth: their eyes by continuall diuing doe grow as red as blood, whereby you may know a diuing woman from all other women.

We were two daies rowing from *Firando* to *Faccate.* About eight or tenne leagues on this side the straights of *Xemina-seque,* we found a great towne, where there lay in a docke, a iuncke of eight hundred or a thousand tunnes of burthen, sheathed all with yron, with a guard appointed to keep her from firing and treachery. She was built in a very homely fashion, much like that which describeth *Noahs* arke vnto vs. The naturals told vs, that she serued to transport souldiers into any of the Ilands, if rebellion or warre should happen.

We found nothing extraordinary after we had passed the straights of *Xemina-seque,* vntill we came vnto *Ozaca,* where we arriued the twenty seuenth day of August; our galley could not come neere the towne by six miles, where another smaller vessell met vs, wherein came the good man or host of the house where we lay in *Ozaca,* and brought a banquet with him of wine and salt fruits to intertaine me. The boat having a fast made to the mast-head, was drawn by men, as our barkes are from *London* westward. We found *Ozaca* to be a very great towne, as great as *London* within the walls, with many faire timber bridges of a great height, seruing to passe ouer a riuer there as wide as the *Thames* at *London.* Some faire houses we found there, but not many. It is one of the chiefe sea-ports of all *Iapan;* hauing a castle in it, maruellous large and strong, with very deepe trenches about it, and many draw bridges, with gates plated with yron.

The castle is built all of free-stone, with bulwarks and bat-tlements, with loope holes for smal shot and arrowes, and diuers passages for to cast stones vpon the assaylants. The walls are at the least sixe or seuen yards thicke, all (as I said) of free-stone, without any filling in the inward part with trumpery, as they reported vnto me. The stones are great, of an excellent quarry, and are cut so exactly to fit the place where they are laid, that no morter is used, but onely earth cast betweene to fill vp voyd creuises if any be. In this castle did dwell at our beeing there, the sonne of *Tiqua-samma*, who being an infant at the time of his fathers decease, was left to the gouernement and education of foure, whereof *Ogoshosamma*, the now Emperour, was one and chiefe. The other three desirous of soveraigntie each for his particular, and repulsed by *Ogoshosamma*, were for their owne safetie forced to take vp armes, wherein fortune fauouring *Ogosho-samma* at the triall in field, two of them beeing slaine, the third was glad to saue himselfe by flight. He beeing con-querour, attempted that which formerly (as it is thought) hee neuer dream'd of, and proclaimed himselfe Emperour, and seazing vpon the true heire, married him vnto his daughter, as the onely meanes to worke a perfect reconcilement, con-fining the young married couple to liue within this castle of *Ozaca*, attended onely with such as had been brought vp from their cradles by *Ogoshosamma*, not knowing any other father (as it were) then him : so that by their intelligence he could at all times vnderstand what passed there, and accordingly rule him.

Right ouer against *Ozaca*, on the other side of the riuer, lyeth another great Towne called *Sacay*, but not so bigge as *Ozaca*, yet is it a towne of great trade for all the Ilands thereabout.

The eight and twentieth day at night, hauing left musters and prices of our commodities with our host, we departed from *Ozaca* by barke towards *Fushimi*, where we ariued.

The nine and twentieth at night we found here a garrison
of three thousand souldiers maintayned by the emperour, to
keepe *Miaco* and *Ozaco* in subiection. The garrison is shifted
euery three yeares, which change happened to be at our being
there, so that we saw the old bands march away, and the new
enter, in most souldier-like manner, marching five a brest, and
to euerie ten files an officer which is called a captain of fiftie,
who kept them continually in verie good order.    First,
their shot, *viz.* calieuers, (for muskets they haue none, neyther will they vse any), then followed pikes, next swords, or
cattans and targets, then bowes and arrowes : next those,
weapons resembling a Welch-hooke called *waggadashes* ;
then calieuers again, and so as formerly, without any ensigne
or colours : neyther had they any drummes or other musical
instruments for warre.    The first file of the cattans and targets had siluer scabberds to there cattans, and the last file
which was next to the captain had their scabberds of gold.
The companies consists of divers numbers, some fiue hundred,
some three hundred, some one hundred and fiftie men.    In
the midst of euery companie were three horses very richly
trapped, aud furnished with sadles, well set out, some couered with costly furres, some with veluet, some with stammet
broad-cloth, euery horse had three slaues to attend him,
ledde with silken halters, their eyes couered with leather
couers.    After euery troope followed the captaine on horse
backe, his bed and other necessaries were laid vpon his owne
horse, equally peased [*poised*] on either side.    Ouer the same
was spread a couering of redde felt of *China*, whereupon the
captaine did sit crosse-legged, as if hee had sate betwixt a couple of panniers : and for those that were ancient or otherwise
weake-backt, they had a staff artificially fixed unto the pan-
nell, that the rider might rest himselfe, and leane backward
against it, as if he were sitting in a chaire.    The captaine
generall of this garrison wee met two dayes after we had met
his first troope, (hauing still in the mean-time met with some

of these companies as we passed along, sometimes one league, sometimes two leagues distant one from another.) Hee marched in very great state, beyond that the others did, (for the second troope was more richly set out in their armes then the first : and the third then the second, and so still euery one better then other, vntill it came vnto this the last and best of all.) He hunted and hawked all the way, hauing his owne hounds and hawkes along with him, the hawkes being hooded and lured as ours are. His horses for his owne sadle being sixe in number, richly trapped. Their horses are not tall, but of the size of our midling nags, short and well trust, small headed and very full of mettle, in my opinion farre excelling the *Spanish* iennet in pride and stomacke. He had his *pallankin* carryed before him, the inside crimson veluet, and sixe men appointed to carrie it, two at a time.

Such good order was taken for the passing and prouiding for, of these three thousand souldiers, that no man either trauelling or inhabiting vpon the way where they lodged. was any way iniured by them, but chiefly entertayned them as other their guests, because they paid for what they tooke, as all other men did. Euery towne and village vpon the way being well fitted with cookes and victualling houses, where they might at an instant haue what they needed, and dyet themselues from a pennie *English* a meale, to two shillings a meal.

The thirtieth, we were furnished with ninetene horse at the emperours charge, to carrie vp our Kings presents, and those that attended me to *Surunga.*

I had a *pallankin* appointed for me, and a spare horse led by, to ride when I pleased, very well set out. Sixe men appointed to carrie my *pallankin* in plaine and euen ground. But where the countrey grew hilly, ten men were allowed me thereto. The guardian whom king *Foyne* sent along with vs, did from time to time and place to place by warrant, take vp these men and horses to serue our turnes, as the postmasters doe here in *England*: as also lodgiug at night. According to the custome of the countrey, I had a slaue appointed to runne with a pike before mee.

Thus we trauelled vntill the sixth of September, before we got to *Surunga*, each day fifteene or sixteene leagues, of three miles to a league as we ghessed it. The way for the most part is wonderfull euen, and where it meeteth with mountaines, passage is cut through. This way is the mayne reade of all this countrey, and is for the most part sandie and grauell; it is diuided into leagues, and at euery leagues end are two small hils, *viz.* of either side of the way one, and vpon euery one of them a faire pine tree, trimmed round in fashion of an arbor. These markes are placed vpon the way to the end, that the hacknie men, and those which let out horses for hire, should not make men pay more then their due, which is about three pence a league. The roade is exceedingly trauelled, full of people, euer and anon you meet with farmes and countrey houses, with villages, and often with great townes, with ferries ouer fresh riuers, and many *Futtakeasse* or *Fotoquis*, which are their temples, scituate in groues and most pleasantest places for delight of the whole countrey. The priests that tend thereupon dwelling about the same, as our friers in old time planted themselues here in *England*. When wee approached any towne, we saw crosses with the dead bodies of those who had been crucified thereupon. For crucifying is heere an ordinarie punishment for most malefactors. Comming neere *Surunga*, where the Emperours court is, wee saw a scaffold with the heads of diuers (which had beene executed) placed thereupon, and by it were diuers crosses with the dead corpses of those which had been executed, remayning still vpon them, and the pieces of others, which after their executioners had beene hewen againe and againe by the triall of others *cattans*. All which caused a most vnsauourie passage to vs, that to enter into *Surunga*, must needs passe by them.

This citie of *Surunga* is full as big as *London,* with all the suburbs. The handi-crafts men wee found dwelling in the outward parts and skirts of the towne; because those that are of the better sort, dwell in the inward part of the citie, and will not be annoyed with the rapping, knocking, and other disturbance that artificers cannot be without.

### WILLIAM ADAMS : HIS LETTER CONTINEWED.

Comming to *Meaco* [? *Osacca*] had the kinge free hoorsses according to need to goo to the courte wher the emperour wass: at which plac of the genneralls ariuall, I made his couming knowen. So the first day after, being sovmwhat weery, rested and sovmwhat in fitting of the kinges pressents. So the next daye following being redy, the gennerall went to his ⌊*the emperour's*⌋ palles [*palace*] : being courteously receued and bid welcoum by the tresvrer and others. So being in the palles set downe, the gennerall called me and byd me tell the ssecretari, that the kinge mati. letter he would delliuer it with his own handes. Vppon which I went and told ye secretari thearof: at which he awnsswered, that it was not the covstoum of the land to delliuer anny letter with the hand of anny stranger, but that he should keep the letter in his hand till he cam into the pressence of the emperor; and then he would tak it from him ovt of his handes and delliuer it to the emperour. Which awnsser I told the generall theearof; at which awnsswer not being contented cassed me to tell the secretari that yf he myght not delliuer it himself he would retourn agayne to his loging. Which second awnsswer I told the secretari; the which awnsser, not thinking well therof, was disconted with me in that I had nott instruckted him in the manners and coustoum of all strangers which had bein yeerly in thir covntri; and made me again to go to the gennerall: the which I did; but the gennerall being verry mvch discontented, it so rested. At which tym, pressently, the emperour came fourth, and the

K

gennerall wass brought befoor him : to whoum the emperour bid him wellcovm of so weery journy, receuing his mati. letter from the gennerall by the handes of the secrittary, etc.

So the generall departed his way, and I wass called in : to whoum the emperor inquired of me of the kinges mati. of Ingland : consserning his greatnes and poovr [*power*], with diuers other questiones which wear to longe to wright. Onlly at ye last he byd me tell the gennerall, yt what request he had, yt he should mak it knowen to me, or to go to his ssecretary; he should be awnssered : which awnsser I re-turned to the gennerall. So the next day folowing the gen-nerall went with me to the ssecrettaris hovss, with whoum he mad known his demandes. The which being written wear caried befor the emperor. The which the emperor reead all his demandes, and hauing reed them told me that he should hau them. Hauing mvch talk with me of his covming, I told him to settell a factory in his land. He asked me in what plac. I told him, hereon, I did think not far from his court, or the kinges courtt : att which he seemed verry glad. And hauing had mvch speech heer and thear, he asked me if part of his covming was not for discouer [*i*] to farther partes to the northwestward, or, northwards. I told him our countri still douth not cees to spend mvch monny in discouer thearof. He asked me whether thear wear nott a way, and whear [? *whether*] it wass not verry short, or, neer. I told him we douted nott but thear is a way, and that veery neeir; at which tym called for a mappe of the wholl world, and so sawe that it wass very neer. Hauing speechis with me, whether we had no knolledg of a land lying hard by his countri, on the north part of his land, called Yedzoo and Mattesmay. I told him I did neuer see it pvt into anny mappe nor gllobe. I told him it myght bee that the wour-shipfull coumpany woould send soum ship, or other, to dis-couer. He told me that in the yeer of our Lord 1611, a ship

The Translation of the Emperor of
Japans privaledges Granted in the
name of the Right Honoured Knight
Sir Thomas Smith Governour of
the East India Company ffor the use
of the voyage &c

**Imprimis** we doe give free license to the King of Englands
subiects Sir Thomas Smith Governour and Compança
of East India Marchants ffor their safety To come into
any of portes or Empire of Japan with their shipps and
marchandize without any hinderaunce to them or their goods
**And** to a buse buy sell and Barter according to their owne manner
without all restraint **And** to tarry so long as they will And dept
at their pleasures

**Item** we Grant unto them three thousand tall boxe marcea
nowe as they stand or stand after tall being into our Kingdome
or shall transport to any forrein part **And** doe by these
presents Authorize the yeard after shipps to make present
sale of their commodities without further Somming or doing
any to the Court

**Item** if their shipp falle in danger to be lost And perish
wee will that the old Subiects not only ... their ...
what shalbe saved to returne it to the Captaine marchant or
their assignes **And** that you permit them to builte in any
part of the Empire where they thinke fitte **And** at
departure to make free saile of their goods howsoever at there
pleasure

**Item** if any of them shall die in these o Dominions the goods
of the deceased shalbe at the dispose of the Cappo: Marchant
**And** all offences Comitted by them shalbe at his said mercys
discretion to punnish **And** our Lawes to take no hould other
of their persons or goods

**Item** we will that yo e Subiects trading with them for
any their Commodities paye them according to agreement
without Delaye or returne of their wares.

**Item** all such their marchandize as yee at present or hereafter
shall bring & make for o serving we will that no abuse
be made them of **But** that present payment be made **And** at
such prices as the Cappo: Marchant can at present sett them sell.

**Item** we will that in discovery of any of other places of Trade
or returne of their shipps they shall want no other or
victualls **That** you o Subiects furnish them for their mony
at their needs shall require **And** that without o further
pass they shall sett out and Goe in Discovery for yeares
or any other part in or about o Empire / from o After
in Corougo this first daye of the 9 th munneth and in the 18 th
yeare of o Davy According to o Computation Sealde with
e brand Seale

mima mottono
xei ye yeas

wass seen of theis cost, on the est syde, in latitude of 38 d., or thearabout, whether that wear anny of our countri ship? I told him I thought not.  He told me agayn it could be no ship of ye Spaynnards going for Novo Spania: for this ship was seen in Apprill, which tym no ship goeth not from the Manillieus [*Manillas*].  He asked me yf I did deesir to go that waye.  I told hym, yf the wourshippful coumpanie should dessir svch a thing, I would willingly ymploy my self in svch an honorabell accion.  He told me yf I did go, he would geue [*give*] me his letter of frindship to the land of Yedzoo, whear his subiects haue frinship, hauing a stronge towne and a castell: thorough which menes haue 30 dayes joourney frindship with thoos pepell; which peopell be, as I do gather, Tartares joyning to the CAM, or borders of Cattay. Now in my sympel iudgment, yf the northwest passag be euer discouered, it wilbe discouered by this way of Jappan; and so thuss, with diuers other speechis most frindli evsed [*used*], I toouk [*took*] my leaue of him.

So the next day folowing, the gennerall mad him self reddy to go for Quanto, a province so called, whear the kinge, the emperors eldest sonn, is ressident, being distant from the emperours court soum 42 lleagues.  To which place we went, hauing in 4 or 5 dayes finnissed according to ye coustoum of the land, the gennerall being verri well entertayned.  So returned to the emperors courte agayne. At which place receuing the emperours commission and priuileges, mad our retourn for Ferrando.[1]

Now consserning my self.  Hauing dispached the gennerall bysiness, I did seek vnto the counsell to speak in my behalf, to get leeau [*leave*] to go hoom for my covntri; but the ssecretari, with no other, would not speak for my liberty to goo for my country, knowing that I had diuers tymes mad [*request*] and he would not let mee goo.  So I neuertheless mad my selfe soumwhat bold.  Finding the emperour in a good

---

[1] NOTE Y. *The Privileges.*

moud [*mood*], I took ovt of my boussom his broode seeall, consserning certtain lands, and layed it dounn beefore him, geuing his mati. most hvmbell thankes for his great fauor vnto mee, dessiring leaue to go for my countri. At which request he looked ernestli vppon mee, and asked me yf I wass dessirrovs to go for my country? I awnssered most dessirovs. He awnssered, yf he should dettain me, he should do me wrong; in so mvch, that in his seruis I had behaued my self well, with manny other woourds of coummendacions, the which I leaue. So I thank God got my lyberty ovt of my long and evill sarues [*service*]. With this toouk my leau of him, bidding me yf I did not think well of going this yeear, I should tarry tell other shipping came, and go as I wovld: telling me yt. yf I cam vp into the countri to bring sertain goodes which he named. So thuss, I thank God, being not littell joyfful retvrned with the gennerall to Ferrando, whear the ship wasse, etc.

So about a 15 dayes of my abod in Ferrando, it was the gennerall plleasur to call for mee, the cāpe marchant with others bein in pressenc, hauing wrytten cartain lynes vppon a sid of paper, calling me to [? *an ac*] count, and to know of mee what my intent wass, whether I would go hom with him, or tarry heer in this countri. I awnsswered him my desir wass to go houm to my countri. He asked me, now with him or no; I awnssered him, I had spent in this countri mani yeares, thorov which I wass poour: for which cass I wass dessirrouss to get soumthing befor my retourn. The reason I would not go with him wass for dyuers injerues [? *injurious things*] doun against me; the which were thinges to me veri strang and vnloked for, which thinges were wrytt I ceass,[1] leuing it to others to mak rellacion thereof. He asked me yf I would serue the coumpani. I awnssered, yees, veri willing. He asked me on what condisscion, whether I would tak the 20*l.* of grattis which the wourshipfull coumpany had lent my

---

[1] *? Regarding the things down against me, I refrain from writing.*

wyfe, and stand to their courtessi. ✷ First, I do most hvmbly thank the wourshipfull company for this deed of Christian charriti in the lending of my poour wyff the 20*l.* If euer I be abell, I will mak sattisfaxcion for the proffit therof, and for the principall hau heer mad sattisfaxcion to gennerall John Sarris, taking the byll of exchang, which diuers of my good frinds had giuen their wourds for payment therof, hauing theear hands firmed, and I thank all myghti God, that hath geuen me abilliti to mak payment therof. The tym wass manny yeares in this covntri, I hau not bin mr. of 20*s.*✷ I awnswered, yf I weer in pressenc of the wourship. coumpani, I would stand to anny thing they should think good of; bvt in this plac, was willing to haue soum sartanty. He still vrged mee with the 20*l.* lent to my wyff of grattis,[1] and stand to the coumpanis good will. I awnssered as at the first, again. Theay asked we what I would for a yeear. I told him, I hau neuer bin hired by the yeear, but by the month. He told me the coumpani did not hire anny man by the monneth, but by the yeear. I told him, I wass not willing to go by the yeer, but by the mounth. He asked me what I would ask a moñeth. I told him of strangers by whoum I hau bin imployed did geu mee 15*l.* the monnth, but I demanded 12*l.* the month. Vppon demand, he bade mee go ovt of the chamber a littell whill, and he would call me again. So I went away, and a littell whill afterward he called me again, and asked me yf I wass ressolued. I told him as at the first. So he bad mee the yeer 80*l.* I told him again, I would not. So in the end I told him not vnder 10*l.* the monnth, I would not serue, alledging I wass vnwilling to pvt the coumpany to svch a great charge, becass I did not see in Japan anny proffit to be mad to quit svch great wages, but rather to be free, for in respect of bennifit I had diuers mens [*means*] ofered me, to be mor to my proffit, which the gennerall knew of: dessir-

---

[1] From entries in commercial books of the period, it appears the term *gratis*, when applied to loans, etc., means *free from interest.*

ing ye gennerall to let mee be free, and to tak other orders, which weear for my furtheranc ; and not to be heer imployed, whear I saw no proffit coum in. Thus in the end, he proffited [? *proffered*] me 80*l*. and the 20*l*. geuen mee free which wass lent my wyff. I awnser him, no. So lett me dept. till the next day, at which tym I promissed to geu him a ressolut awnsser. So the next day, in the morning, sent for me again, [*asking*] whether I was ressolued, I sayd ass affor. So he awnssered me, I did exact vppon them to hau them to geu mee what I list. I told him again my mening was not so, for I could better my selfe a great dell more, onlly I wass not willing to searue, where, by my sarues I could not win so mvch for my masters, for which cass onlly and nothing ells. So demanding me still ernestly, proffered me 100*l*. the yeer; the which, in conssideracion I would not geu discontentment, but granted vnto it. So vppon this he did aske me how I would be paid it. I told him, heer in Japan. He said, none in his ship did receue not aboue a 3 pt beffor he cam hom : at which I awnssered, it might be so, bvt my cass was otherwyss, for I haue promyssed my sserues [*service*] no longer but svch tym as God shall send the Cloue in to Ingland, or awnsser of her ariual, and return of the wourshipfull companis awnsser, whether they will discouer to the norwest, or not. Thearfor, for me tarry so longe, and not to receu [*receive*] no wages heir, I would not mayntain my self with aparill and expences, with ovt receuing soom monny to mayntain my self in credit and clothes. So I agreed : which God grant his blessing vppon my labors, that I may be a proffitabell saruant vnto your wourship : which I hop in all myghti God I shalbe, etc.

Now consserning this discouerie to the norward. Yf it stand with your wourshipps liking, in my judgment neuer hath bin better menes to discouer. My ressons : First, this Kingdoum of Jappan, with whom we hav frindship : the emperador hath promyssed his assistance to you, his letter of frindship to the countri of Yedzoo and Matesmaye, whear his subiects are ressident. Secondly, langwiges, that can speak the Corea and Tartar langwage, for Japan langedge not to be reckined. For shipping : yf your wourship send not, yet you may hau bylded, or cass to be bylded, svch shipes or pinñces necessary for svch discoueri with lesse charges. Things ar heer good cheep, as tymber, plank, irroun, hemp, and carpenteres : only tarre heer is none ; rosen annouf, but verry deer. Thees thinges I hau experienc of, becass I hau byllt 2 shipes in this country for the emperor : the on of them sold to the Spaynnard vppon occacion, and the other I sayld in my selff vppon dyuers voyages uppon this cost. Now, the on of them that wass sold to the Spaynnards, wass vppon this occassion : that a great ship of 1000 tovnes, which cam from ye Manilia, which was cast away vppon this cost, whear in was the gouernor of Manilia, to whoum the emperor lent hir to carry him to Akapulca, a place in Nova Spaynia ; which ship theay found so good as theay neuer returned agayn, butt sent so mvch monny ass shee wass wourth, and afterwards wass imployed in the vyages from Nova Spaynia to the Phillipines. Sso that neuertheless by my profession I am no shippwright, yet I hop to make svch shipping as shalbe necessary for anny svch discouery. Now men to sayll with only excepted, the peopell are not acquaynted with our manner. Therfor, yf your wourshipps hau anny svch pvrposs, send me good marriners [*navigators*] to sayll with ; and yf you send but 15 or 20, or leess, it is no matter, for the peopell of this land are verri stoutt seea men, and in what way I shall go in, I can hau so manny as I will. Now for vytelling. Heir is in this land annouf and svch plenty, and so good cheep, as is in Ingland, as thoss who haue bin heer can satisfi your wourshipp therin. So that I say agayn, the wantes be coordish [*cordage*], pouldaues [*canvas*], and tarr, pich, or rossen, and coumpasses, rounning [*hour*] glasses, a payr of gllobes for demonstracion, and soum cardes [*charts*] or mapes, contayninge the wholl world. Thees thinges yf

your wourship do furnish me with, you shall find me not neg-
legent in svch an honorabell surues [*service*]: by God's grace.
Thus mvch I hau thought good to wrytt to your wourshipp,
being soumwhat longe in making the particullers apparent of
this di̇scource; which discource, I do trust in all myghti
God, should be on of the most famost that euer hath bin,
etc.

Now conserning the great kindnes which your wourshipps
hath shewed to me, in lending my wyf monny. I do still
crau your wourship coumpassion. What monny your wourship shall lend, by God's grace I will mak svch sattisfaccion
as shalbe to your dessir. Thearfor, I do again intreat your
wourshipes to lend my wyf 30*l.* or 40*l.*, tell it be the will of
God I coum hoom; and eyther heer to pay it, or els wher,
as you shall cõmand me, etc.

I do embolden my self to coummend me vnto your wourshipes: praying God all myghty to bless your wourship with
continewance of his grace, in health and prosperitie; and in
the lyf to coum euerlasting feliciti. Amen.

> By your vnwourth saruant and vnknown ffrind, yeat
> faythfvll to coummand tell death

William Addames.[1]

---

[1] E. I. Mss. *Japan Series.*

## Appendix to Letter No. IV.

*CONTRACT made with CAPT. WM. ADAMS, at Firando, in Japon, the 24th of November, 1613.*

*WHEREAS* ye. R. honourable companye, ye. marchants of London trading [*into*] ye. East Indyes, of there greate loue and affection to you Capt. Addams, haue appointed and set out this shipp called ye. Cloue pr. Japan; bilding there hoopes vppone ye. foundation of your long experyence in these partes, for the settling of a benyficiall ffactorye. And hauing since my arriuall not onlye obteyned ye. emperor's grant with large priualiges for ye. same, but also procured your freedome, which, till this present, could not be obteyned. *IT* now resteth what course you will take; wheather to retorne for your countery, or remaine heare ye. companyes servant, in what manner you hould your selfe best able to doe them seruice: what sallory you will haue; and in what manner to be paid. Viz. to haue the 20*l*. pr. exchange imprested vnto you, and to stand to ye. curtesie of ye. companye for further guirdon, or to com to a sertaine agreement pr. such a some as my selfe and ye. ffactors appointed to staye heare shall thinke fitting, till advize out of England. And hearin I intreate you chearfullye to deliuere your resolution to each pointe: for yt. the tyme of yeare inforseth my departure. And I should be heartalye sorrye yf in what I may giue you content, there should happen the leaste defect.

*WHERVNTO* he made answer, that his desyre is to goe home for his native contrey of England, but not in this shipp: only his stayinge is for a certen tyme to get somthing,

L

hauing hetherto spent his tyme soe many yeares in vayne, and wold not now goe home with an emptie purse. And that he is willinge to do the companye the best service he can in any thinge he may serue them in, eather pr. sea or land, to the benyfit of the English ffactory in Japon, or else wheare, as shall be thought fyting by the Counsell of the English ffactors their [*there*] resident, vntill the retorne of the next shipp, or ships, after the certen news of the Cloues arivall in England. Yet is not willinge to take the 20*l*. empresse before mentioned, and to stand to the wourshipfull companeyes courtsie for the rest ; but rather to com to agreement now, that he should hau to stand vpon a certentie. And demanded twelue pownds str. per moneth : sayinge, the Fflemynge did geue hym fyfteene pownd, when they first emploid hym into these p͂tes ; and herevpon went forth ; willing the Generall and rest, that they should bethinke them selues : for yf they wolde not geue him soe much, theare were others that wold ; and therefore wished them not to be his hindrance. And soon after retorninge, our Generall offred hym ffowreskore pownd a yeare. But he answered, that vnder one hvndred and twenty pownds per anno. he wold not. Then he was offred to haue the 20*l*. lent to his wife geven gratis, besids the 80*l*. per anno. But he stood still to his formeir offer of 120*l*. per anno. ; and soe departed, wishing vs to bethink our selues better, till the morrow morning. At which tyme the Cownsell afforsaid beinge assembled againe, Capt. Adams, beinge present, was of his owne good will, contented to be entertayned into the wourshipfull companyes service for the stipend, or sallery, of one hvndred pownds str. pr. yeare, to be paid at the end of two yeares, or, at such tyme as news shall com out of England of the arivall of the Cloue pr. any one ship, or ships ; Only in the meane tyme his desire was, that yf he stood in neede of twentie pownd str. to lay out in aparell, or any other necessaries, that he might be furnished therewith.

Sealed & deliuerd in the presence of

Ric Cocks

Tempest Peacocke

Richarde Wickham

By me my

*AND SOE IN WITNESSE* of the truth, he hath here-vnto put his hand and seale, promesinge not to vse any trade for his owne private benefytt per sea or land, to be preiudtiall to the benefytt of the Company. *Dated at Firando in Japon, the 24th day of November,* 1613.

By me *WM. ADDAM.* [L. S.]

Sealed and dd. in the putes [?] of us

> *RICH. COCK.*
> *TEMPEST PEACOCK.*
> *RICHARDE WICKHAM.*

This agreement with *Mr. Addams,* was made with the consent of vs, *Richard Cock, Tempest Peacock,* and *Rich. Wickham,* whose names are aboue written for witnesses.[1]

-------

## Letter No. V.

THERE is a second letter from William Adams, dated in December 1613, but to whom addressed is not apparent. It is a faithful epitome of the "vearey larg" letter above given : and there are only three portions that need be cited : viz. I. *As to the vessel first lent to, and eventually purchased by, the Governor-General of the Phillipine Islands :* II. *As to Adams continuing in Japon :* III. *The conclusion.*

I.

I my seelf hau bylt 2 shipes in Jappan, the on [e], by occassion sold to the Spaynnards, went for Nova Spania. Which ship, on [e] viage vppon this cost I mad with her : being of burden 170 tovnes.

[1] E. I. Mss. *Japon Series.*

II.

Your woourship shall vnderstand I had thought to a
coum hom in the Cloue, but by som discovrtissis offred me
by the generall, changed my mind: which injuries to wryt
of them I leau; leauing to others, God sending the ship hom,
to mak rellacion.[1]

III.

Senc the tym I saw your wourship, I hau passed great
misseries and trowbells. God hau the prayss to whoum it
douth belonge, that hath delliuered me ovt of them all. To
writt of the particullers, it wear for me very longe, thearfor,
in short, I leau the rehearsall tell further tym. Thus, with
my most harty and humbell sallutacions to you and to your
good wyf, I seeas [cease]; dessiring your wourship to sallut
me to Sr. Thomass Smyth, and tell him on my behalf, he
shall find me in his servis, so trusti as euer faithfull Inglish
man, that euer hath serued the coumpany. And as consserning the affares in Jappan, let him tak no cair [care]. His
factory is so saf; and so sver [sure] his goods, as in his own
houss. This I dare insver so long as I do lyue, And whatsoeuer the wourshipfull company shall hav need in Japan, it
shalbe accomplished. This I dare insver: for the emperour
and the kinge hath mad me such promis, which I do know
shalbe accovmplished. I pray you sallut me vnto my good
frind Mr. William Bourrall, shipwryt, who I heer is on of
the company: whous good kindnes hath bynn to my pour
wyf, in speking to lend her the forsayd 20*l*. [? *of*] which, I
thank God [?*I*], hau heer mad payment: and I pray him in my

---

[1] "Yf at your departure from Japon, the said William Adams shall
ymportune you to transporte him into his natiue countrie, to visitt his
wife and children, we pray you then to accomodate him with as convenient a cabben as you may, and all other necessaries which your shipp
may afford him." (*Instructions to Captain Saris from the Governor, etc.
of the Company*, April 14, 1611. E. I. Mss)

behalf still to continew his Christian loue and pitty, which without dowt God will reward. I pray remember my humbell dvtty to my good Mr. Nicholass Diggens, and thank him for his great former loue to me, etc.

Thuss hauing no tym, I cess, covmmending you with yours to the protexion of God : who bless your wourship in this lyf; and in the world to covm euerlasting lyfe. Amen.

By your unwourthy frind and seruant to covmmmand,

WM. ADDAMES.

Yf you send for Japan anny shipping : that present that shalbe sent to the emperour in it, lette them send soom Rousse [*Russian*] glass of the gretest sort : so mvch as may glasse him a rowm of 2 fadoom 4 squar, and what fine lames [*lambs*] skenes [*skins*], [*? you will*], and 2 or 3 peces of fyne holland, yf it be more I leau it to your discression : with 3 or 4 payr of spaktakle glasses. And for marchandis, he deessired to haue soum 1000 barres of steill 4 squar, in length sovm 8 or 9 foout ; which goods the Hollanders haue brought and sold to the emperour at 5*l*. starling the picoll, which is Inglish waight 125 powndes.           W. A.[1]

---

# Obserbations.

PROBABLY under the impression that he had been overreached by *Adams,* in regard to the terms of his engagement with the Company, *Captain Saris* may have exhibited some discourtesies : since in the document, designated a *"Remembrance",* which he left for the guidance of Captain Cock in the management of the factory, the following disparaging remarks occur,

[1] E. I. Mss. *Japon Series.*

viz., "And for Mr. Adams he is onlye fittinge to be mr. of the junke, and to be vsed as linguist at corte, when you have no imployment pr. hym at sea. It is necessarye you stirr hym, his condition being well knowne vnto you as to my selfe : otherwayes you shall hau littell seruice of hym, the countrye offording great libertye, wheare vnto he is mvch affected. The forsed agreement I haue made with hym as you know could not be eschudd, ye. Flemmings and Spaniards making false proffers of great intertaynement, and hym selfe more affected to them then his owne natyon, we holye destitute of language. . . . . You shall not need to sende for anye farther order to ye. Emperour for the setting out of the junke [*intended to proceed to Siam*], it being an article granted in the charter, as by the coppie thereof in English left with you will appeare. Yet will Mr. Adams tell you that he cannot departe without a licence, which will not be granted except he go vp. Beleue him not ; nether neglect that busines : for his wish is but to haue the coumpanye bear his charges to his wife [*meaning his native wife, who resided on the property granted to him by the Emperor, on the way to the court.*] Yet rather then that he shall leaue you, and bitake himself to the Spaniards, or Fflemmings, you must make a vertue of necessitye, and let hym go." [1]

In all this, *Captain Saris* was wrong and unjust. 1. *William Adams did not need stirring.* After an experience of twelve months, Captain Cock states : " I finde the man very tractable, and willinge to do your wourship the best seruis he can, and hath taken great paine about repairing our juncke, the *Sea Adventure*, otherwayes she would not haue byn ready to haue made the Syam voyage this yeare." [2]

---

[1] E. I. Mss. *Japon Series.*

[2] *Captain Cock to the Gour, etc., of the E. I. C⁰*, 25 Novʳ, 1614. The Cape Merchant, on a subsequent occasion, bears testimony to the tractability of William Adams in the following words : " Mr. Wickham, I praye you haue a good care to geve Captain Adams content, which you may easilyc doe yf you vse hym with kynde speeches, and fall not into

II. *It is not to be assumed that any offers made by the Flemmings and Spaniards to William Adams were not bonâ fide.* *The Flemings* had had too much experience of the value of his good offices, not to be solicitous to secure the continuance of his services.[1] *The Spaniards* had had too much experience of the effects of his opposition to their views, not to be desirous of cultivating his good-will.[2] *Both parties* were perfectly aware of his ready access to the presence,[3] and of the influence he exercised over the Emperor : which was fully demonstrated by the extensive privileges he obtained for the English : " such as the Portuguese, even at the time of their highest interest with the Japonese, were unable to procure on any terms whatever."[4] III. *Adams did not prove*

termes with hym vpon any argvment. I am perswaded I could lyve with hym 7 yeares before any extraordenary speeches should happen betwixt vs." (*Cock to Wickham, proceeding to his station at Sorongo and Edo,* Jan. 16$\frac{13}{14}$. E. I. Mss.). Some months afterwards, the Cape Merchant recurs to the subject, and concludes his admonition to Mr. Wickham, with the following sensible remark : " Fayre words are as soon spoaken as fowle, and cause a man to pass thorow the world as well amongst fowes as frinds." (*From the same to the same, proceeding with Adams to Siam,* 25 Nov. 1614. E. I. Mss.). From various passages in Captain Cock's Diary, Mr. Wickham appears to have been somewhat "humoursome", and apt to " fall into termes" with his associates, especially when he had " pottle in pate".

[1] The good offices rendered by Adams to the Flemings, which were the chief means of their becoming established in the Empire, are detailed at length by *Charlevoix* (t. iv, p. 125, and pp. 258 and 264), who prefaces his narrative with the following remark : " *Le Pilote Anglois, Guillaume Adams, qui étoit homme de mérite,* s'introduisit à la cour de Surunga si bien, qu'il y devint en quelque sort le favori du souverain."

[2] *Charlevoix* (t. iv, p. 292) observes : " Ce Pilote disservit d'une manière cruelle les Espagnols, et tous le Chrétiens"; *i. e.,* in the phraseology of Captain Cock, the " *Romish Christians*"; and cites instances. This is also the case with *Capt. Cock.*

[3] " The truth is, the emperour esteemeth hym mvch, and he may goe and speake with hym at all tymes, when kynges and princes are kept ovt." (*Cock to the Gouernour, etc., of the Company,* 25 Feb. 16$\frac{15}{16}$. E. I. Mss.)

[4] *Scheuchzer, Introduction to Kæmpfer's Hist. of Japan,* page xlix. Also *Charlevoix,* t. iv, p. 291.

*himself more affected to the Flemings and Spaniards than to his
own nation.* There is not an instance to be found in Captain
Cock's Diary, of Adams having afforded any assistance to the
Flemings, except when their interests and those of his own
nation were identical. Of his disposition towards the Spaniards,
enough has been said. In fact, Adams nobly redeemed the
pledge he gave to Sir Thomas Smith, that he should find him
" so trusti as ever faithful Inglishman, that euer hath serued
the coumpany." He was staunch to his countrymen, resisting
alike the overtures of the Flemings, the Spaniards, and the
Japonese.[1]  IV. *Adams did not pretend it was necessary to go
up to the Court* to obtain a license for the junk to proceed to
Syam; and *he did not go up to the court* before the junk sailed,
either that the Company might bear the expenses of a visit
from him to his wife, or for any other purpose. As before
stated, he was usefully and zealously engaged in fitting up
the junk ; and when the vessel was ready for sea, he sailed
in her forthwith.

The generall was also wrong in another particular : the
extent of the privileges conferred on the English by the
" charter". Captain Cock corrects the error into which he

---

[1] " Thus much Captain Adams tould me. Also that the emperour gaue
hym councell not to seale [*sail*] in Japan jonks on noe voyage, but rather
stay in Japan ; that yf the stipend he had geuen hym were not svffitient, he
would geve him more. But he answered, his word was passed, and therefore yf he performed not his word, yt would be a dishonour vnto hym."
Captain Cock tested the sincerity of Captain Adams' professions. The
Cāpe Merchant proceeds to say :  " Yet, truly, at his retorne to Firando,
I offered to hau quit hym of his promis, and to hau sent hym to Edo, to
be neare the emperour vpon all occations. Yet would he not be perswaded therevnto." (*Cock to the Gouernour, etc.*, dated 25th of February,
16$\frac{15}{16}$. E. I. Mss.)   On another occasion it is reported :  "And being at
court, the admerall of the sea was very ernest with Mr. Wm. Adams, to
haue hym pilot of a voyage they pretended to the northward, to haue
made conquest of certen islands (as they said) rich in gould ; but Captain Adams exkewsed hym selfe, in that he was in your worship's seruice,
and so put hym ofe." (*Cock to the Gouernour, etc., of the Company*, dated
1st of January, 16$\frac{16}{17}$. E. I. Mss.)

had fallen in the following terms : " Neither can we set out any junke, without procuring the yearely license of the Emperour : otherwise no *Japon* mariner dare go out of *Japon* vpon paine of death, only our owne shippes from England may come in, and goe out again when they will, and no man gain-say it."[1]

## Letter No. VI.

To the hounarabell *Sir Thomas Smyth*, knight, gouernour of the Est Indes Coumpani in Loundoun. Per Mr. [. . . . .], whoum God presserue.

*Written in Firando in the kingdoum of Japon, the* 14 *of Jennevari* [1616-17].

RIGHT wourshipfull Sir, finding my self altogether unwourthy to writt vnto your wourship, yeet lest you should condemn mee of ingratitude, I hau imboldened my self to writt theis few lines to gev your wourship to vnderstand how for the space of three yeeares I hau byn ymploied by your woorship Cāpe Marchant, Mr. Richard Cock, 2 viages for Siam, etc. In the yeare of our Lord 1615, 2 dayes after my departure from Firando a most grieuous storme took me, called a horricane, of violent wind, by which I was in great danger to looss both liues, ship and goods, for the space of 3 daies baylling in 4 rooumes,[2] hauing with mee at that tyme of officers, marriners, marchants and passingers [? *some*] 40 sooules ; the which being wearied with a long storm, could

---

[1] *Cock, to Saris in England. Purchas*, vol. i, p. 407.

[2] The Japonese, like the Chinese vessels, are built in compartments, with water-tight bulk-heads. In this country, the *divisions in a coal barge* are still called *rooms*.

M

not longer enduer it; but the principall of them cam to mee and held vp ther handes, praying mee to do my best 'to saue ther liues. Now at this pressent I had 2 of your woorship saruants, the one called Mr. Richard Wickham, who for the pressent viage wass Cāpe Marchant, the other called Edmon Sarris, his assistant : to which twoo I made the complaynt of our men knowen, whoo allso seeinge the great extremiti wee were in, dessired mee the like. The which thing greved me not a littell (being not aboue 20 lleags from the cost of China) to go for China, beinge most bitter ennemys to the Japanners (thear wee could not trym our ship) : that I wass fayne to take an other cours, and derectted my courss for sartayne ilands called the LEQUES,[1] which through the bless-ing of God 3 dayes aftere arriued in saffetie, to all our great reioycing : for which God be praysed for euer. Now in theese ilands wee found maruelous great frindship : for both generous [? *people of rank*] and ordenari peopell frindly. But in conclusion, beefor wee could vnlade our ship, tak out our mast, and trym her agayn, the monsson was past, that wee could not prosseed of our voyage: but in the end returned for Japan agayne.

Now in the yeere of our Lord 1617 [? 1616], hauing trymed our ship, agayne prosseeded for Siam, and thorough the fauour of God mad a prosperoose vyage; and at my returne to Japan I found 2 ships arriued abought 15 dayes biffor mee, the on called the Thomas, the other the Advice : of which I wass most joyfull to see.

So pressently of my arriuall, the Cāpe Marchant was reddie to go to the court, hauing wayted sartain dayes in hoop of my couming. So within 5 daies of my arriuall, according to wind and wether departed, and went with the Cāpe Marchant beffor the Emperour, with which in 5 daies delliuered his pressent. So hauing delliuerd his pressent, 2 dayes after sent mee to the country to procure those things

[1] The Loo CHOO groupe.

## 1616

Coppie off the Articles (or priviledges) granted to the
English nation, by Ongosha Samme Emperour of Japon

1. Wee Endowe vnto all men, that the English nation through
out all Japon, in what part thereof soever they Arive wth
theire shipping, shall wth all conuenyent speed (they haue
Leysure) to theire towne (and port) off ffriends, there to make sale
off theire merchandiz, defending all other places and partes whatsoeuer
in Japon, not to receaue any off theire said not merchdiz aforesaid
sent at ffriendes onely / &c.

2. But yf it fortune through Contrary wyndes (or bad wether) theire
shipping arive in any other port in Japon, that they shalbe
friendly vsed, in paying for what they take (or buy) not thowt
exacting, any Anchorage, Custom, or other extraordenary matters
whatsoeuer &c ~

3. That yf the Emperour nedeth any thing theire shipping bringeth
that it shalbe reserved for them in paying the worth thereof /

4. That noe man shalbe (or Constraint) theng lyf to buy nor sell
wth them, neyther theng lyf the like wth the Japons, but
that both partyes deale the one wth the other in ffriendly sort

5. That yf any of the English nation chance to die, in any part
off Japon, that, the good, monies or merchandiz or whatsoeuer
else / is found to be in his Custody; at the color of his
death, shall be holde to be or belong to them (or them) vnto
whome the said or Cargo mght of the English nation sayeth
it belongeth vnto / &c.

6. That yf there be any difference (or Controuersy (be it off
life and death or otherwaise) amongst the English, about
theire Cargos or aland, yt shall be at the disposing off the
Cap: or Cargo mght to make an end thereof, wthout that
any other Justice in Japon, shall bring them or meddell in the matter

7. The Conclusion is, to Comand all Tonos (or kings) gouernors,
and other officers in Japon whatsoeuer, to fe the premises
afforsaid Accomplished / &c

which he required, which was the renewall of the old Emperour's priûliges [*privileges*] with a gowshon [*license*] for his
juncke for Siam: which things were granted with all kinde
speeches, but in conclusion were not performed; as afterwards appeared. For hauing taken his leaue of the court,
and being bovnd to Meaco, by the way coummeth an express
with letters from Mr. Richard Wickham from Meaco, with
letters how that all strangers goods was forbiden to make
sale of any, and that covmmandment was geuen to all marchants that were strangers, should go for Firando and Lan-
gasacki. Vppon which strange newes, the Cãpe Marchant,
Mr. Cock, thought it necessary to go to the court agayne, to
know the occasione, and to see yf he could remedy it. So
returned to the court agayne, and evsed me as his messenger
therein. And returning agayne, examined agayne his coum-
mission, or, priûlleges; and indeed found an artikell altered:
which wass, that in the old Emperour, his priûlleges, thorough
his whool domynions, our Inglish factori might trad[*trade*], by
[*buy*] or sell, wher they thought good, in thease new priûlleges
weare granted but in two pllaces, which weare nomynated,
that wass in Firando and Langasachi. So about this byssiness Mr. Cock hath taken no small care to a reformed it.
So I beinge daylie ymploied in this byssiness, could not get
it refformed; but in fyne this generall awnsswer, that wass:
that this wass the first yeare of the Emperour's raign, and as
his eddict wass gone all ouere Japan, it was not a thing
pressently to be called back agayne; that wee should be
content till next yeear, at which tyme request being mad by
thoes that shall coum vp to geue the present, doutted not
but it should be geuen. So with this absolut awnsser, the
Cãpe Marchant returned to Meaco. Ther dispaching svch
bissiness as he had to do, returned to the shipping in Firando, with svch factoris as weear aboue.[1]

Now your woorship shall vnderstand the casse [*cause*] of

---

[1] NOTE Z. *The Modified Privileges.*

thees things as followeth. In the yeear of our Lord 1615
heer was great warres : for Quambaccodono [*i. e., Faxiba, or
Taico Sama*] a two yeears before his deth had a ssoone,
which vntill this [. . . . .] beeing the 24 yeare of his age,
and hauing aboundance of riches, thought him selfe strong
with [. . . . . .] diuers nobles to a rooss [?] with him, which
was great likly. Hee mad warres with the Emperour [. . . .],
allso by the Jessvits and Ffriers, which mad this man Fiddaya
Samma belleeue he should be fauord with mirrackles and
wounders ; but in fyne it proued to the contrari. For the
old Emperour [. . . . . .], against him presentlly, maketh his
forces reddy by sea and land, and compasseth his castell that
he was in ; although with loss of multitudes on both sides,
yet in the end rasseth the castell walles, setteth it on fyre,
and burneth hym in it.[1] Thus ended the warres. Now the
Emperour heering of thees jessvets and friers being in the
kastell with his ennemis, and still from tym to tym agaynst
hym, coummandeth all romische sorte of men to depart ovt
of his countri, thear churches pulld dooun, and burned.
This folowed in the old Emperour's daies. Now this yeear,
1616, the old Emperour he did [*died*]. His son raigneth in
his place, and hee is more hot agaynste the romish relligion
then his ffather wass : for he hath forbidden thorough all his
domynions, on paine of deth, none of his subiects to be
romish christiane ; which romish seckt to prevent eueri wayes
that he maye, he hath forbidden that no stranger merchant
shall abid in any of the great citties. On svch pretence many
jessvets and ffriers might seket [? *in secret*] teach the romissh
relligion. Thees are the casses of our Inglish ffactori, and
all other strangers are not suffred abou in the countri.[2]

Now consserning my owne part, your wourshipp shall vnderstand I am this yeear bound to COCHE CHINA : yf my God

---

[1] *Master Adams* writes too peremptorily. The fate of Fidaya Sama
remains a mystery to the present day : though a general impression
exists, that he escaped, and received protection from the king of Arima.

[2] NOTE A A. *The Fate of the English Factory.*

will permitt me. Thees ressones hath mad mee tak it in hand. 3 yeers past your Cãpe merchant, Mr. Richard Cock, sent a ffactori thether, but men nor goods returned not; as thē report on of them killed thear, and the other couming from Japan cast awaye. Now my selfe being no waye abell to mak that my hart dessireth, of anny sattisfacion for your wourshipps great kindnes to my poor wyf in my absenc, and allsso, heer in Japan, your woorship ffactor Mr. Richard Cock, his lou and most frindly affactcion : I say hath mad mee to tak this joorney in hand, to sse yf by my menes I can get thooss priuelleges wherby your woorship may get a free trad or ffactori agayne; and allsso to know by what menes Mr. Pecock lost hys lyf.[1] Mr. Cock had thought to a sent Mr. Wm. Nellson with mee, but hauing svch need of his pressence, that indeed hee could not miss hym. Vppon which occacion I go my selfe alloun, desiring the protexion and favor of all mightie God heer in.

Thus being vnwoorthy, I hau imboldened my selfe to wryt thees feaw lines to let your woorship to vnderstand of the trowbelles of thees parts in brif : only knowing assvredly Mr. Cock hath moost largly wrott your woorship of all mat-ters. Therfor, this pressent my hvmbell devtye remembred, I ceess : praying God for your woorship longe lyf and moost happi daies; and in the lyf to covm euerlasting felliciti for euer. Amen.

Your woorship vnwoorthy saruant to comand in all dutifull sarvis that I cann,

WM. ADDAMS.[2]

---

[1] Great pains were taken to ascertain the circumstances under which Mr. Peacock met with his death. It is uncertain whether he was slain accidentally, or by treachery. His death, the non-appearance of his com-panion, and the loss of all the property entrusted to their charge, are alone certain.

[2] E. I. Mss. *Japon Series.*

## Conclusion.

THE foregoing is the last communication from William Adams that has been preserved, if any other were sent. The two following extracts have each an interest, but of a totally dissimilar character. One represents Adams in his prosperity, an object of honour and esteem : the other announces the occurrence of " the last scene of all", the termination of the singular career of this " *homme de mérite*", as justice forced an antagonist to term him.

In 1616, Captain Cock went up to Edo about the " Privileges". In his Diary,[1] under date the 26th of September, narrating the circumstances connected with his return, he states : " We departed towards Orengava this morning abt. 10 a clock, and arived at Phebe some 2 houres before night, where we staid all that night : for that Captain Adames wife and his two children met vs theare. This Phebe is a Lordshipp geuen to Capt. Adames pr. the ould Emperour, to hym and his for eaver, and confermed to his sonne, called Joseph. There is above 100 farms, or howsholds, vppon it, besides others vnder them, all which are his vassalls, and he hath power of lyfe and death ouer them : they being his slaues ;[2] and he hauing as absolute authoretie over them as any tono (or king) in Japon hath over his vassales. Divers of his tenants brought me presents of frute : as oringes, figges, peares, chistnutts, and grapes, whereof there is aboundance in that place." Continuing his Diary, the next day, the 27th of September, Captain Cock remarks : " We gaue the tenants of Phebe a bar of coban to make a banket after our departure from thence, with 500 gins to the servants of howses, the cheefe of the towne accompanying vs

---

[1] E. I. Mss. *Japon Series.*     [2] NOTE B B. *Slavery in Japon.*

out of thēir precincts, and sent many servants to accompany vs to Oringava (which is about 8 or 9 English miles) ; all rvning before vs on foote as honeyer [? *honour*] to Captain Adames. After our arivall at Oringava, most of the neighbours came to vizett mee, and brought frutes and fysh, and reioiced (as it should seeme) of Captain Adames retorne."

The next extract is from a letter addressed by Captain Cock to the Governor and Committees of the East India Company, dated the 13th of December 1620. It is to the following effect : " Our good frend Captain Wm. Addames, whoe was soe long before vs in Japon, departed out of this world the vj of May last ; and made Mr. Wm. Eaton and my selfe his overseers : geuing the one halfe of his estate to his wife and childe in England ; and the other halfe to a sonne and doughter he hath in Japon. The coppie of his will, with an other of his inventory (or account of his estate) I send to his wife and doughter, per Captain Martin Pring, their good frend, well knowne to them long tyme past. And I haue delivered one hvndred pounds starling to diuers of the James Royall Company, entred into the pursers book to pay two for one in England, is two hvndred pounds starling to Mrs. Addames and her doughter, for it was not his mind his wife should haue all, in regard she might marry an other hvsband, and carry all from his childe ; but rather that it should be equally parted between them : of which I thought good to adviz your wourship. And the rest of his debts and estates being gotten in, I will either bring, or send it per first occasion offred, and that may be most for their profitt : according as the deceased put his trust in me and his other frend Mr. Eaton."[1]

It only remains to be observed, that the WILL OF WILLIAM ADAMS, *in Japonese*, is preserved among the records of the Honourable the East India Company ; and that a trans-

[1] E. I. Mss. *Japon Series.*

lation has not been traced. The INVENTORY is also extant. The title runs thus:

*" IN THE NAME OF GOD, AMEN.*
*1620, May the 22d day.*

*THE INVENTORY OF THE ESTATE OF THE DE-CEASED, CAPT. WM. ADAMES, taken at Firando, in Japan, after his death, pr. me Richd. Cock, and Mr. Wm. Eaton, factors, in the English Factory at Firando, in Japan, left by testament his oversears, viz., of all the monies, debts, merchandiz, and moveabls, being as hereafter followeth."*

The succeeding extract shews that William Adams had accumulated about £. stg. 500 at the period of his death, viz.

*" The totall is :*

| | ta. | m. | co. |
|---|---|---|---|
| In ready money | 0365 | 0 | 9 |
| In bills of debt | 0890 | 0 | 0 |
| In merchandiz, rated at | 0638 | 7 | 0 |
| In moveables, sould for | 0078 | 4 | 5 |
| | 1972 | 2 | 4 |

|  | ta. | ma. | co. |
|---|---|---|---|
| | 1972 | 2 | 4 " |

---

| | | s. | d. | |
|---|---|---|---|---|
| ¹ 10 Condrins | = 1 Mas = | 0 | 6 | } *English.* |
| 10 Mas | = 1 Taie = | 5 | 0 | |

# MEMORIALS OF JAPON.

---

## NOTES.

NOTE A.

## Name, Discovery, Situation, Division, Revenues, Population, Trade, and Commerce.

*Name.*—By *Marco Polo*, the Empire is named *Zipangu;* and by the Chinese, *Gipuanque :* or, " The Empire proceeding from the Sun". *Japon* or *Japan,* appears to be a corrupt form of the Chinese term, introduced probably by the Portuguese or Italians. By the inhabitants, the empire, after the principal island, is designated *Nipon,* or euphoniously *Nifon,* which has the same signification as the Chinese term. *Tenka* is another name by which the empire is recognized : which signifies, " The sub-celestial realm". From this designation, the sovereign originally derived one of his titles : that of *Tenka Sama, i. e.,* " The Lord of Tenka", or of the sub-celestial-empire.

*Discovery.*—The merit of this act is claimed by *Fernando Mendez Pinto,* who, justly or unjustly, has obtained unenviable notoriety for want of veracity. Pinto alleges, that in the year 1542, he was making a voyage with Samipocheva, a celebrated Chinese corsair of the period, and that the junk on which they were embarked was stranded, during a storm, on the coast of *Bungo,* in the island of *Kiusiu,* one of the Japonese groupe. In addition, he relates many wonderful adventures that befel him, during his alleged sojourn in the country. In the same year, it is also said, three Portuguese merchants, *Antonio Mota, Francisco Zeimoto,* and *Antonio Pexota,* while proceeding from Macassar to China, were driven by stress of weather on the shores of *Cangosima,* in *Satsuma,* another of the Japonese islands ; and to these parties is attributed the opening of commercial intercourse between the empire and the western-nations.   St. François Xavier, the apostle of the Romish Christians in the east, is the first European that may be considered to have located himself in Japon.   He commenced his missionary labours A.D. 1549.

*Situation.*—The empire of Japon lies in the North Pacific ocean, off the coasts of Tartary and Corea: excluding Yesso on the north, and the Loo Choo groupe on the south: between 30° 14′ and 41° 35′ of latitude north; and between 128° 4′ and 142° 10′ of longitude, east from Greenwich.   The empire consists of a vast number of islands : stated, by native authorities, to be upwards of a thousand.   The principal island is *Nipon,* and the islands next in extent and importance are *Kiusiu, Sikokf,* and *Adwasi,* which lie to the southward of Nipon.

*Divisions.*—Primarily, the Empire consists of eight *Tracts.* These are subdivided into sixty-eight *Provinces :* which are re-divided into six hundred and thirty-nine *Districts.*   The first division was effected by the Daïri Suisuin, A.D. 590; and the second by one of his successors, in 681.   The number of provinces was originally sixty-six, but during the sixteenth century, Taico Sama added two : the islands of *Iki* and *Tsuss* lying between Japon and Corea: of which he took possession by force of arms.   *Five of the provinces* are dependent on a political arrangement.   They are situated round *Miaco,* and are designated, " *Gokinai goka kokf"*, *i. e.,* " The Imperial-domains," or literally, " The five provinces of the Imperial-revenues."   The collections of revenue made in them, are appropriated solely to the service of the emperor.

*Revenues.*—From official sources, *Kœmpfer* ascertained, that, in 1690-91, the produce of the Gokinai amounted to 148 *mans,* 1200 *kokfs of rice :* equivalent to about £. *stg.* 1,851,500 ; and that the other provinces yielded 2180 *mans* and 5000 *kokfs of rice :* equivalent to about £. *stg.* 27,256,250. The expenditure of the emperor, M. Caron states, also on official authority, to have amounted in 1664, to "23,845,000 cockiens de 4 fleurins pièce."

The *financial system* of Japon is distinguished by the absence of an element that is disagreeably obtrusive in the financial systems of most other countries. In the strict sense of the term, *Taxation does not exist.*

The territory of which the empire consists is invested entirely in the crown. The revenues are derived solely from the rents of land; and the land is held either directly under the crown, or under the princes or nobles who have been invested by the crown with territorial rights; and who in return pay rent, accompanied by the performance of certain feudal services. Tenants holding direct from the crown, pay to the emperor's stewards, four parts out of ten of the produce of the soil: whether of rice, corn, or pulse; reserving the residue for their own use. Such as hold under the prince, pay six parts out of ten.[1] To adjust the respective rights of landowner and tenant, certain government officers, called *Kemme*, are employed. They are represented to possess some skill in mathematics, and are held in estimation, being allowed to wear two swords: by which they are placed in the same rank with the nobility and soldiery, the most distinguished classes in the empire. Before the fields are sown, they are surveyed by the *kemme*, and an estimate is formed of what they are calculated to produce. When the crops are nearly ripe, the fields are re-surveyed. In ordinary seasons simple inspection is deemed sufficient; but the result is represented to be surprisingly accurate. Should the crops, however, promise to be extraordinarily large, a square piece of ground is selected, and the produce being ascertained, the sample forms the basis on which the entire contribution is calculated.

[1] Four parts in ten, and six parts in ten, are the *standard* rates; but remissions are made on account of the qualities of the soil; which are thus designated: 1, best; 2, middling; 3, poor; with the subdivisions of: 1, next to best; 2, next to middling; 3, next to bad. There are also some trifling variations in the rates in the different provinces.

With regard to untilled lands, considerable fairness is exhibited. The party undertaking to bring them into culture, is exempted during the first two or three years of occupancy, from any payment on account of rent. On the other hand, all occupiers of land are liable to ejectment if they neglect the cultivation of their holding for the space of a year. *Kæmpfer* alludes to the first provision, as "one among many excellent laws which relate to agriculture." What the other laws are, he does not state. This omission is to be regretted, as it is possible the Japonese, altogether a singular race, may entertain some curious, if not instructive notions on the subject.

In the cities, towns, and villages, the rent is calculated at so much "*p. mat*" for frontage : without reference to the depth of the premises, which is quite discretional.

The rent paid by the people is not altogether lost to them. The amount of produce transferred to the sovereign appears to be greater than his needs require ; and the surplus above his wants is carefully stored up. During periods of famine, or of short crops, the imperial-garners, and also those of the princes, are thrown open. Such as have the means to purchase, are supplied at a moderate rate ; and those who are destitute of means are supplied gratuitously. The opportunity of profiting by the misery of their fellows, is not afforded to greedy speculators. Similar consideration seems also to be shown on minor occasions. From a manuscript record, dated in 1664, it appears, that a great fire occurred in Nangasacki, by which "ye whole towne was destroyed excepting four streetes, killing 56 people, and half burning 34"; and that "the gouernour caused rice to be boyled continually at the corner of euery streete to feede the people, and the Emperour sent 200 chests of siluer to the cittizens to build vp their houses."[1]

---

[1] A chest of silver, according to the Dutch calculation, is equal to 1000 taies, or thails, of 5s. each.—*Kæmpfer*, vol. i, p. 362. Edn. 1727.

Princes guilty of extortion, or even negligent in exercising proper control over their officers, are deprived of their revenues, removed, disgraced, and otherwise punished.

*Population.*—The extent of the population is rather to be imagined than defined : yet, although so little is known specifically on the subject, perhaps no country affords more accurate materials for deciding a question of this nature : since, for a long succession of ages, a yearly census has been taken, and regularly preserved. While *Kæmpfer* was at *Miaco*, in 1690, the annual *aratame*, as it is termed, was taken, and the following is the result :—

BUILDINGS :

| | |
|---|---:|
| Temples of the Buddhist creed | 3893 |
| Temples of the Sinto creed, the native religion | 2127 |
| Palaces of the nobility | 137 |
| Bridges | 87 |
| Streets | 1858 |
| Houses | 138,979 |

PERSONS : *ecclesiastics,*

| | |
|---|---:|
| Buddhist priests | 37093 |
| Sinto priests | 9203 |
| Jammabos : or mountain priests, fanatics | 6073 |
| | 52,169 |

*Laymen,* classed according to their respective creeds . . . . . . . 477,557

529,726

The above amount is exclusive of temporary sojourners and of the members of the Court of the Daïri, which forms a distinct quarter of the city, including twelve or thirteen streets, and which teem with people : though to what extent is not known.[1]

The *entire population* of the same city is stated by *Don*

[1] *Kæmpfer, Hist. of Japan,* vol. ii, p. 486. Edn. 1727.

*Rodrigo de Vivero y Velasco*, to have been 1,500,000 in 1608-9: that of *Jedo*, 700,000; and that of *Sorongo*, 600,000. The same authority states, that between *Jedo* and *Sorongo*, a distance of one hundred leagues, a large city, town, or village, occurred at every quarter of a league, with an average number of inhabitants for each place of 100,000 ; and that from *Sorongo* to *Miaco*, also about one hundred leagues, the inhabited places were equally numerous and populous. Abundance, he says, reigned every where, provisions so cheap, that the poorest could purchase them.[1]

*Kæmpfer*, about a century after, observes : " The country is populous beyond expression, and one would scarce think it possible, that being no greater than it is, it should nevertheless maintain and support such a vast number of inhabitants. The highways are an almost continued row of villages and boroughs. You scarce come out of one, but you enter another ; and you may travel many miles, as it were, in one street, without knowing it to be composed of many villages, but by the differing names that were formerly given them ; and which they afterwards retain, though joined to one another. It hath many towns, the chief whereof may vie with the most considerable in the world for largeness, magnificence, and the number of inhabitants. One of the chief is called *Kio*, or *Miaco*, that is, *the town*, or *metropolis*, by way of pre-eminence, being the seat of the ecclesiastical-hereditary emperor. . . . . . *Jedo*, properly the capital of the whole empire, and the seat of the secular-monarch, is so large, that I may venture to say it is the biggest town known. Thus much I can affirm from my own certain knowledge, that we were one whole day riding a moderate pace from *Sinagawa*, where the suburb begins, along the chief street, which goes across, a little irregularly indeed, to the end of the town."[2]

[1] Summary of the Narrative of *Velasco*, in the *Asiatic Journal*, for July 1830.
[2] *Appendix*, pp. 55, 56.

*Trade and Commerce.*—"How much is carried on," *Kœmp-fer remarks,* "between the several provinces and parts of the empire! how busy and industrious the merchants are everywhere! how full their ports of ships! how many rich and mercantile towns up and down the country! There are such multitudes of people along the coasts, and near the seaports, such a noise of oars and sails, and numbers of ships and boats, both for use and pleasure, that one would be apt to imagine the whole nation had settled there, and all the inland parts of the country were left quite desart and empty."

To the great extent of the internal trade of Japon, testimony is also borne by *Captain Cock,* in the diaries of his journeys between Firando and Jedo : while allusions are constantly made to the great wealth of many of the traders. In connexion with the latter point, the following account is extracted from *Doeff's work,*[1] and refers to a late period, 1806. The author, who was President of the Dutch Factory at Desima, observes : "There is *a silk-mercer* here [at Jedo], *named Itsigoya,* who has shops in all the great towns throughout the Empire. If you buy any thing of him here, take it away to another town—say to Nagasaki—and no longer like it, you may return it, if undamaged, to his shop there, and receive back for it the whole sum paid at Jedo." The author adds : "The wealth of this man is astonishing, as appears by what follows. During my stay at Jedo, there occurred a tremendous fire, that laid every thing, our residence included, in ashes, over an area of about three leagues and a half. Itsigoya lost on this occasion his whole shop, together with a warehouse, containing upwards of one hundred thousand pounds weight of spun silk. . . Notwithstanding this, he sent *forty* of his servants to our assistance during the fire, who were of great use to us. The second

[1] Quoted in "*Manners and Customs of the Japonese in the Nineteenth Century.*"

O

day after the conflagration, he was already rebuilding his premises, and paid every carpenter at the rate of ten shillings (English) a day."

### The industrious character of the Japonese.

The charge made in the text against the Japonese, of " slouthfulness and negligence" in agricultural matters, is not sustained by the representation of other writers. Commencing with *Captain Cock* in 1611, corroborated by *Kœmpfer* in 1691-92, and supported by the testimony of *Broughton, Krusenstern,* and of the *Dutch authors* of recent times, the Japonese may be pronounced to be, in the cultivation of the soil, " uncommonly careful and industrious"; and to exhibit a most commendable " spirit of labour and industry".

The fact is, the features of the country, in an agricultural point of view, are not generally promising. Mountains, rocks, morasses, and arid plains predominate. Yet over these disadvantages, the inhabitants, by the exertion of skill, energy, and perseverance, have triumphed. By judicious drainage, swamps have been reclaimed. By skilful irrigation, barren sands have been rendered fertile. The sides of mountains, impracticable for cattle, have been scaled by man : manure has been carried up; and the most unpromising spots made to yield abundant crops. All who have recently visited the Empire, concur in representing it to be the richest in agricultural produce of any country in the world.

### Tempestuous Storms.

Numerous instances might be cited from the Diary and Correspondence of the Members of the English Factory at

Firando in Japon, of violent tempests. The following occurs in a letter addressed by Richard Cock, the captain merchant, "to the wourshippful Thomas Wilson, Esquire, at his house, at Britaine Burse, at the Strand", Decr. the 10th, 1614, viz. " of late here is newes come from Edo, a cittie in Japon as bigge as London, wherein the chief of the nobillitie in Japon haue beautifull houses, that by means of an exceeding tuffoon, or tempest, all, or the most part of them, are defaced : the whole cittie being ouer-flowen with water, and the people forsed to flie vp into the mountaines ; . . and the Kings pallace, being stately builded in a new fortresse, the tyles being all gilded on the outside, were all carrid awaye with a whirlewinde, so that nonn of them are to be fownd." [*E. I. Mss.*]

NOTE D.

Earthquakes and Volcanic Phenomena.

In the province of *Oumi*, south-west from *Miaco*, there is a *lake* called *Oitz* or *Oumi*, which, though comparatively narrow, extends in length from N. to S., between 130 and 140 English miles. According to the national annals, this piece of water appeared in one night, and was caused by the sinking of the land, which occurred during an earthquake in the year 285 B.C.

*Earthquakes* are frequently alluded to in the Diary and correspondence of Captain Cock. An extract from the Diary follows :

" 1618 : *Novembr. 7th* [at Edo].

This mornyng cold, calme wether, with a hor frost. Dry wether all day; and night following.

About 10 a clock happened a greate earthquake, which caused many people to rvn out of their houses; and abowte the lyke hower the night following happened an other.

Calme cold wether with a hor frost, a stiffe gale of winde most parte of the day after, at S. W. erly. Yet dry both day and night. [*Novemb. 8th.*]

### Nota.

This contrey is much subiect to earthquakes, and that which is comonely marked thē allwais happen at a hie-water (or full sea). So it is thought it chanseth per reazon there is much winde blownen into hollow caves under grownd at loe water; and the sea flowinge in after and stopping the passage out, causeth these earthquakes, to fynd passage, or vent, for the wind shut vp." (*E. I. Mss.*)

*Volcanos* form a remarkable feature in the topography of Japon. There is one on a small island not far from *Firando*, which in Kæmpfer's time had been burning and trembling for many centuries. There is another, also on a small island opposite to *Satzuma*, to the southward of the *Straits of Van Dieman*. At *Aso*, in the province of *Figo*, there is a mountain perpetually burning, which shews a brilliant light by night. Near *Simabara* is UNSEN (*Kæmpfer*) or WUNZENDAKE, (*Siebold*), a misformed, widely extended, but not very high mountain. Kæmpfer, describing it in 1690, says : " At all times the top is bare, whitish from the colour of the sulphur, and withal resembling a caput mortuum, or burnt out massa. It smokes little; however, I could discern the smoke arising from it at three miles distance. Its soil is burning hot in several places, and besides so loose and spongious, that a few spots of ground excepted, on which stand some trees, one cannot walk over it without continual fear, for the creaking, hollow noise perceived under foot. Its sulphurous smell is so strong, that for many miles round there is not a bird to be seen; when it rains the water bubbles up, and the whole mountain seems as it were boiling."

About the middle of March 1793, the entire summit of this mountain fell in. Torrents of water gushed forth from all parts, and a dense vapour resembling smoke, overspread the country. The phenomenon, which continued for a few days only, was succeeded early in the following month, by an eruption of BIVO-NO-KOUBI, a mountain rising from the eastern declivity of Unsen. The flame, sparkling and of a reddish colour, varied with brown flashes, ascended to a great height, and set on fire the trees in the immediate vicinity. Spreading rapidly over hill and dale, covered with the materials of combustion, and augmented in intensity by streams of burning lava that rolled down the sides of the mountain, the conflagration spread desolation over a wide tract of country. May came, and brought with it additional disasters. Early in the month, *Simabara* was violently convulsed with an earthquake, that affected in various degrees the entire island of *Kiusiu*. Stupified with apprehension, and seemingly deprived of the powers of motion, a portion of the population awaited with idiotic indifference the destruction by which they were threatened. Others excited to phrenzy, carrying in their arms their sick or aged relatives, or their tender babes, rushed to and fro, in vain seeking a place of safety, uttering loud wails and lamentations, or fervently imploring protection from the *Kami*, their gods. Time passed away, and the danger proved less than had been apprehended. Still the minds of all men were troubled : kept in a state of continual perturbation. Convulsions followed each other in rapid succession, though with mitigated violence. It was not till the first day of the fourth month (June) of the fifth year *Konau-sei* (our 1793), that the apprehensions which had been entertained, were realized to their full extent. As the people were at their noon-tide repast on that day, a violent convulsion took place. During an hour and a half, shock followed shock in rapid succession : each shock exceeding its precursor in violence. Just in front of the vortex of the convulsion stood a castle, built of massive stone-work, covering a large and populous village. The castle had been protected from the torrents of lava by a rampart of rocks; and it now withstood the fury of the earthquake by its own extraordinary strength. But the village, with all its inhabitants, was instantaneously engulphed, amidst the piercing shrieks of human beings, and the wild cries of animals. Upheaved from their beds, ponderous rocks tore down the mountain's side, overthrowing or crushing to atoms every obstacle encountered in their impetuous descent. Loud bellowings beneath the earth, commingling with fierce roarings in the air, produced a horrid din, that needed not other terrific accompaniments to appal the hearts of the stoutest. A lull at length ensued. It endured a short space. Then the commotion was renewed. Another mountain, named MIYIYAMA (*Kæmpfer*), or MYOKENYAMA (*Siebold*), burst forth in eruption. The main portion of the mountain was blown into the air, and falling into the sea, caused so great a rise in the waters, that the country all about, including a large city at the base of the mountain, was at once submerged. As the sea rose it was met by torrents of water that gushed from fissures rent in the sides of the mountain, by which the fierceness of the inundation was increased. Mighty and irresistible whirlpools were created. Human beings, cattle, houses, and trees, were involved in universal wreck and ruin. The graveyards were torn up. The sepulchres were destroyed. Huge stones used to close them were carried away by the torrent; and the exhumed corses were ejected from their resting places to become the sport of the tumultuous waves. In an incredibly short space of time, a fair and flourishing country was reduced to the state of a desert. The province of FIGO opposite to *Simabara* did not escape. It suffered in an extraordinary degree. Its form appeared to be totally changed: scarcely to be recognized. A great number of vessels riding at anchor in the vicinity went to the bottom. Such was the incredible number of carcases of men and animals, and so great the mass of wreck of different descriptions, that vessels could scarcely make way between them. Upwards of fifty-three thousand persons perished, according to the official records.

In 1783, the volcano ASAMAGA-DAKI, to the north-west of *Jedo*, wrought direful effects in the province of *Sinano*. The eruption commenced on the 1st of August, and terminated on the 4th of the same month ; but violent shocks of earthquakes were incessant till the 8th, extending in one direction sixty miles, and in another ninety miles, English. Twenty-seven out of thirty-one villages were destroyed. The inhabitants strove to escape, but were prevented by innumerable chasms which were opened in the ground. Or, they escaped from being engulphed, only to be consumed by flames that sprung up from the earth. The waters of the rivers *Yoko* and *Karow* boiled. The course of the *Yone*, one of the largest rivers in Japan, was obstructed, and the boiling water inundated the adjacent country, causing awful devastation. Driven from their lairs in the mountains, wild beasts descended into the plains, and preyed on the hapless villagers. Such of the wretched people as were not entirely devoured were horribly mangled. The land was strewed, and the rivers were choked up with dead bodies : but the exact amount of the loss of life has never been ascertained. [*Kœmpfer. Titsingh. Siebold.*]

### NOTE E.

### Mineral Productions.

*Gold* is found in various localities. That procured from *Sado* has the reputation of being the finest; and it is stated, the ore will yield from 1 to 2 oz. of fine metal, per $1\frac{1}{4}$ lb. The mines in *Soronga* are stated to be very rich, the copper ore raised, also, being impregnated with gold. The ore from *Satzuma* yields from 4 to 6 oz. per $1\frac{1}{4}$ lb. These are the principal mines. *Gold-dust* is also found in some of the streams. *Tin* is found in *Bungo* in a remarkably fine state; but it is not held in any estimation. *Iron* is confined to three provinces, but there it is most abundant : it is but little used. *Silver* is abundant. *Copper* is super-abundant, and preferred to iron. Of *Coal*, of good quality, there is no scarcity either in the northern or southern provinces : it is generally made into *Coke*. *Sulphur* is very abundant; and *Salt* is manufactured from sea-water.

*Sowas* is a compound metal, copper with a small proportion of gold intermixed. It is represented to be very beautiful ; and is highly prized. [*Kæmpfer. Charlevoix. Siebold.*]

NOTE F.

𝔓unctuality in entertaining 𝔖trangers.

It may be considered that sufficient evidence in corroboration of this representation is distributed throughout the volume; but there appears to be an interest in the following narrative, which renders it worthy of being cited. It affords a curious illustration of Japonese manners at the period it was written, and exhibits the relations subsisting between a Japonese Sovereign and his subjects in a most favourable point of view.

The narrator is *Captain Cock,* in a letter to England, dated December, 1613. He says : " The thirtieth day [*of October*], the Captain *Chinesa* (our landlord) came vnto mee, and told mee of a generall collection which was made throughout euery house in the Towne [*Firando*], to send presents of eatable commodities to the kings, for the more honour of a great feast they have tomorrow, with a comœdie, or play. And so by his councell (with aduice of others) I ordained two bottles of *Spanish* wine, two roasted hennes, a roasted pigge, a small quantitie ruske [*biscuits*], and three boxes banketting stuff [*sweet-meats*], to send to their feast tomorrow. And before night the yong king sent one of his men vnto mee, to furnish them with *English* apparell, for the better setting out of their comœdie, namely a pair of Stamel-cloath breeches. I returned answere, I had none such, neither did know any other which had : notwithstanding, if any apparell I had would pleasure his highnesse, I would willingly geue it him. And within night both the kings sent to me, to bring Master *Foster*, the master [*of the Clove*], and be a spectator of their comœdie tomorrow. The one and thirtieth before dinner, I sent our present aforesaid to the kings by our jurebasso [*interpreter*], desiring their highnesses to pardon the master and my selfe, and that we would·come to them some other time, when there were lesse people : but that would not serue the turne, for they would needs haue our companie, and to bring Master *Eaton* (afterwards one of the factors) along with vs : which wee did, and had a place appointed for vs, where we sate and sawe all at our pleasures. And the old king him selfe came and brought vs a collation in sight of all the people ; and after, *Semidone* [chief lord of the council] did the like in name of both the kings ; and after, diuers noblemen of the king's folowers made vs a third collation. But the matter I noted most of all was their comoedie (or play), the actors being the kings themselves, with the greatest noblemen and princes. The matter was of the valiant deeds of their ancestors, from the beginning of their kingdome, or commonwealth, vntill this present, with much mirth mixed among, to giu the common people content. The audience was great, for no house in toune but brought a present, nor no village nor place vnder their dominions but did the like, and were spectators. And the kings them selues did see that euery one, both great and small, did eate and drinke before they departed."

The promoter of this entertainment was Foyne Sama, the king of Firando, the hospitable entertainer of the English on the arrival in Japon. Regarding him, Captain Cock observes in a letter, dated in 1620: "This king (or Tono) of Firando, hath but six mangocas [of rice : equivalent to something more than £. Stg. 56,000]; yet it is esteemed as much as the greatest earldome in England, he being stinted at 4000 souldiers, or men at armes; 2000 to keepe his owne countrie, and 2000 to serue the emperour at demand; but he is able to set out many thousands if need require." Laying aside all state, however, he would oft times visit the English-house at the supper-meal, carrying himself merrily, and partaking with hearty good will of such cheer as he found provided. His simplicity of manners was such, that he would solicit, and receive with grateful acknowledgments, "a peece, or two, of poudred beefe, or porcke, sod with turnips and onions"; and a bottle of wine, sent to him when he was sick, was received with hearty thanks.

Much to the credit, too, of this good old man, his good-will was not confined to the chiefs of the mission. It was extended to the subordinates. On one occasion, he noticed a party of the people from the Clove labouring hard in landing the great guns from the ship, and he proffered them assistance. This being declined, he presented the party with a barrel of wine and "certain fish", to testify his approbation of their exertions. [*Purchas.*]

NOTE G.

**Birds.**

*Poultry* is most abundant ; but the cock-birds are seldom killed, being held in great esteem, especially by the religious orders, because they measure time, and are believed to prognosticate changes in the weather. *Tame* and *wild-ducks* literally swarm. One species, called *kinmodsui*, is remarkable for the splendour of its plumage, and its singular form. *Wild-geese* are no less common than wild-ducks. The *crane* is regarded as a bird of good omen, and is always addressed by the title of "*O Isuri Sama*": i. e., "*My great lord crane*". To receive one of these birds as a present, is esteemed an honour. Of *herons*, there are several varieties; they are used in fishing; and one species rivals the crane in size. *Hawks* are abundant, and are used in taking game. *Pheasants* are common: one variety displaying a tail nearly equal to the height of a man, with plumage not inferior to that of the peacock. *Storks* remain in the country all the year round. *Nightingales* when they sing well, sell as high as 20 cobangs of gold : equivalent to about £. Stg. 26. *Larks* sing better than in Europe. *Pigeons* are innumerable; but they are not harboured in houses : experience having proved the dung to be liable to spontaneous combustion. There are also *wood-cocks, falcons, ravens,* with most of the smaller birds common to Europe.

*Birds peculiar to the country.*—The *foken,* or *fototenis,* is "a night bird", of most delicious flavour ; costly in price, and only served at the tables of the nobility on extraordinary occasions. The *misage,* or *bisage,* is a voracious sea-bird, of the hawk breed. This bird selects a hole in a rock for the deposit of the fish it takes : which is found to keep as well as pickled fish, and is much prized. Their store-houses are eagerly sought by the people, and the discoverer, if he proceed with moderation, derives considerable profit from the produce. [*Kæmpfer. Charlevoix.*]

## NOTE H.

### Education.

*Saint François Xavier,* writing from Japon towards the close of the sixteenth century, mentions the existence of four "academies" in the vicinity of Meaco, at each of which education was afforded to between three and four thousand pupils ; adding, that considerable as these numbers were, they were insignificant in comparison with the numbers instructed at an institution near the city of Bandoue; and that such institutions were universal throughout the Empire. [*Charlevoix.*]

*Meylan*, writing at the commencement of the present century, observes, that children of both sexes and of all ranks are invariably sent to rudimentary schools, where they learn to read and write, and to acquire some knowledge of the history of their country. To this extent it is considered necessary the meanest peasant should be educated, if not more highly. [*Manners and Customs of the Japonese in the Nineteenth Century.*]

*On the visit of H. M. ship Samarang*, in 1845, it was ascertained that a college existed at Nangasaki, in which, in addition to the routine of native acquirements, foreign languages were taught. Among the visitors on board the ship, many spoke Dutch. One young student understood English slightly, could pronounce a few English words, caught readily at every expression, and recorded it in his note-book. Some understood a little French. All appeared to be well acquainted with geography; and many appeared to be conversant with guns and the science of gunnery. The desire to acquire information, is represented to have been excessive. [*Narrative of the Voyage*, vol. ii, pp. 14-15, etc.]

NOTE I.

### Martial Character.

*Kæmpfer* observes: " The Japonese are not wanting something, which I don't know whether I shall call it boldness, or heroism." This characteristic may be traced from the early conflicts of this nation with the invading Tartars, in A.D. 1275, through their incessantly occurring intestine wars, to the heroic action near Simabara, A.D. 1638, in which the insurgent Catholic converts of Arima distinguished themselves. Forty thousand of these men threw themselves into a fortress, which art had made strong, but which time had rendered scarcely defensible. Although a formidable army was sent against them by the Emperor, they could not be reduced without European aid; and their reduction was only effected by almost total annihilation. The Dutch lent an armed ship, from which, and from batteries erected on shore, upwards of four hundred balls were thrown against the fortress in less than a fortnight. The crumbling walls were reduced to powder, and the imperial troops swarming through the breaches, put the wretched remains of the garrison mercilessly to the sword. Upwards of thirty-seven thousand victims are stated to have fallen during the entire conflict.

*Sir Edward Michellborne* records the fact of the " Japons not being suffered to land in any port in India with weapons, being accounted a people so desperate and daring, that they were feared in all places where they came"; and he graphically narrates the attempt made by a party of rovers to capture the ship in which he had embarked, and was proceeding on a voyage towards the East Indies, in the year 1604. The ship in question was named the *Tiger*, of two hundred and forty tons burthen, and commanded by *Captain John Davis*. She was accompanied by a pinnace, of forty tons, called the *Tiger's Whelp*. The rovers, when fallen in with, were in a small junk in a very leaky condition: which they had stolen. Their own vessel, with her armament and stores, had been wrecked. The demeanour of the rovers was so quiet, that suspicion was lulled, and they were invited on board the English vessel, while a party of the English were despatched to overhaul the junk. Upwards of twenty of the rovers accepted the invitation; and they had not been long on board, before, on a signal, apparently preconcerted, the crew left on the junk assailed the English sailors; of whom many were killed, and the rest driven over-board. "Those that were aboord my ship," the narrator says, " sallied out of my cabbin, where they were, with such weapons as they had,

finding certain targets in my cabbin, and other things, that
they vsed as weapons.   My selfe beeing aloft on the decke,
knowing what was likely to follow, leapt into the waste, where
with boate swaines, carpenter, and some few more, wee kept
them vnder the halfe-decke.   At their first coming forth of
the cabbin, they met *Captaine Dauis* coming out of the gun-
roome, whom they pulled into the cabbin, and giuing him
sixe or seuen mortall wounds, they thrust him out of the
cabbin before them.   His wounds were so mortall, that he
dyed as soone as he came into the waste.   They pressed so
fiercely to come to vs, as we receiuing them on our pikes,
they would gather on our pikes with their hands to reach vs
with their swords.   It was halfe an houre before we could
stone them back into the cabbin: in which time we had
killed three or foure of their leaders.   After they were driuen
into the cabbin, they fought with vs at the least foure houres,
before wee could suppress them, often fyring the cabbin,
burning the bedding, and much other stuffe that was there.
And had wee not with two demy-culuerings, from vnder the
halfe-decke, beaten down the bulke-head and the pumpe of
the ship, wee could not have suppressed them from burning
the ship.   This ordnance being charged with crosse-barres,
bullets, and case-shot, and bent close to the bulke-head, so
violently marred them with boords and splinters, that it left
but one of them standinge, of two and twentie.   Their legs,
armes, and bodies, were so torne, as it was strange to see
how the shot had massacred them."   The narrative concludes
with these remarks: " In all this conflict they neuer would
desire their liues, though they were hopelesse to escape:
svch was the desperatenesse of these *Japonians*."   [*Purchas.*]

   That patriotism was combined with valour in early times,
the following instance will demonstrate.   In 1630, the Dutch
held the island of Formosa; and a Japonese vessel, belonging to Satzuma, coming to trade, the governor, *Peter Nuits*,
treated the crew with great harshness and severity.   This

was considered by their countrymen as a national affront, and was taken up as such. Seven of the young men attached to the Prince's guard volunteered to revenge the insult; and having obtained permission, proceeded to carry their project into execution. They set sail from Satzuma, and after a happy voyage, arrived at Formosa. Being admitted to an audience, they drew their cattans, seized on the person of the governor, and carried him off prisoner to their vessel. This audacious act was performed at mid-day, and in the midst of his guards and domestics, who were deterred from attempting a rescue by the threats of the Japonians to stab their captive to the heart, should any opposition be offered. [*Kœmpfer, Appendix*, vol. ii.]

The total cessation of internal broils, and the non-existence of external wars, were followed by the deterioration of the military character. The pitch to which the demoralization had risen was such when Yousi-Moune, the eighth Cubo-Sama, succeeded to power, that the soldiery disgraced themselves by painting their faces, staining their lips, and dressing like women. The indignation of the new Cubo-Sama was excited by this effeminate conduct on the part of the troops; and he issued strict orders, that the training, by which they were originally rendered robust and hardy, should forthwith be resumed. The orders were rigidly enforced, and with excellent effect. The warriors soon became so expert in shooting with bow and arrow, that, riding at full speed, many would not fail to hit a mark a hundred times in succession. So great also was the skill they acquired in other exercises, that one man would defend himself successfully with his pike against five or six antagonists; while another would keep at bay, fencing with his cattan, a bevy of assailants. Swimming had been neglected, because the men feared that exposure to the sun on coming out of the water would embrown their fair features. This exercise Yousi-Moune revived. He instituted swimming matches, which took place periodically in his presence, and he gave prizes to the most skilful.    On one of these occasions, a man named Yamamoto-Kintarou, crossed the river Asakousa, eight hundred and forty feet broad, thirty-six times in succession; and another, Awasou, kept his whole body above the navel, out of water.    In short, under the rule of this Cubo-Sama, dexterity in gymnastic exercises was the only sure way to military promotion.    [*Titsingh.*]

### Neat and Fine Habits.

*Kæmpfer* observes :   " They are very nice in keeping themselves, their cloaths, and houses, clean and neat."    It may be added, that, to every house of any pretension to respectability, an apartment termed a "*Fro*" is attached : which is fitted up with vapour, warm, and cold baths.    One or the other of these, the Japonese use every morning, and also when their daily occupations are over.    The nature of the Japonese costume obviates any trouble in undressing. It is only necessary to unfasten the girdle that encircles the waist, and the ample habiliments of the wearer drop at once to the ground.    A minute description of the fro, with the process of heating, is given in *Kæmpfer*, vol. ii. pp. 424-5. To this practice of constant bathing, the German author attributes the generally robust health, and longevity of the people in the Empire.

### Family Intercourse.

The love, obedience, and reverence, manifested by children towards their parents are stated to be unbounded : while the confidence placed by parents in their children is represented to be without limit.    Parents select their children to be arbitrators in their disputes with others, and submit implicitly to their decisions. It is also a constant practice with parents to resign their state and property to a son when he shall have attained a suitable age, remaining for the rest of life dependent on him for support; and abuse of this trust is said to be unknown. This practice exists even in the Daïri, and is resorted to by the Mikado, that he may enjoy the pleasure of contemplating his child in the enjoyment of rank and honour. [*Kæmpfer. Charlevoix. Titsingh. " Manners and Customs of the Japonese, etc."*]

NOTE L.

**Additional traits of Character, Manners, and Customs.**

The Japonese have adopted white as the colour denoting grief. They regard black teeth and black nails as beauties, and stain them accordingly. The left side, being that on which the sword is borne, is deemed the most honourable; and respect is paid by placing persons on the left hand. On entering a chamber, to pay a formal visit, a cloak of ceremony is put on, which is removed on retiring. On occasions of state, their servants precede them; and when they retire from the presence of a superior, they turn the backs on him. Invalids are allowed to gratify their appetites in any manner they please; on the principle, that the desire is dictated by nature. In cases of cholic, acu-punctuation is adopted, to disperse flatulency: to which the disorder is attributed. The abdomen of the pregnant female is tightly compressed with a bandage: in order to facilitate parturition. The chambers of those sick with the small-pox, are hung with scarlet cloth; and the attendants are also clothed in red.

The women of Japon are represented to be intelligent, and agreeable in their manners: to make affectionate wives; and to be examples of conjugal fidelity. They resent dishonour;

and there is more than one instance recorded, of death having been inflicted on her dishonourer, by the injured woman. As an evidence of determination of character, the following anecdote is related. A man of rank went on a journey, and a noble in authority made overtures to his wife. They were rejected with scorn and indignation; but the libertine, by force or fraud, accomplished his object. The husband returned, and was received by his wife with affection, but with a dignified reserve, that excited his surprise. He sought explanations but could not obtain them at once. His wife prayed him to restrain himself till the morrow, and then before her relations and the chief people of the city, whom she had invited to an entertainment, his desire should be satisfied. The morrow came, and with it the guests, including the noble who had done the wrong. The entertainment was given, in a manner not unusual in the country, on the terraced roof of the house. The repast was concluded, when the lady rose and made known the outrage to which she had been subjected, and passionately demanded that her husband should slay her : as an unworthy object, unfit to live. The guests, the husband foremost, besought her to be calm : they strove to impress her with the idea that she had done no wrong : that she was an innocent victim, though the author of the outrage merited no less punishment than death. She thanked them all kindly. She wept on her husband's shoulder. She kissed him affectionately. Then suddenly escaping from his embraces, rushed precipitately to the edge of the terrace, and cast herself over the parapet. In the confusion that ensued, the author of the mischief, still unsuspected, for the hapless creature had not indicated the offender, made his way down the stairs. When the rest of the party arrived, he was found weltering in his blood by the corse of his victim. He had expiated his crime by committing suicide in the national manner : by slashing himself across the abdomen with two slashes, in the form of a cross.

The system of self-immolation, of which an example is given above, constitutes a singular trait in the national character. In some cases it is compulsory: in others voluntary. All military men, with the immediate dependents of the Emperor, and all persons holding appointments under the government who may be guilty of certain crimes, are under the necessity of ripping themselves up, on receiving an order to that effect. In contemplation of such an event, all persons affected by the ordinance, carry with them when they are travelling, in addition to their ordinary habiliments, and the dress worn in cases of fire, a suit appropriate to the occasion. It consists of a white robe and a kerrimon (or cloak) of ceremony, made of hempen cloth, and destitute of the armorial bearings that are usually displayed. The outside of the house where the ceremony takes place is also hung with white. The ceremony itself is thus regulated. On the order of the Sovereign being communicated to the offender, he forthwith despatches invitations to his friends for a specified day. The visitors are regaled with Zakhi (a strong water distilled from rice), and when a certain quantity has been drunk, the host takes leave of his friends, preparatory to the second reading of the order for his death. This being done, usually among the highest, in the presence of the secretary and the government officer, the condemned man makes a speech, or offers some complimentary address to the company. Then inclining his head forward, he unsheathes his cattan, and inflicts two gashes on his abdomen, one horizontal, and the other perpendicular. A confidential servant, who is stationed for the purpose in the rear, immediately smites off the head of his master.

The deed, as before observed, is in some instances voluntary: in case of consciousness of guilt entailing death on the offender: to avoid disgrace: or to gratify revenge. In regard to the latter point, *M. Caron* relates a remarkable instance, which occurred within his own knowledge. It appears that two high officers of the court met on the palace-stairs and

jostled each other. One was an irascible man, and immediately demanded satisfaction. The other, of a placable disposition, represented that the circumstance was accidental,
and tendered an ample apology: representing that satisfaction could not reasonably be demanded. The irascible man,
however, would not be appeased, and finding he could not
provoke the other to a conflict, suddenly drew up his robes,
unsheathed his cattan, and cut himself in the prescribed
mode. As a point of honour, his adversary was under the
necessity of following the example, and the irascible man,
before he breathed his last, had the gratification of seeing
the object of his passion dying beside him.

To perform this act with grace, dexterity, and precision, is
considered a high accomplishment; and the youth of Japan
bestow as much pains, under efficient tutors, to acquire the
art, as European youths take to become elegant dancers, or
skilful horsemen.

Music, dancing, and the drama, are favourite amusements.
Mummers and mountebanks parade the streets. Domestic
performances are also common. The mendicants exhibit
touches of humour : a troop apparently of " halt, lame, and
blind", will one moment solicit alms in doleful strains, and
the next, throwing off disguise, leap about and chant merrily,
in return for the guerdon that may have been bestowed on
them : or, calculating that they are more likely to gain their
object by mirth, than by persisting in the assumption of distress, the unreality of which can be easily detected. During
fine weather, junketting parties into the country are universal.
The more wealthy place themselves under the direction of a
professional master of the ceremonies. He amuses the company by retailing the tattle of the town, by his " quips and
cranks", and by a certain degree of buffoonery. Yet should
any of the party in the exuberance of their spirits encroach
on decorum, he immediately interposes his authority, and
is implicitly obeyed.

Regarding the disposition of the people, the following passages that occur in the diary of *Captain Cock*, the chief of the English factory at Firando, may be cited. Under the date of the 27th of October 1615, the writer says : " We set the maste of our junke, *Sea Adventure*, this day. At the doing wherof, were 3 or 400 men present. All the neighboures (or rather all the towne) sending their seruants ; and came them selues (them that were of accointance), and brought presents, *nifon cantange* (after Japon maner) of wyne, and other eating comodety, abord the juncke, wishing a prosperouse voyag : all the officers hauing eache one a present of a little barso of wyne." And on the 28th of December of the same year, it is recorded : " The China capten buylte, or reard, a new howse this day, and all the neighboures sent hym presents, *nifon cantange ;* so I sent hym a bottell morosack, 2 bottells Spanish wyne, a dried salmon, and halfe a Hollands cheese. And after went my selfe with the neighboures : where I saw the seremony was vsed, the carpenter of the king [of Firando] doing it ; and it was as followeth. *First,* they brought in all the presents sent, and sett them in ranke before the middell post of the howse, and out of eiche one took something of the best, and offred it at the foot of the post ; and powered wyne vpon eache severall parcell ; doing it in great humilitie and silence, not so much as a word spoaken all the while it was doing. *But* beinge ended, they took the remeander of the presents, and soe did eate and drinke with much mirth and jesting, drinking them selues drunken, all, or the most parte. *They* tould mee, they believed that a new howse being hallowed in this sort, could not chuse but be happie to hym which dwelled in it ; for soe their law taught them, ordayned by holy men in tymes past." In further evidence of the kindly disposition of this people, their treatment of the Dutch from 1799 to 1817 cannot in justice be omitted. Shut out for this period from nearly all intercourse with their native country, the factors of Dezima were frequently destitute of the means of paying

their daily expenses, and of procuring the necessary articles
of food. But it is written, "This formidable calamity was
alleviated by the liberality of the native government, which
at once ordered the factory to be supported in their temporary
distress by the Nangasackè treasury; and the governor sent
regularly twice or thrice a week to inquire whether their pur-
veyors duly supplied them, or if they were in want of anything." *Doeff*, resident at the time in the factory, says:
"They made every exertion to relieve, as far as possible,
the disagreeableness of our dismal situation. The spy,
[? *purveyor*] Segè Dennoxen, among other things, took great
pains to distil us some gin. He succeeded tolerably; though
he could not get rid of the resinous taste of the juniper
berries; but he produced corn-brandy, that was really excellent."

To sum up the character of the Japonese. They carry notions
of honour to the verge of fanaticism; and they are haughty,
vindictive, and licentious. On the other hand, brawlers,
braggarts, and backbiters, are held in the most supreme con-
tempt. The slightest infraction of truth is punished with
severity; they are open-hearted, hospitable, and as friends,
faithful to death. It is represented, there is no peril a Japonese will not encounter to serve a friend: that no torture
will compel him to betray a trust; and that even the stranger
who seeks aid, will be protected to the last drop of
blood. The nation, with all their faults and vices, evinced
qualities that won the hearts, and commanded the esteem of
the missionary-fathers. Saint François Xavier concludes one
of his letters by saying: " I am loth to finish when I discourse
of Japons, who verily are the delight of my heart." Father
Lewis Froës, too, after a residence of some years at the court,
eloquently defends the people against detractors: he emphatically pronounces them to be " as gifted a nation as any in
Europe"; and energetically declares, that no one will gainsay
him but those who have not had the means of forming a

correct judgment. [*Kœmpfer. Charlevoix. Titsingh. " Manners and Customs, etc." Montanus. Ogilby. E. I. Mss.*]

## NOTE M.

### Beasts.

These include *bears :* with *hyenas* according to Titsingh, though Kæmpfer does not mention them; *wild dogs; deer* in abundance; *monkeys,* and *foxes* in considerable numbers. The latter are held to be in league with the devil, but, it is said, " the fox-hunters are expert in conjuring and stripping this animated devil, the hair and wool being much coveted for writing and painting pencils." [*Kœmpfer.*] There are also *hares* and *rabbits. Rats* and *mice* swarm. The former are taught very diverting tricks by the jugglers. The *cats* are very beautiful, of a whitish colour, with large yellow and black spots, and a very short tail, as if it had been purposely cropped. " They don't care for mousing, but love mightily to be carried about and caressed, chiefly by women." [*Kœmpfer.*] *Dogs* abound. The *horses* are small, but of good quality, some breeds being equal to the Persian in form and speed. *Buffaloes* are of a very large size, and used in the cities as beasts of burden. *Oxen* are used entirely for agricultural purposes, and for draft. The repugnance which is stated to have been felt to killing these animals in early times, still exists. Captain Sir Edward Belcher, on his visit to Nangasaki (1845), requested to be supplied with some bullocks, but could not obtain them. When he inquired the reason, he received the following characteristic reply : " The Japanese do not eat *cows;* they do their duty, they bear calves, they give milk; it is sinful to take it, they require it to rear their calves, and because they do this, they are not allowed to work. The *bulls* do their work; they labour at the plough, they get thin, you cannot eat them, it is not just to kill a beast that does its duty; but the *hogs* are indolent,

lazy, do no work, they are proper for food." The hogs supplied to the Samarang "were overwhelmed with their own
fat, and weighed about 150 lbs." [*Narr. of the Voyage.*]

*The animals peculiar to the country* are the *fanuki,* something resembling the fox, and the *itutz* and *tin,* two small
animals of a red colour, that live under the roofs of the
houses, and are very tame.

NOTE N.

### Fish and Marine Productions.

The seas by which Japon is surrounded teem with animal
life : supplying a boundless store of food to the inhabitants ;
and, through the fisheries, affording employment to vast numbers, both of males and females. The *fisherwomen* are a peculiar race. Their homes are literally on the waters. Boats
are their only habitations. They swim like the natives of
the element, and in diving, the males are inferior to them in
skill. "By diving," it is said, "they will catch fish which
by net and lines have been missed, and that in eight fathoms
depth." They are no less hardy and daring than skilful.
Armed with a long keen knife, or a spear, they plunge boldly
into the waters, and fearlessly meet the whales, porpoises, and
other large fish, by which they are constantly encountered.

The seas of Japon yield seventy species of fish, with many
varieties of each species. Most descriptions common to
Europe are included.

Of *whales,* six varieties are enumerated. The flesh of most
varieties is esteemed good and wholesome : so much so, that
to the use of this kind of food, the fishermen and common
people attribute their healthiness, and the capability they
exhibit, in an extraordinary degree, of enduring exposure to
cold and foul weather. In other respects, the whale is most
valuable to the Japonese. Excepting the large shoulder
bone, every part of the fish is converted to some useful pur-

pose. The flesh and the intestines (called, from their remarkable length, *fiakfiro*, or hundred fathoms) are either roasted,
boiled, fried, or pickled, and used as an article of food: which
is the case even with the sediment of the blubber, when it
has been twice boiled for the oil. The cartilaginous bones
are also eaten, either boiled when fresh, or dried for future
use. The nervous and tendinous parts, both white and yellow, are worked into strings, cords, and ropes; some being
used for musical instruments, but most in the apparatus for the
manufacture of cotton goods. Several small things are made
of the jaw-bones, fins, and other bones, particularly the fine
steelyards used for weighing gold and silver. The Japonese
have a mode of *whale-fishing* peculiar to themselves, which
was introduced, in 1680, by a wealthy and ingenious *fisher-
man* of *Omura*, named *Gilaijo*, and which is not resorted to
generally, only on account of the expensiveness of the tackle
that is required. The apparatus is made of strong rope,
two inches thick, made into a net, in which, by dexterous
management, the fish is entangled by the head, and is
thus more easily captured than by means of the harpoon
alone.

The *satisfoko* is peculiar to Japon. It varies in size from
two to six fathoms, having two long teeth, or tusks, standing
out, upwards, from the mouth. They are much used to ornament the tops of buildings. According to the account *Kæmpfer* received from the fishermen: "this fish is a cunning and
mortal enemy of whales, killing them by creeping into the
mouth, and devouring their tongues; as he hath a way, as
he creeps in, to put his head and teeth in such a way, that
they are no hindrance to him."

The *furube* is another native fish, which possesses the power
of distending, or blowing itself out to the shape of a ball.
There are three varieties: two most delicate in flavour, but
dangerous to eat on account of their poisonous qualities, unless cleansed with scrupulous care. By imperial ordinance,

R

the soldiery are forbidden from using this fish as food; and if any one in office should chance to die in consequence of indulging in this luxury, his son is precluded from filling the post vacated by his deceased parent, which he would otherwise be entitled to occupy in the ordinary course of succession. The third variety is a mortal poison, and is eaten solely as an agreeable means of committing suicide.

The *sea-horse* or *sea-dog* is a singular fish, thus described : " He is much about the length of a boy ten years of age, without any scales or fins, with a large head, mouth, and breast, and a large thin belly, like a bag, which will hold a large quantity of water. He hath thin sharp teeth in the chaps, much like a snake. The inner parts are so minute, that they are scarce visible. He hath two cartilaginous feet, not unlike the hands of a child, under the belly, by which means he creeps, in all likelihood, or walks, at the bottom of the sea. All his parts are eaten, none excepted." This fish, *Kæmpfer* represents to be abundant in the markets.

The *tai* is one of many varieties of a species of carp. It is regarded as the emblem of happiness, and is dedicated to *Ibis*, the Japonese Neptune. This fish has a most beautiful appearance : possesses a most exquisite flavour ; and is an indispensable dish at the imperial feasts, and at other entertainments of high order. At certain seasons this fish is very scarce, and has been known to fetch as much as a thousand kobans of gold, equal to about 1,300*l*.

In the estuaries, two varieties of *salmon* are found, exclusive of other sorts in the fresh-water lakes. Of *cod*, there are two varieties. Of *eels*, there are many sorts, including the conger. The *rays* measure from two to three fathoms in length, and there are many other descriptions of *flat-fish* of an unusually large size. The *bonito, sardine,* and *herring,* are kinds different from the European. The *pilchard* and *smelt* are exceedingly plentiful. The *flying-fish* is esteemed a delicacy, but is rarely caught.

*Shrimps, lobsters,* and *crabs* abound. One variety of the latter is of " singular structure, with a long serrated prickle, or sword, standing out from the head, and a roundish, smooth back." Another variety is exceedingly large. *Kæmpfer* bought the hind claw of one in a cook-shop at Sorongo, which he describes as being " as long, and full as big, as a man's shin bone."

Of *sepiæ,* there are three kinds : one said to be of such dimensions, that it can scarcely be lifted by two men. When dried, they form a staple article of food. *Turtles* are abundant, and, on the southern and eastern coasts, they are represented to be of sufficient size "to cover a man from head to toe."

*Oysters, cockles,* and *muscles,* exist in profusion; so also does the *haliotus.* This mollusc is pickled and exported to China in large quantities. *Krusenstern* and his companions "thought them no bad food; and they may well form part of a ship's provision, as they will keep during several years." They are relished as an article of food in the British Channel-islands, as well as in Japon and China.

Among other marine productions, *algæ* are most abundant; and the utmost attention is paid to the selection and curing of proper sorts for food : probably as they prepare the delicacy called "*laver*" on the western coasts of England. One variety is largely exported from Yesso to Nipon. [*Kæmpfer. Broughton. Krusenstern.*]

NOTE O.

**Produce of the Fields.**

The principal produce of the fields is included in the general term "*Gokokf,*" or, "*The five fruits of the field,*" and consist of, 1. *Kome* or *rice,* superior to that produced in any other country, and which is kept for many years by being immersed in muddy water, and the sediment allowed to dry on. 2.

*Oomuggi* (great corn), or *barley ;* the general food of cattle, though occasionally used in the kitchen; and a variety of which, with purple-coloured ears, presents a beautiful appearance when waving under a bright sun. 3. *Koomuggi* (small corn), or *wheat ;* extremely cheap, and of no estimation. 4. *Daidsu,* or *Daid-beans ;* from which *soeju,* or *soy,* is made; and which is also highly esteemed as an article of food. 5. *Adsuki,* or *sodsu,* or *so-beans* (similar to *lentils*) ; made into flour, baked with sugar, and prepared in cakes.

Other productions are *awa,* or *Indian corn ; kibi* and *fije,* two varieties of millet; *pease ; turnips* of extraordinary size, as well as *radishes. Meylan (Manners and Customs of the Japonese in the Nineteenth Century)* states, it is not uncommon for a radish to attain the weight of 15 lbs., or sometimes 50 and 60 lbs. *Horse-radish, carrots, gourds, melons, cucumbers, fennell,* and some sorts of *lettuce,* which are cultivated with care in European gardens, grow spontaneously in Japon. *Parsley, cummin, succory,* and the common lettuce of Europe, have been introduced, and thrive, *Kœmpfer* says, " extraordinarily well." The garden *parsnip* is unknown, but a wild variety is abundant. *Mushrooms* are found everywhere. The Japanese have the art of depriving poisonous plants of their noxious qualities, and of rendering them edible. Amongst plants of this description that they use for food, are the *konjakf,* a species of *dracunculus ;* the *warabi* or *fern ;* and *ren,* or *faba Egyptiaca.*

*Cotton* and *hemp* are grown wherever the ground can be spared. The *hemp-nettle* is abundant, and much used. *Plants* from which *oil* are extracted for culinary purposes, abound. *Tobacco* is good and plentiful. The plant was introduced into Japon at the beginning of the seventeenth century. At the time James the First, of England, issued his " *Counterblast,*" it appears from Captain Cock's *Diary,* (*E. I. Mss.*), that Ogosho Sama, Emperor of Japon, was issuing edicts against, and subjecting to severe punishments the growers and consumers of, the "weed." James and Ogosho Sama are dead. The "drinking of tobacco", however, survives.[1]

## Chia, or Tea.

This plant is called by the Japonese *tsjaa*,[2] and by the Chinese *the'h*. It is cultivated only round the edges and borders of fields, without any regard to the soil: or in places which would otherwise be waste; and the produce of Japon is therefore generally inferior to the Chinese. The only plants cultivated with anything like care, are those grown at *Udsi*. This is an imperial property; and the produce is appropriated solely to the use of the Emperor. *Kæmpfer* computes all the charges of cultivating, gathering, preparing, and sending this description of tea up to the court, at not less than from thirty to forty *taies* (from £. stg. 7 : 10 to £. stg. 10) per *catti*, of about a pound and a quarter English. At the same time, he says, the chief purveyor does not hesitate to charge at the rate of one hundred *taies* (£. stg. 25) per *catti*; and in illustration of the subject, observes: "In our audience at court, it is customary to treat us with tea"; and adds, "I remember one gentleman, then in waiting, presented a dish to me, with the following compliment: '*Drink heartily, and with pleasure, for one dish costs one itzebo*,' or from twelve to thirteen shillings sterling."

The Japonese process of making tea, and the ceremony of

[1] *Captain Cock*, in his Diary (E. I. Mss.), mentions the destruction of four or five hundred houses in a town, occasioned by the carelessness of a smoker. Conflagrations, when they occur in Japon, are awfully destructive; and the edict of Ogosho Sama against smoking, may have originated from a desire to prevent the waste of property which might be occasioned by perseverance in the habit.

[2] In noticing this beverage, *Captain Cock* (E. I. Mss.) constantly makes mention of "CHAW-CUPS", which may give some idea of the true pronunciation of the word. The orthography of the word in *Ogilby* is "CHOA".

drinking tea, present some features of novelty. Tea in Japon is made in three different ways. The first is by simple infusion, in the ordinary and well-known mode. The second is by grinding the leaves (either the day before, or the day on which they are to be used) in a hand-mill, made of a peculiar stone; and the powder thus produced is placed in a box, which is added to the rest of the tea-table furniture. At meal-time, the "dishes" being filled with hot water, the box is opened, and with a small neat spoon, as much of the powder is taken out as will lie on the point of a pretty large knife, and put into every dish. After this, it is mixed and shaken with a "curious denticulated instrument till it foams, and is so presented to be sipped while it is hot." This tea is called *koitsjaa*, i. e., *thick tea*, and is that which the great men and rich people in Japon daily use. The third way is by perfect boiling. Before daybreak, one of the domestics rises, hangs the kettle over the fire, and puts in (either when the water is cold, or after it is heated) two, three, or more handsfull of *bantsjaa* leaves,[1] according to the quantity required for the day. At the same time he puts in a basket exactly fitting the inside of the kettle. By this means, the leaves are kept down to the bottom, so as to prevent any impediment being offered to drawing off the fluid. A bag is sometimes substituted for the basket, which answers the purpose equally well. The kettle is kept boiling throughout the day. The contents are at the service of the passers-by, as well as of the family; and a basin of cold water is placed near the kettle, so that persons in haste may cool the drink, and be enabled to slake their thirst at once, with a hearty draught. Many of the peasantry also boil their rice in a decoction of tea, which is considered to produce a dish no less nutritious than econo-

---

[1] It is only the *bantsjaa leaves* that are boiled. Their virtues are more fixed than in any other kinds; and they contain a quantity of resinous matter that cannot be well extracted by simple infusion. [*Kœmpfer.*]

mical. One portion of rice thus cooked, it is said, will go as far as three portions dressed in the ordinary way.

When, through age, the leaves have lost their virtue for use as a beverage, they are used to dye silk-stuffs, to which they give a brown or chestnut colour.

With regard to the ceremony observed at tea-drinkings, *Kœmpfer* observes: " It is a particular art to make tea, and to serve it in company; which, however, consists more in certain decent and agreeable manners, than in any difficulty as to the boiling or preparation. This art is called *sado* and *tsianoi*. "As there are people in Europe," he continues, " who teach to carve, to dance, to sing, and other things of the like nature, so there are masters in Japon who teach children of both sexes what they call *tsianoi*; that is, to be-have well when in company with tea-drinkers, and also to make the tea, and to present it in company with a genteel, becoming, and graceful manner."—(*App.*, vol. ii, pp. 3-16, ed. 1727.)

## NOTE Q.

### Trees.

Arbores vel ad amœnitatem, vel ad fructum serunt haud absimiles nostris. . . . . Plurima vero variis locis exsurgit cedrus, tantæ proceritatis et crassitudinis, vt inde fabri basi-licarum columnas, et cuiuslibet quamuis capacis onerariæ malos efficiant. *(Ortelius, sub voc. Japonia, Theatrum Orbis Tenarum, Antv.* 1595.) The missionary *Almeyda,* in 1565, visited the temple of *Cosanga,* in the vicinity of the city of *Nara.* The approach was through an avenue of pines and cedars intermixed, " qui faisoient une fort belle symétrée, et dont les têtes se joignoient tellement, que le soleil n'y pouvoit percer." Some of the cedars, the trunks of which were quite symmetrical, measured " cinq brasses"[1] in circum-

---

[1] BRASSE, f. *A fadome.* Cotgrave, Dictionary, 1611.

ference. The roof of the temple was supported by ninety columns of cedar, of prodigious height, perfectly round, and measuring eighteen feet and a half in girth. This temple was built, about seventy years before, on the ruins of a more magnificent edifice, that had been destroyed by fire. The bases of some of the original columns remained, and indicated larger dimensions than those of the growing trees already noticed. (*Charlevoix*, t. ii, pp. 248-9, edit. 1754.) *Captain Sir Edward Belcher*, of H.M.S. *Samarang*, was supplied gratuitously, in 1845, at Nangasaki, with a quantity of spars. "The *small spars* (for studding sail-booms, etc.) were of cedar, measuring about ninety-six feet in length, by fourteen inches at the butt." (*Voyage*, Lond. 1848, vol. ii, p. 13.) *Kæmpfer*, in 1691, saw a camphor-tree on the island of *Kiusiu*, celebrated for its size and great age ; but he could not ascertain the exact dimensions. One hundred and thirty-five years afterwards, in 1826, Siebold visited the tree, and found it still healthy and rich in foliage. "He and his pupils measured it, and he gives 16·884 metres (about fifty feet) as its circumference, adding, in confirmation of this enormous size, that fifteen men can stand inside," the trunk being completely hollowed out. (*Manners, etc., of the Japonese in the Nineteenth Century*, Lond. 1841, p. 95.) A drawing of this tree is given by Siebold, in his pictorial illustrations.

The following are other trees that grow in Japan.—The *mulberry* presents three varieties. Of two, the black and the white, the fruit is insipid, and not eaten. These trees are cultivated solely with the view of feeding silk-worms. They are abundant, especially in the northern provinces, and afford the means of support to large numbers of industrious manufacturers. The third variety is called *kadsa*. From it are manufactured paper, ropes, cloth, and various other useful articles. The *urusi* is a noble and most valuable tree : from it is procured the varnish which has given celebrity to the Japon-ware. An inferior quality of varnish is obtained from the *forasi*. The *bay-tree* is described as a spurious kind of *cinnamon-tree*, degenerated owing to the quality of the soil. The *tsianoki*, or *tea-plant*, is abundant. *Sansio* is a spinous, moderately sized tree: the bark and husks of the fruit being used as substitutes for pepper and ginger; and the leaf, which has a pleasant aromatic flavour, being also eaten. Of the *kaki*, or *fig*, there are two native varieties, differing from the European; but the latter, which was introduced by the Portuguese, has improved both in size and flavour. *Chestnut-trees* are plentiful: the fruit superior to that produced in Europe. The *pears* resemble winter pears, growing to a large size: seldom weighing less than a pound, and invariably cooked before they are used as food. *Walnut-trees* grow in the northern provinces. The same parts produce the *kaja*, a tall description of *taxus*: from the nut of which, not unlike the *areca*, an oil much used in medicine is expressed, much resembling oil of sweet-almonds; and when burned, the smoke produces a soot, from which the best and most expensive kind of ink is prepared. Of *oaks*, there are three varieties; two differing from the European; and the acorns of the largest description are boiled and eaten by the peasantry. *Pome-citrons* "are grown in the gardens of the curious." *Oranges* and *lemons* are abundant. The best kind of the latter is called *mican*: in size and shape resembling a peach, and having a fine aromatic flavour, though rather sour. Another sort, called *kinkan*, is not much larger than a nutmeg, which it also resembles in form; very sour, and much used in cookery. There are *vines*, but the grapes do not ripen. *Peaches, apricots*, and *plums*, are abundant. Of the latter, there are two kinds, differing from the European: both granulated like mulberries. The *cherry* is only grown for its blossoms, which is also the case sometimes with apricot and plum-trees. *Kæmpfer* saw cherry-blossoms as large as roses. *Meylan* saw plum-blossoms four times as large as cabbage-roses. The Japonese take great delight, and are exceedingly skilful, both in enlarging and dwarfing

s

plants. The branches of some trees, springing at the height
of seven or eight feet from the trunk, are led out occasionally across ponds, and supported on props, so as to afford a
shade of three hundred feet in diameter. A box has been
seen, four inches long, one and a half wide, and six high, in
which were growing and thriving a bamboo, a fir, and a
plum-tree, the latter in full blossom. The price of this
curiosity was 1,200 Dutch gulden, or about £100. *stg.* The
*cypresses* and *cedars* are planted by the sides of the roads,
over the ridges of hills and mountains, and in sandy and
barren places, so economical are the Japonese of their good
ground. These trees can only be cut down with the permission of the magistrates ; and to prevent waste, a young tree
must be planted for every one that is felled. The *jusnoki* is
a kind of iron-wood, extensively used in building. The
*bamboo* is most plentiful ; and, as everywhere else in Asia, is
made to serve a great variety of purposes. One of the
species is called *fatsiku.* The roots are converted into the
walking-sticks known in Europe by the name of *rattans,* a
corruption of *rottung.* When dug out of the ground, the
whole art of preparing and fitting them for use, is cutting off
the surplus parts at the upper and lower ends, and removing
the young roots and fibres that surround the joints, which is
effected by knives, peculiarly tempered for the purpose. By
this operation, the small circular holes that produce the singular appearance of the stick are produced. [*Kæmpfer. Thun-
berg. Siebold. " Manners and Customs, etc."*]

NOTE R.

### Change of Names.

This practice is frequently alluded to by *Captain Cock,* in
his *Diary ;* and he mentions, on several occasions, the circumstances of his re-naming native children at the request of
their parents. To girls the name of *Elizabeth* was usually

given. The *Dutch writers*, up to a late date, also notice that the "honour," as it is esteemed, is frequently solicited of their countrymen. The custom being adopted by the Sovereigns of Japon, some confusion in reading Japonese history is occasioned.

NOTE S.

## The Laws and Administration of Justice.

THE LAWS OF JAPON are exceedingly simple in their construction, and they possess the additional merit of being intelligible. They consist of edicts issued in the name of the Emperor, which announce, concisely, that the commission of a specified act will constitute an offence, and that the commission of the inhibited act will be followed by punishment. The laws are also fairly promulgated. On the issue of every new edict, the Magistrates, in the first instance, assemble the residents within their respective jurisdictions, and proclaim, *vivâ voce*, the will of the Emperor. Next: the document is extensively circulated in a printed form; and, what is material, the state of education is such in the Empire, that the population can read and comprehend the matter published for their guidance. Finally: the edict is exposed for a permanency, in a public place appropriated to the purpose, in every city, town, and village, throughout the land.[1]

[1] "I have often admired, in my journeys through this country, the shortness and laconism of these tables, which are hung up on the roads, in places particularly appointed for this purpose, to notify to the public the emperor's pleasure, and to make known the laws of the country; for it is barely mentioned, and in as few words as possible, what the emperor commands to be done or omitted by his subjects. There is no reason given how it came about that such and such a law was made; no mention of the law-giver's view and intention; nor is there any certain determined penalty put upon transgression thereof. Such conciseness is thought becoming the majesty of so powerful a monarch." [*Kæmpfer, Appendix*, vol. ii, p. 68.] "The Japanese do affect breuite," is also the remark made by *Captain Saris*, about a century before.

*The Proceedings under the Laws* are as simple as the laws themselves. The Japonese system does not admit any technical and complicated forms; and, consequently, there is no professional class required to elucidate, or, the case may be, further to perplex what is already obscure. In the Empire, a party feeling himself aggrieved appeals direct to the Magistrate. The case is stated in the presence of the accused, and he is heard in reply. Witnesses are examined. Sentence is then passed, and generally carried into execution *instanter*. In trivial cases, the parties are usually ordered to retire and settle the difference, either between themselves, or with the assistance of mutual friends; and the matter may be considered to be adjusted. It is perfectly well understood, that persisting in the dispute would lead to unpleasant consequences. Should both parties appear to be blameable, the Judge makes his award accordingly, and neither escapes without censure. When false accusations are preferred, the false accuser is punished; and should malice be apparent, the punishment is augmented in proportion. In cases of great intricacy and importance, the Magistrate has the option of referring the matter to the Chief Justice at Miaco, or to the Emperor in council; but when a decision is once given, there is no appeal.[1] Towards the conclusion of the seventeenth century, *Kæmpfer* makes the following remarks on the Japonese system of administering justice. He says : " Some will observe, that the Japonese are wanting a competent knowledge of the law. . . . . But I would not have the reader imagine that the Japonese live entirely without laws. Far from it. Their laws and constitutions are excellent, and strictly observed." Coming down to the present century,

---

[1] " No superior court hath it in his power to mitigate the sentence pronounced in another, though inferior. ... Although it cannot be denied, but this short way of proceeding is liable to some errors and mistakes in particular cases ; yet I dare affirm, that in the main, it would be found abundantly less detrimental to the parties concerned, than the tedious and expensive law-suits in Europe." [*Kæmpfer, Appendix*, vol. ii, p. 64.]

competent authorities concur in bearing testimony to the purity with which justice is administered in the Empire : to the great solemnity and strict decorum with which the proceedings are conducted before the Tribunals : to the ardent desire manifested by the Magistrates to elicit the truth; and to the remarkable acumen they display in detecting falsehood." [1] If the representations on the subject be not overcharged, the Judicial Institutions of the Empire appear to realize, in a great degree, the maxim propounded by one of our most profound thinkers, that " *Truth is but Justice in our knowledge, and Justice but Truth in our practice.*" [2]

In the theory of PUNISHMENTS, it is not considered " *qu'un homme pendu est un homme perdu.*" [3] As a principle, *death* is the punishment for all offences. It does not, however, appear to have been adopted either from caprice, or through wanton disregard of human life ; but may be traced rather to an erroneous conception of the means of doing equal justice. It is maintained, that justice would be violated, unless all persons, whatever their ranks, guilty of similar offences, were punished in an equal manner; and it is conceived that death is the only penalty that affects alike Prince and Peasant. "Justice," says William Adams, "is very severe, having no respect to persons." Accordingly, the only favour exhibited in regard to the man of rank, is that of his being permitted to anticipate the act of the executioner by the commission of suicide. But though sanguinary in principle, the laws are greatly modified in practice. The power of inflicting death appears to be permissive, not compulsory, on the magistrate ; and, accordingly, a very wide discretion is exercised. From this discretion murder alone is excepted, including homicide of any kind, even in its least aggravated

[1] *Doeff, Fischer, Siebold*, etc.: quoted in " Manners and Customs of the Japanese in the Nineteenth Century."

[2] *Milton*, " Answer to Eikon Basilike."

[3] *Voltaire*, " L'Homme aux Quarante Ecus."

form. This appears to have arisen from the disposition of the population, represented to have been originally, but probably now tempered by altered circumstances, " no less fiery and changeable than the neighbouring sea is stormy and tempestuous." On the principle of equal justice, *pecuniary fines* are not tolerated.[1] Recourse is had to *imprisonment* as a punishment, which is rendered more or less severe according to the place in which incarceration takes place. One description of prison is called *roya*, or *cage*. Here due provision is made for cleanliness and ventilation, and a fair proportion of wholesome food is provided. The other description of prison is denominated *gokuya*, or *hell*. It is a dungeon, generally within the walls of the governor's house, into which from fif-

---

[1] " It is thought pernicious and unjust in the highest degree (and certainly not without reason), that the laws should be made only for the poor ; and that the rich, by being enabled to buy off the punishment, should have it in their power to commit what crimes they please." [*Kœmpfer, Appendix*, vol. ii, p. 68.] In *Aulus Gellius* (Noc. Att. 1. 20, c. 1. *Disceptatio ... de legibus Duodecim Tabularum*), there is an anecdote of a truculent fellow, who availed himself of the provision, " SI. INIVRIAM . FAXIT . ALTERI . VIGINTI . QVINQVE . AERIS . POENAE . SVNTO.", to gratify his splenetic humour. He perambulated the streets, accompanied by a slave, bearing a well filled purse ; and having taken an opportunity of committing an assault, ordered the stipulated penalty to be paid to the injured party. The question put by one of the interlocutors, " Quis enim erit tam inops, quem ab injuriæ faciendæ lubidine viginti quinque asses deterreant ?" is not quite pertinent. Two pence to a man who is worth a groat only, is a heavy penalty, the liability to which may deter him from indulging in a mischievous, or worse propensity; but such will not be the case with the man of abundant means. By inflicting the same penalty on the man of one groat as on the man with many groats, the provisions of the law are enforced, without any reference to an act of justice. In the case of a man " not worth a groat", the case may be worse. When incarceration is consequent on inability to pay the pecuniary fine, an increase of punishment is inflicted. It must be considered, that the difference between the money penalty awarded for the offence, —that is to say, two pence,—and the extra punishment, must be assigned not to the wrong done, but to the *inopsial* condition of the wrong doer ; which, however consistent it may be with law, cannot be regarded as concurrent with justice.

teen to twenty persons are usually thrust, or at least more, ordinarily, than the place can conveniently accommodate. The door is never opened but for the admission or release of a prisoner. A hole in the wall serves as the means of ejecting the filth, and of receiving food. Except from a small grated window at the top, there is neither light nor ventilation. Books, pipes, all kinds of recreation, are prohibited. No beds are allowed, and, as a mark of disgrace which is acutely felt, the prisoners are deprived of their silk or linen waist girdles, for which bands of straw are substituted. A singular regulation is connected with these hells. The diet is limited in quantity, and execrable in quality; but, on a certain condition, prisoners who have the means, or who have friends willing to assist them, are allowed to be provided with good and sufficient food. *The condition on which this indulgence is granted, is, that it shall be shared equally by all the inmates of the dungeon.* It is utterly repugnant to the Japonese notions of justice, that a criminal of wealth, or influence, should fare better than those who may be destitute. *Banishment* seems not to extend beyond the persons of the nobles attached to the imperial court, with some political offenders of high rank. These parties are deported to certain barren islands, from whence escape is impracticable. Food is provided for them, but they must work for their living. Their usual employment is the manufacture of silk goods, which are represented to be of an exceedingly fine description, and to be highly prized. *Corporal punishment* is inflicted frequently, and with great severity. *Torture* is resorted to but rarely, principally in cases of religious apostasy or political delinquency.

The substance of the following proceeding, derived by Titsingh from a native source, is given in his *Illustrations of Japan* (London, 1822), and will afford an idea of the manner in which the discretionary power vested in the magistrate may be exercised.

A man was charged by his master, a trader in Osacca, with having robbed him of five hundred kobans, equivalent in sterling value to about £700. The charge was made before the Governor. The accused solemnly protested his innocence; and the accuser, supported by the testimony of other servants, as solemnly maintained the truth of the charge. Circumstances were against the prisoner; but the evidence was of that doubtful nature, that the Magistrate did not feel himself warranted in convicting or discharging the man. He, therefore, to use a familiar phrase, remanded him. At the end of some days, the Magistrate called the parties before him again; and he remonstrated with the accuser, but ineffectually. At length, he required the charge, and the demand of the accuser, to be submitted to him in writing. This was done in the following terms: "Tchoudjet, servant to Tomoya, has robbed his master of five hundred kobans This we attest by this writing, and we demand, that, by way of example, he be punished with death. We, the servants and relatives of Tomoya-kiougero, have confirmed this writing, by affixing our signatures and our seals. The second month of the first year *Gen-boun* (1736)." The Governor, Kavatche-no-kami by name, read the paper attentively, and then said to Tomoya: "Good. Nor am I absolved from responsibility. Depart. Be assured, justice shall be done." So Tomoya and his party went away rejoicing. A short time afterwards, a convicted felon confessed himself guilty of the robbery with which Tchoudjets had been charged; and Tomoya, with all his people, were straightway summoned into the presence of the Governor. "What is this thing ye have done?" said the Governor, addressing the party, sternly; "Know ye not, that your false accusation hath tended to cause the death of an innocent man? Know ye not the law, that ye have put your own lives in jeopardy? that thou, thyself, Tomoya, thy wife, and thy people, may be delivered over to the executioner? And behold me, should I not die the death, because I have

NOTES. 137

not looked with greater care into this matter? Prepare
for doom." Thunderstruck, the terrified wretches threw
themselves on their knees, and implored for mercy. The
Magistrate beheld their abject state for some time in silence.
He kept them in agonising suspense, willing to give them a
lesson they should not speedily forget. At length he ex-
claimed: "Be of good cheer. The man is not dead. I
doubted his guilt, and I have kept him in concealment, hoping that, in process of time, his innocence might be brought
to light. Most sincerely do I rejoice that my precaution
hath proved of avail. Let Tchoudjet be brought in." The
order was obeyed, and the Governor, resuming his address,
said: "Tomoya, behold an innocent man, who might have
fallen a victim to thy unjust accusation. A grievous injury
hast thou inflicted on him. Thy life I spare, because his has
not been taken; but for what he has suffered through thy
injustice, thou owest him reparation. Pay unto him, then,
the sum of five hundred kobans, and henceforth cherish him
as a faithful servant. Go thy ways. Justice is now done."
In due course, this proceeding was reported to the Emperor.
What had been done by Kavatche was approved, and he
was in a short space of time appointed to the lucrative and
high posts of Inspector of the Chamber of Accounts, and
Governor at Nangasacki, where his good qualities endeared
him to the people, his memory being held in reverence in
the time of the European narrator of the transaction.

NOTE T.

### Embassy from Japon to Rome.

DE MISSIONE *Legatorum Japonensium ad Romanam Curiam,
rebusque in Europa ac toto Itinere animadversis, Dialogus, ex
Ephemeride ipsorum Legatorum collectus, et in Linguam Lati-
nam versus ab Evardo de Sande, Societatis Jesu, cum facultate
ordinarii et superiorum, anno 1590.* (Quarto.)—" This rare

T

and curious Treatise, which was printed at Macao, in China, both in Latin and Japonese, lays open at once the state of Europe and the Indies, as it was at that time. The Jesuits, proud of the success of this embassy, which was entirely a work of theirs, intended that the Japonese should be informed, as it were, by the ambassadors themselves, of the favourable reception they had met with in Europe, and the remarkable things they had seen on their voyage and return. And certainly it contains as complete an account, as it was then possible to give, of the state of Europe, its largeness and division, its government, monarchial, aristocratical, or democratical; of the pomp and magnificence of the European princes, the splendour of their court, their riches and power; of the manners, customs, and way of life, of the nobles and inferior sort of people; of the flourishing condition of trade and commerce; of the way of carrying on war in Europe, both by sea and land; of the principal towns in Europe, particularly of Lisbon, Evora, Villaviziosa, Madrid, Pisa, Florence, Rome, Naples, Padua, Verona, Mantua, Cremona, Milan, Genoa, being the places which the ambassadors themselves had passed through, and where they had been shown, in the most ample manner, what was curious and remarkable; of the power and authority of the pope at Rome, the magnificence of his court, the ceremonies observed upon his demise and burial, as also upon the election of a new pope, the splendour of his coronation, the pomp of his going to take possession of S. John de Lateran; of the power and grandeur of Philip II, then king of Spain, and the largeness of his dominions in Europe and both the Indies; of the republics of Venice, the nature of its government, the situation, riches, and antiquities, of that town and commonwealth; of the numerous conquests and discoveries of the Portuguese in the Indies; of several countries in the Indies, particularly the Empire of China; and a variety of other things, too many to be here mentioned. It was wrote by way of Dialogues, wherein the ambassadors *Mancius* and *Michael,* their two companions *Martinus* and *Julian, Leo,* a brother of the Prince of *Arima,* and *Linus,* a brother of the Prince of *Omura,* are introduced as interlocutors. The author hath not omitted, in proper places, to give some account of the Empire of Japon itself, and particularly to compare the manners and customs of that country with those of Europe. In short, were the whole work now reprinted, I do not doubt but that it would yet meet with a favourable reception." [*Scheuchzer, "Introduction to Kæmpfer's History of Japon,* 1727.*"*]

*Charlevoix,* in his list of authors that have written on Japan, mentions another work on this subject, entitled: RELATIONE DELLA VENUTA *de gli Ambasciatori Giapponesi à Roma fino alla partita di Lisbona, con le accoglienze fatte loro da tutti i Principi, per dove sono passati : racolte da Guido Gualtiere : Roma,* 1585, 8vo. [*Grenville Coll., B. M.*]

There is also a work in Latin on the subject, edited by *Hen. Cuyckius ; Anv.* 1593. 8vo. Some further particulars will also be found in a volume by *Scip. Amati ; Roma,* 1615. 4to.; entitled *Historia del Regno di Voxu de Giapone,* etc. etc. [*Grenville Coll., B. M.*]

NOTE U.

## Reverses of the Dairi, or Mikado.

SIN MU TEN OO, *i. e.,* "The Supreme of all men, or the Divine conqueror", is the first Daïri,[1] or Mikado, named in the chronicles of the Japonese Empire. The origin of this

[1] "DAÏ-RI......signifie *le grand intérieur,* c'est à dire, le palais impérial. C'est le terme ordinaire dont on se sert pour désigner l'empereur, parce qu'il est défendu de prononcer son nom, qui d'ailleurs est ignoré de son vivant par la multitude." (*Titsingh's Translation of " Nipon o Daï itsi Ran, ou Annales des Empereurs du Japon";* note, p. 442, *by Klaproth.* Paris and London, 4to., 1834). The signification of the word Daïri, as given by Klaproth, may be correct. The rest of what is stated is not supported by any authority, and its correctness is open to doubt.

personage is involved in obscurity. According to the tradition of the country, he was descended from the gods. He is also represented to have been a Chinese conqueror; and a chieftain, born in one of the inferior islands of the Empire, by whom Nipon was subdued. *Kæmpfer* propounds the theory : that for many ages, the Japonese led a nomade life, "erring from place to place with their families and cattle": that from "following a course of life not unlike that of the patriarchs, where the several families lived under the command and authority of their fathers, or else obeyed the most prudent among themselves", they gradually became civilized, the process being advanced by constant intercourse with the Chinese, till at length they were prepared to submit to the individual authority of some man of "happy genius".

Whatever may have been the origin of Sin Mu, it is certain he was a man of "happy genius". To him is attributed the civilization of Japon : the introduction of a chronological system : the division of time into years, months, and days : the institution of laws; and the establishment of a regular form of government. It is indisputable that his posterity exercised supreme sway in Japan for a long succession of ages; and that now his descendants, in a direct and unbroken line, though deprived of their political rights, are regarded by the nation as objects of affection, esteem, and veneration.

*Yoritomo*, in the twelfth century after Christ, first infringed on the rights of the Mikado. He was a warrior of repute, and allied by blood to the imperial family. In the first instance, he distinguished himself by his loyalty. He crushed a wide-spread rebellion which threatened to hurl the Emperor from the seat of power. He afterwards signalized himself in a different way. In reward for his exertions, he was invested by his Sovereign with extraordinary powers, and he gained extraordinary influence in the state. Availing himself of the opportunities his condition afforded him, and yielding to the aspirations of ambition, he appropriated to himself the most valuable prerogatives of the Mikado, and without openly pretending to the dignity, exercised the rights of an independent Sovereign. *Faxiba*, or *Taico Sama*, in the sixteenth century, completed the design which Yoritomo had commenced, and reduced the Mikado to the state of a splendid pageant.

The character that formerly marched at the head of mighty armies, sharing in their peril and participating in their glory, is now esteemed so sacred, that, lest his person should suffer pollution, he may not stir beyond the precincts of his palace, except on the shoulders of men; and within his palace, he may walk only on the most exquisitely wrought mats, lest his foot should come in contact with lowly earth. Neither may the air breathe on him, nor may the rays of the sun fall on him. To every part of his person is such holiness ascribed, that it would be deemed a foul offence were he to cut his hair, trim his beard, or pare his nails. But to prevent his being inconvenienced by this ordinance, recourse is had to a pious fraud. When he sleeps, or affects to sleep, his attendants *steal*, as it is termed, the exuberances of nature; and on the presumption of his being insensible, the object of this care is absolved from the consequences of an act, which, if performed by himself, would be deemed little less than sacrilege. At one period, the Mikado was under the necessity of sitting on the throne in imperial state for many hours daily; and during this period he was required to assume the rigidity of a statue, not being permitted to move either his hands, arms, legs, eyes, or indeed any part of his person. This irksome duty, probably the result of some politic manœuvre, was imposed on him as the means of securing the peace and tranquillity of the realm: " for if unfortunately he turned himself on one side or the other, or if he looked a good while towards any part of his dominions, it was apprehended that war, famine, fire, or some great misfortune, was near at hand to desolate the country." [*Kæmpfer.*] In modern times, however, a convenient discovery has been made, that the crown is the palladium, which by its immobility secures the safety of the Empire; and no doubt greatly to the relief of his sacred Majesty, this peculiar task has been transferred from him to his head-gear.

The prescribed aliment of the Mikado is rice. Every grain prepared for his use, is scrupulously selected by an officer specially appointed for the purpose; and whose duty it also is, to take care that the diurnal allowance is strictly uniform in quantity, neither diminished nor increased in the slightest degree. On every occasion, the food of the Mikado is dressed in a new vessel, and every meal is served on new ware. Such of both kinds, as have been once used, are destroyed. Formerly, the Mikado was served on common clay, but porcelain appears to have been substituted in recent times.

The vestments of the Mikado and his wives differ from the costume adopted by the rest of the nation. They differ in colour, materials, and form; and so extravagantly ample are they in dimension, that locomotion is rendered inconvenient. No dress is worn a second time; and all the cast-off habiliments, after being preserved a specified period, are burned. They are deemed too sacred for others to use.

To provide against the failure of issue, the Mikado is allowed twelve consorts, exclusive of a number of females in the capacity of attendants, that make up the mystic number of eighty-one, or nine times nine. If, on the decease of a Mikado, there should chance to be no issue, the nearest of kin, without distinction of sex, succeeds. Before the Seogouns assumed the imperial power, the succession of the Mikado not unfrequently produced serious convulsions in the state; but now, " a Mikado may die, or resign, and another be put in his place, without anybody but the court knowing of it, till the affair is over." [*Kæmpfer.*]

A court still exists, consisting entirely of the descendants of *Sin Mu Ten Oo*, the family being designated *Ten Sio Dai Sin*. On account of their reputed celestial descent, the members of the court claim and receive a greater degree of homage than any portion of the community: even the highest princes in the land being considered inferior to them in station. The degrees of rank among this class of nobility are accurately defined: carefully preserved; and distinctly indicated, by characteristic dresses.

To the court there is attached a council of high officers; even ministers for political and military affairs being retained. There are also professors well skilled in the Chinese language, whose duty it is to acquire a knowledge of all that is new, and to give circulation to whatever may tend to benefit the country. There are astrologers and astronomers, who study and comprehend the works of La Lande and La Place, whose works have been translated for their edification. There is a sub-council, that regulates education throughout the Empire; and there is also a special minister, whose duty it is to receive and examine the reports, which are periodically submitted, in relation to the numbers and condition of the population: including information connected with agriculture, manufactures, roads, bridges, water-ways, and forests. History, poetry, and music, generally, are studied by the members of the court, both male and female; and, it is said, with no mean success. The former are, also, represented to be proficient in athletic exercises. What the religion professed by the Mikado is, it is difficult to define. He is *understood*, while living, to be attached to the Sinto doctrine, the original faith of the country; but when he dies, his exequies are performed by the Bhoodist sect, in conformity with their rites.

The revenue of the Mikado is derived from three sources, viz.: the income of the city of Meaco, " and all its appurtenances": an allowance from the Seogoun; and the emoluments derived from the sale of patents of nobility, the only substance of prerogative he retains. Whether the revenue is insufficient for the purpose, or whether the Mikado appropriates an undue share to his own purposes, is not apparent; but great distress is represented to exist among the members of the court, estimated to include several thousand individuals. "The great ones run themselves into debt, and the inferior officers and servants must work for their living. Accordingly, they make and sell baskets of straw, tables, straw shoes for men and horses, and other mean things of this nature." [*Kæmpfer.*]

### NOTE V.

### Government and Policy of Japon.

The Empire of Japon presents the anomaly of two co-existing Sovereigns, each maintaining a state independent of the other: both the objects of homage on the part of the people; and neither indicating any dissatisfaction at the degree of allegiance that is tendered to him. One of the Sovereigns, the *Daïri*, or *Mikado*, rules, it has been seen, by "right divine", by virtue of attributed descent from the gods. The other Sovereign, the *Seogoun*, or *Cubo-Sama*, rules by the "right of might", by virtue of his ability to maintain power wrested by his predecessors from the Mikado. Sovereign *de jure*, the *Mikado* is supreme in rank, yet insignificant in political importance. The *Cubo-Sama*, Sovereign *de facto*, is inferior in station, but uncontrolled in political authority.

The government of Japon is essentially feudal in its constitution. It is also despotic: not, however, according to the European acceptation of the term. "We must especially abstract," it has been observed,[1] "from that idea one of its

---

[1] "*Manners and Customs of the Japonese in the Nineteenth Century.*"

greatest evils, namely, its arbitrariness. Liberty is, indeed, unknown in Japon; it exists not in the common intercourse of man with man; and the very idea of freedom, as distinguished from rude licence, could, perhaps, hardly be made intelligible to a native of that extraordinary empire. But, on the other hand, no individual in the whole nation, high or low, is above the law; both sovereigns seeming to be as completely enthralled by despotism as their meanest subjects, if not more so. Law and established custom, unvarying, known to all, and pressing on all alike, are the despots of Japon. Scarcely an action of life is exempt from their rigid, inflexible, and irksome control; but he who complies with their dictates, has no arbitrary power, no capricious tyranny to apprehend." In this representation there is much truth.

### NOTE W.

### Career of Faxiba, or Taico Sama.

*Taico Sama,*[1] the most celebrated character in the annals of Japon, is represented to have been ill-favoured, if not absolutely repulsive, in person. He was below the average height, and corpulent to excess; but, withal, endowed with immense strength, extraordinary activity, and a spirit of daring beyond conception. On one hand he had six fingers: his eyes were so prominent, that they seemed ready to start from their sockets: his chin was destitute of the manly appendage of a beard; and his features, altogether, were of so singular a

---

[1] *Taico Sama* was known by various names, viz.: 1, *Toyotomo;* 2, *Toquixiro;* 3, *Cicuquidono;* 4, *Faxiba;* "dont la signification," *Charlevoix* observes, "faisoit allusion aux armes ou quelque dévice du Roi de Nauguto": who had been in rebellion, and was reduced to submission by Faxiba, on whom the Seogoun, Nobounanga, conferred the title. 5, *Quabancondono,* which by some writers is said to mean " *The Lord of the Treasure*". *Captain Cock* states (*E. I. Mss.*), it is equivalent to the "*Cæsar*" of the Romans. 6, *Taico Sama* signifies " *The most high and sovereign Lord.*"

mould, that he obtained the unenviable cognomen of "*The Ape*".[1] Yet these disadvantages were overcome by the transcendant qualities of his mind.

*Taico Sama* commenced his career as a hewer and carrier of wood. From this menial occupation he was taken into the service of an officer attached to the court of Nobounanga, the Seogoun. What his occupation was is not known, but he found means of displaying superior intelligence, and was transferred by his master to the military service. In the capacity of a private soldier he attracted the attention of the Seogoun, who had the reputation of being a shrewd interpreter of character, and in this instance gave a striking proof of his discernment. The rich vein of talent concealed under an unpromising surface, did not escape his penetration, and the humble soldier was unhesitatingly promoted. "O'ervaulting ambition" does not appear to have been a defect to which Taico was subject. His advancement was rapid, though gradual: step by step, as his merits developed themselves in succession. At length he obtained a separate command, and in an incredibly short space of time, was recognized as one of the most skilful generals in the Empire. His patron, the Seogoun, now reaped the fruits of his discernment; and Taico zealously strove to repay his Sovereign the favours he had received from him. It was owing to his skill and valour, that the cause of Nobounanga was maintained against a host of powerful opponents, whose exertions were devoted to thrust him from power. But though powerful against hosts, Taico was unable to restrain individual malice. Nobounanga fell beneath the blade of an assassin: leaving, as his successor, a grandson, a youth possessed of little influence and less talent.

Presently, on the death of Nobounanga, the most disaffected, turbulent, and ambitious, constituting the largest pro-

---

[1] According to *Charlevoix*, *Titsingh* says "*Saroutsoma*", or "*Monkey Face*".

portion of the Princes and Nobles of the land, flew to arms: contending among themselves for the seat of power. For a time, anarchy reigned triumphant; but at length Taico, who had been fighting the battles of his late Sovereign in a distant part of the land, arrived, by a succession of rapid marches, at the scene of action; and, falling suddenly on the contending parties, put their forces to the rout, and their dreams of ambition to flight. The leader of a numerous and well-disciplined army, which under his generalship had proved invincible: supported by devoted followers unwilling to submit to any authority but his: Taico felt his power, and installed himself the successor of Nobounanga.

The superiority of the Mikado was at first acknowledged by the new Segoun, but the subjection was a trammel to which he did not long submit. After a few months had elapsed, he declared himself independent and absolute. Irresistible in might and skill, he crushed every attempt at opposition; and ruling the Princes and Nobles with a rod of iron, he reduced them to a state of abject submission. Adding policy to force, he declared war against Corea, which in the lapse of ages had regained its independence; and despatched a force of 200,000 men for the reconquest of that country.[1] In this army, the most dangerous characters in the Empire were absorbed. Few of the leaders returned to their native land,

---

[1] The first conquest of Corea was effected during the reign of *Dsiu Guuck Woo Gu Oo,* who at the age of thirty years was left a widow, and succeeded her deceased husband as Daïri, A.D. 201. Assuming the command of the army, this martial lady passed over the straits, and despite of a vigorous resistance, succeeded in effecting a landing in Corea; where she fought many battles with signal success, and laid the foundation for the conquest of the country; although being required to retire prematurely to Japan on account of her pregnancy, she was prevented from witnessing the final success of her arms. Living to the age of one hundred years, the reign of this heroine was unusually protracted; and, according to the annals of the country, it was no less glorious. At her death, she was "related" among the *camis,* or gods, with the honorary title of *Kassi no Dai Mio Sin.*

and the few who did return were not in a condition to excite
any apprehension, on the part of the Sovereign, for the peace
of the Empire. So far successful, he proceeded to devise
means by which the turbulent spirits in the realm might be
kept in subjection for the future. The measures he adopted
remain part of the policy of Japon to the present day, and
have proved most efficient. As a legislator, as well as warrior and politician, Taico also distinguished himself. He
introduced laws which bear the impress of great severity, but
they were necessary to meet the exigencies of the times, and
were adapted to the temper of the people: which at that
period, whatever it may be now, is represented to have been
"no less fiery and changeable, than the neighbouring sea is
stormy and tempestuous." [*Kœmpfer*.] When introduced,
these laws produced the most beneficial results, and, being
judiciously administered, are not less efficacious in the present day.

Magnificence and profusion were two of the leading cha-
racteristics of this Seogoun; but as he taxed the aristocracy,
and left the people unburthened with imposts, the plebeian
part of his subjects were well content that he should indulge
in expensive wars, which contributed, in their estimation,
to the glory of the nation; and also in the exhibition of
gorgeous spectacles, which were no less gratifying to them,
than agreeable to their Sovereign.

The renown of Taico was not confined within the limits of
the Empire. It extended to China, and was acknowledged
in Europe. His alliance was courted both by the Emperor
of the former region, and by the King of Spain. In reply
to the overtures of an Ambassador despatched by the Viceroy
of the Spanish Indies, by command of the King of the
mother-country, the Segoun gave the following brief account
of his career: "The kingdom of Japon", he says, "contain-
eth above sixty states, or jurisdictions, which from long time
had been sorely afflicted with internal broils and civil wars;

by reason, that wicked men, traitors to their country, did conspire to deny obedience to their sovereign lord. Even in my youth did this matter grieve my spirit, and from early days I took counsel with myself how this people might best be made subject to order, and how peace might be restored to the kingdom. That so mighty a work might be brought about, I especially essayed to practise these three virtues which follow. Therefore I strove to render myself affable to all men, thereby to gain their good-will : I spared no pains to judge all things with prudence, and to comport myself with discretion : nothing did I omit to do that might make men esteem me for valour of heart and fortitude of mind. Now, by these means, have I gained the end I sought. All the kingdom is become as one, and is subject to my sole rule. I govern with mildness, that yields only to my energy as a conqueror. Most especially do I view with favour the tillers of the ground; they it is by whom my kingdom is filled with abundance. Severe I may be deemed; but my severity is visited, alone, on those who stray into the paths of wickedness. Thus hath it come to pass, that at this present, peace universal reigns in the Empire; and in this tranquillity consisteth the strength of the realm. Like to a rock, which may not be shaken by any power of the adversary, is the condition of this vast monarchy under my rule."

Taico Sama is not to be charged with over-estimating his own merits. In his representation, he is corroborated by *Kæmpfer*. That staunch Protestant observes : "The ambition and insolence of the princes of the empire was successively grown to such a height, that at last it became almost impossible for the ecclesiastical emperors to restrain and control them. In vain did they for *four ayes* together send the crown generals against them, at the head of numerous armies. And yet *this great work was brought about by Taico in about ten years' time, not so much indeed by force of arms, as by his prudent conduct and good management.*" Testimony, not less conclusive, to the merits of Taico Sama, is also borne by *Charlevoix;* and he derived his information entirely from Catholic sources.   In a style of admirable candour, the learned Jesuit gives the following review of this Seogoun's reign.   "Never", he says, "was Japon better ruled than under Taico; and the condition of the country at that period affords a proof, that the Japonese, as well as most other nations, only require to be subject to a man who knows how to govern, to conduct themselves peaceably and obediently. Vice was punished : virtue was rewarded : merit was acknowledged; and occupation was found for the restless, or they were coerced into quietness.   Excepting the persecution of the Christians, in which, however, the Emperor exhibited a degree of moderation hardly to be expected from a man of his character, no just complaint can be urged against his government.   It is true, he was not an object of affection ; but he was feared and admired."[1]   Moreover, the traditions of the

[1] In another place, *Charlevoix* observes : " It cannot be denied, that with Taico commenced that terrible persecution which even now makes the Christian world recoil with horror.   But of upwards of 200 missionaries, and 1,800,000 converts in Japan, during his reign, he put to death not more than twenty-six or twenty-seven ; and he did not, in these cases, have recourse to any of those extraordinary cruelties, by which his successors were signalized.   If his motives for condemning these parties to death be scrutinized, it will be evident they were not of a sanguinary nature.   I cannot then perceive how he can justly be represented as one of those cruel tyrants that delight in shedding blood, or as a ferocious and untameable beast.   Such expressions might perhaps be excused in a letter from some zealous missionary, written in the bitterness of disappointment, at witnessing the destruction, for ever, of his hopes of raising the Kingdom of God on the ruins of Idolatry.   But an historian, who is accountable to the public for the truth of his narration, should cast aside passion, as well as prejudice." [*Hist. du Japon*, tom. 3, pp. 245-46.   Paris, 1754.]   The latter portion of these remarks appear to be directed against M. Caron, at one time attached to the Dutch factory, who represents Taico to have been a second *Tiberius.*   M. Caron had been foiled by the Emperor in some commercial speculations, which, could he have carried out, would have benefited the Dutch, though at the expense of the Japonese.

country seldom fail to do justice to the memory of a sove-reign, whether meriting applause or reprobation. To the present day, the name of Taico Sama is revered throughout Japon; and his actions continue to be the theme of admira-tion. [*Kæmpfer. Charlevoix. "Nipon o Daï, by Titsingh and Klaproth."*]

## NOTE X.

### The Privy Council and State Officers.

*The following List* of the *High Officers of State* in the *Empire of Japon,* appears in an " Inuentorye of the presents given by the English and Hollanders, in comp$^a$ to the Emperor of Japon, and others his Lords and Gentry, at his courte in Eado, the 14 of Oct. 1620."

### LORDS OF THE COUNSELL.

I. *Doyono Couoi Dono* [*Tono,* or *Lord*], Chancelor of his Ma$^{ties}$ kingedome.

II. *Fondo Corbeque Dono.* Ex-chancelor; but nowe im-ployed by his Emperours Ma$^{tie}$ in all waightie matters tuchinge the State.

III. *Sacay Ota Dona.* One of his Ma$^{ties}$ Counsell, and next in place to the forenamed Couoidono, although in a lower ranke.

IV. *Ando Truxima Dono.* One of his Ma$^{tie}$ Counsell, and in place and authoritie equall vnto Sacay Otadono.

V. *Itami Quinosuque Dono.* Beinge as Counsell and rent-master to the Emperour's Ma$^{tie}$; also the charge of all the Emperour's goods and such like.

VI. *Matiudoro Jemon Dono.* One of the six Lords of his Ma$^{ties}$ Counsell.

The chancellor and ex-chancellor entertained each two

secretaries : the other members of the Counsell each one secretary.

*Chayano Xirosiro Dono.*   One very familliar with the Emperor ; and hath the charge for bringeinge of all strangers before the Emperour, and taketh care for their present [*quick*] dispatch.

*Itaque Suuo Dono.*   High Judge and Ruler of the Cittie of Meaco.

*Ytagura Yga Dono.*   Late high Judg of Meaco, and father to him that is nowe.

*Caruye Dono.*   One that keepeth the Emperour's chapes [*chops, ordinances,* or *orders*].

*Miruno Quennoecu Dono.*   He which sealeth all the chapes before the Emperour.

*Muçai Xoguen Dono.*   The Lord Admirall of Japon.

The latest information on this subject is the following : " The numbers of the council of state are differently given by different writers ; but the best authority (*Siebold*) makes them thirteen—to wit, five councillors of the first class, uniformly selected from the princes of the empire, and eight of the second class, similarly selected from the nobility : if their offices cannot be termed actually hereditary, as there occasionally seems reason to think them.   Other ministers are mentioned, who do not appear to be comprehended in the Council : there are the temple lords, who seem to be laymen, though the actual regulators of all religious matters ; and the two ministers, called by some writers, commissioners for foreign affairs, by others, lieutenants of police, or heads of the spies." [1]

---

[1] " *Manners and Customs of the Japonese in the Nineteenth Century,*" (pp. 202-3).   London, 1841.

## NOTE Y.

### The Original Privileges.

The following document is printed from the official copy,[1] of which a *fac-simile* is introduced in the text, p. 67. There is a version printed in " *Purchas his Pilgrims*", vol. i, lib. IV, p. 376. London, 1624. There is another version printed in the " *Minutes of Evidence*", appended to the " *Report of the Select Committee of the House of Commons on Commercial Relations with China*, 1847"; but it is not to be commended for its fidelity. Alluding to these " PRIVILEGES", a witness on the 18th of May 1847, stated to the Committee : " I have discovered in the British Museum a copy of that treaty [in the native character], a translation of which I beg to give in." In answer to the question, " How has the treaty been translated?" the same witness replied : " *The translation is along with the original in the British Museum.*" The witness should have explained, that the only ' *original*' in the library of the British Museum, is a *typographical fac-simile,* introduced by Purchas, in the Narrative given by Captain Saris of his proceedings in Japon [*Pilgrims*, vol. i, p. 375]; and which is to be found in other book-collections besides the National Library.

### The Translation of the Emperor of Japan's Privileges : granted in the name of the right honoured knight, Sir Thomas Smith, Governor of the East India Company.

Imprimis.—We give free license to the king of England's subjects, Sir Thomas Smith, Governor, and Company of the East India Merchants, for ever : safely to come into any our

[1] E. I. Mss. *Japon Series.*

ports, or Empire of Japan, with their ships and merchandize, without hindrance to them, or their goods; and to abide, buy, sell, and barter, according to their one [? *own*] manner with all nations; and to tarry so long as they will, and depart at their pleasure.

Item.—We grant unto them free cust [*oms*] of all such merchandize as they have, or hereafter shall bring into our kingdom, or shall transport to any foreign part; and do by these presents authorize the hereafter ships to make present [*immediate*] sale of their commodities, without further coming, or sending to our court.

Item.—If their ships shall be in danger to be lost and perish, we will that ye, our subjects, not only assist them, but [? *if*] aught shall be saved, to return it to the captain, merchant, or their assigns; and that ye permit them to build in any part of our Empire where they think fittest; and at departure to make free sale of their house, or houses, at their pleasure.

Item.—If any of them shall die in these our dominions, the goods of the deceased shall be at the disposal of the Captain Merchant; and all offences committed by them, shall be at the said merchant's discretion to punish; and our laws to take no hold, either of their persons, or goods.

Item.—We will, that ye our subjects, trading with them for any of their commodities, pay them according to agreement without delay, or return of their wares.

Item.—All such their merchandize which at present, or hereafter shall be brought meet for our service, we will, that no arrest be made thereof; but that present [*immediate*] payment be made, and at such prices as the Captain Merchant can at present [*at that time*] sell them for.

Item.—We will, that [? *if*] in discovery of any other places of trade, or return of their ships, they should have need of men or victuals, that ye, our subjects, furnish them for their money as their need shall require; and that with out any further pass, they should set out and go in discovery for Yeadzo [*Yesso*], or any other part in or about our Empire.

𝔉rom our 𝔄astle in 𝔖orongo, this first day of the 9th month, and in the 18th year of our Dary [*Daïri*], according to our computation.

𝔖ealed *with our broad seal,*

*MINNA MOTTONO YEI YE YEAS.*[1]

### NOTE Z.

### 𝔗he 𝔐odified 𝔓rivileges.

#### 1616.

*COPY OF THE ARTICLES (OR PRIVILEGES) GRANTED TO THE ENGLISH NATION, BY SHONGO SAMME: EMPEROR OF JAPON.*

1. Be it known unto all men, that the English nation throughout all Japon, in what part thereof soever they arrive with their shipping, shall with all convenient speed (they can) retire to the town (and port) of Firando, there to make sale of their merchandize, defending all other places and parts whatsoever in Japon, not to receive any of their goods nor merchandize ashore, but at Firando only.

2. But if it fortune through contrary winds (or bad weather), their shipping arrive in any other port in Japon, that they shall be friendly used, in paying for what they take (or buy), without exacting any anchorage, custom, or other extraordinary matters whatsoever.

3. That if the Emperour needeth any thing their shipping

---

[1] *MINNAMOTTO-NO-YEYE-YASOU, i.e.*

*Minnamotto:* a distinctive appellation, similar to a Christian name.

*No:* copulative, or introduced for the sake of euphony.

*Yeye-Yasou* [also written *Jejas*]: the family name.

*Titsingh,* " Illustrations of Japon".

bringeth, that it shall be reserved for him in paying the wor [*th there*] of.

4. That no man force (or constrain) the English to buy nor sell with them, neither the English the like with the Japons, but that both parties deal the one with the other in friendly sort.

5. That if any of the English nation chance to die in any part of Japon, that the goods, monies, and merchandize, or whatsoever else is found to be in his custody at the hour of his death, shall be held to be [?], or belong to him (or them), unto whom the Captain, or Captain Merchant of the English nation, sayeth it belongeth unto.

6. That if there be any difference (or controversy)—be it of life and death, or otherwise—amongst the English a board their ships, or a land, it shall be at the disposing of the Captain, or Captain Merchant, to make an end thereof, without that any other justice in Japon shall touch them, or meddle in the matter.

7. The conclusion is, to command all tonos (or kings), governors, and other officers in Japon whatsoever, to see the premises aforesaid accomplished. [*E. I. Mss.*]

The good faith maintained by the government of Japon in regard to the disposal of the effects of deceased Englishmen, will have been rendered apparent by the arrangement connected with the property of William Adams, already noticed. Similar good faith in connexion with the provision contained in the sixth article of the "Privileges", will also appear in the following extracts : which also exhibit some interesting and curious traits of English character in that age.

EXTRACT I.

1621. July 7th.

   *The Admerall, Captain Robert Adams,* with the rest of

the Commanders, came ashore to the English howse at *ARAYNMENT OF JNO. ROAN, FOR MVRTHER.* Firando, and satt in *Councill* about the murthering of a Hollander, called *John Peterson*, by an Englishman, viz. :

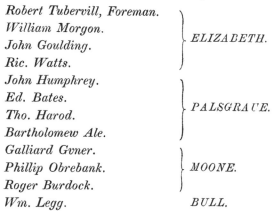

| Robt. Adames. | | | Joseph Cokram. | | |
| Charls Clevenger. | | | Wm. Eaton. | | *ENG.* |
| Edmund Lennis. | *SEAMEN.* | | Edmund Sayer. | | *MERCH.* |
| Jno. Monden. | | | Jno. Osterwick. | | |
| Arnold Browne. | | | Ric. Cock. | | |

With M. *Vaux,* a Hollander, whoe spoke English, to be interpreter, or heare what 4 Duchmen aledged against *John Roan,* the mvrtherer of *Jno. Peterson :* whoe all 4, with *virá voce,* accused the said *Roan* to doe the acte in their sight, and stabed hym into the leafte brest and soe to the hart (with a knife), that he never spoke word, but fell downe dead; the wounde, after being seen and serched by *M. Owen* and *M. Eaton,* chirugions, whoe saw the corps taken out of growne [*ground*] 3 daies after it was buried.

The *Jurie* empaneled were named as follow, viz. :

Robert Tubervill, Foreman. ⎫
William Morgon. ⎪
John Goulding. ⎬ *ELIZABETH.*
Ric. Watts. ⎭

John Humphrey. ⎫
Ed. Bates. ⎪
Tho. Harod. ⎬ *PALSGRAUE.*
Bartholomew Ale. ⎭

Galliard Gvner. ⎫
Phillip Obrebank. ⎬ *MOONE.*
Roger Burdock. ⎭

Wm. Legg. *BULL.*

And the names of men witnessing against *Roan,* viz.:

John Ave, an Englishman.

> *Derick Harmonson,* a Duchman.
> *Evert Lubbertson,* Duchman.
> *Jno. Johnson,* Duchman.
> *Jno. Henrickson,* Duchman.
> *Yozemon Dono,* a Japon, in whose howse it was done, at Cochie.

1621.   July 9th.

This day, *John Roan,* of Bristoll, marrenar, was condemned by the xij. men before nomenated, for killing *John Peterson,* a Duchman; and hanged at the yard arme abord the shipp Elizabeth.   He confessed before his death, that he kild the said man, being in drink, and not knowing what he did, wishing all the shipp's company to take example by hym, and to beware of woamen and wyne, which had brought hym to that vntymely death.   He died very resolutely, and received the sacrament by M. *Arthur Hatch* [*Preacher*], before he went to execution. *A MAN HANGED.*

*Capt. Robt. Adams* was forsed to put the roape about his neck with his owne hands, for non of the shipp's company would doe it, yf he should hange them; and soe tould hym to his face.[1]

EXTRACT II.

1621.   September 27th.

We are geven to vnderstand, *Richd. Short* and other Englishmen are rvn away to the enemy [*the Portuguese*], at Nangasaq.

„       October 1st.

*Aluaro Munos* came to Firando and tells me *Richard Short* was staied at Nangasaq, at his first arivall, for a Padre; but after released when they knew whoe he was.

„       October 3rd.

A bark of Japons being sent after the rvnawaies with

<hr>

[1] *Diary of Capt. Richard Cock.* E. I. Mss.

speed, overtook them, and kept them from proceeding forward, till *M. Sayers* came after. Soe they brought back vj. men rvnawaies. viz.:

|  |  |
|---|---|
| *Edward Harris*, boteswaine. | } |
| *Thomas Gilbert.* | } *of Pepcorns men.* |
| *Christopher Butbee.* | } |
| *Alexander Hix.* | |
| *John Vnderwick.* | } *of the Bulls men.* |
| *Wm. Harris.* | } |

And the master of the bark which caried them away is taken prisoner, with an other Japon of Nangasaq, that entised them to rvn away, and the King of Firando will put them both to death, as is reported.

1621. October 8th.

This day were arrayned vj. English rvnawais, most of them being duble rvnawais and som fellons, and therefore by generall consent, according to marshall [*martial*] law, condemned all to be hanged: 3 of them being of the Bull's men, and the other 3 of the Pepercorn's men, as doth apere the 3 day of this month of October, when they were retorned. And one *James Martyn,* accused by som to be the author of this mischeefe, he being a Scotsman, and fownd to be a cheefe bellows blower and sterrer vp of all mvtanies heretofore, soe the *Admerall Robt. Adams* sent a comition out to aprehend hym, and bring hym ashore, and soe put hym in prison to answer for hym selfe.

„  October 9th.

The *Admerall Captn. Adams,* with all the comanders and merchants, saving my selfe and M. *Osterwick,* went to Cochie to see the execution of the condemned men; and 4 of them were executed.[1]

---

[1] *Diary of Captain Richard Cock.* E. I. Mss.

*Here followeth the ARRAYNEMENT of the OFFENDERS,
and the JUDGMENT of the COUNCELL.*

**Whereas,** vppon the 5th of this present month of October,
we vnderstood of six mareners belonging to the shipp Pep-
percorne and Bull; namely, *Edward Harris, Boateswaine,
Thomas Guilbart, Alexander Hix, Christopher Badbe, Wm.
Harris,* and *Luke Vnderwick;* had hired a Japon bote of
Cochie, and were runn away towards *Nangasaque,* vnto the
Portingals, who are our mortall ennimies in all they can pre-
vaile against vs.

**We therefore** made all dillegence possible, and sent after
them, and tooke them before they came to there apoynted
place, and brought them back to Ffirando prisoners.

**Wherefore,** this present 8th of October, yt plesed the
*Worll Robart Adams to assemble his priuate Councell* at the
English ffactory, in Ffirando, together *with the merchants* of
the said ffactory, *and other honnest men* whome he plesed to
admit of *from the shipps :* who beinge all met together, the
*Worll Robart Adams* caused the prisoners to be sent for, and
examened them one after another : what was there intent
and meninge when they run away, and who perswaded them
there vnto, and what was there greuances : whether they
wanted other meat, or drinke, or any other necessaries, or
were abused by there comanders. Vnto which they answered
in generall, as per there particuler examenation, that they
wanted nether meat nor drinke, nether had beene any waies
abused by there comanders, but that the cheefe occation of
there runinge to the Portingals was, they were enticed there
vnto by a Portingall servant of Nangasaque, who went from
Coche with them in the bote, and is lykewise taken with
them, and remanith as yet our prisoner.

Hauinge taken eury of there examinations aparte, they
were returnd againe to the preson howse : and by comande of

the *Wor<sup>ll</sup> Capt. Adams,* there [*their*] examinations was red ouer
againe vnto *his Councell* and the rest there present : desiring
them all to weigh and conseder reightly of the fackt which
they had comitted ; and what danger might haue befallen vs
yf they had not beene prevented of there wicked designes.
For first, we cannot hould them to be better then trators to
our most gratius kinge and cuntre, by runnynge vnto the
ennimy to betray his ma<sup>ties</sup> shipps and subieckts into there
hands, and raisors of mutany in the highest degre, seekinge
by all possible meanes the ouerthrowe of our voyage by
there runninge away and seducinge others there vnto : espe-
tiolly beinge here in a cuntry far remote from England, and
all redy [*already*] in want of men : and none of this cuntry
people admitted to serue in our shippinge, by procuration of
our enymie to the contrarie. All which beinge duly considered
together, with the power of my comission granted under our
moste gratius kinges brode seale of England, deliuered vnto
me in force by our honourable imployers for executinge of
justice, and martiall law, vppon deseruinge offenders, which
at present inviteth me to put in execution, the better to liue
in pece and good gouernment with the rest ; therefore, nowe
for the better executinge of justice vppon these aforesaid
offenders, I, *Robart Adams,* requiar the assistance of you all
here present, freely and truly, as God Almighty shall guide
your harts, to consedar seriously of the fackt comitted, and
accordingly to deliuer in your wardickt : whether you shall
find them guilty of deth for the fackt comited or not, which
in my oppinion can noe waies be guiltlesse, but haue
deserued punishment in the highest degree.

𝕿𝖍𝖊 𝖆𝖋𝖔𝖗𝖊𝖘𝖆𝖎𝖉 𝖕𝖗𝖊𝖒𝖒𝖊𝖘𝖊𝖘 hauinge beene duly considered,
and discussed vppon by vs all in generall here present, we
find that the foresaid offenders, *Edward Harris, Thomas
Guilbart, Christopher Badbe, Wm. Harris, Alexander Hix,* and
*Luke Vnderwick,* for there [*their*] foresaid wicked and vngodly
fackt comitted, haue, according to the lawes of God and our

Y

cuntry, deserued, and are by vs *found guiltie of deth*, to be inflicted vppon them; and for better execution thereof, we, whose names are herevnto subscribed, doe freely giue our consents to the *wor^ll our Comander, Captaine Robart Adams*, to pronounce the sentance of deth vppon the foresaid offendors ; and that they receue accordingly present execution.

Wherevppon, *the Wor^ll Robart Adams pronounced the* 𝔰𝔢𝔫𝔱𝔞𝔫𝔠𝔢 𝔬𝔣 𝔡𝔢𝔱𝔥 vppon the foresaid *Edward Harris, Thomas Guilbart, Christopher Badbe, Wm. Harris, Alexander Hix*, and *Luke Vnderwick*, to be hanged vntil they should be ded at the maine yeard arme of the shipp they belonged vnto.

𝔚𝔥𝔦𝔠𝔥, 𝔞𝔠𝔠𝔬𝔯𝔡𝔦𝔫𝔤𝔩𝔶, this present day of the date hereof, 𝔦𝔰 𝔢𝔵𝔢𝔠𝔲𝔱𝔢𝔡 vppon fower of the principall offenders ; namely, *Edward Harris, Thomas Guilbart, Wm. Harris*, and *Alexander Hix ;* and for the other two, by name *Christopher Badbe*, and *Luke Vnderwick*, yt hath pleased *Captaine Robart Adams*, with the free consent of his priuate Councell, *to repriue*, and for present giue them their liues, hopinge the example of justice executed vppon the other fower will breede a terror and feare in the harts of all others to comitt the lyke offence, which God of His mercie grant.

Actum the 9th of October, in the English howse at Firando, in Japon.

|   |   |   |   |
|---|---|---|---|
| *a.* | *Richard Cock.* | 1. | *Robart Adams.* |
|  | *Wm. Eaton.* | 2. | *Charles Cleuenger.* |
|  | *John Osterwick.* | 3. | *Edmonde Lennis.* |
|  |  | 5. | *Joseph Cockram.* |
| *b* | *Wm. Morgan.* | 6. | *Mathew Morton.* |
|  | *Rich. Watts.* | 4. | *John Munden.* |
|  | *Robt. Tuberuile.* | 7. | *Arnold Browne.* |
|  | *Wm. Gordon.* | 8. | *Christopher Bogan.*[1] |

*a.* Members of the Factory.

*b.* Probably some of the " honest men . . . from the shipps."

*c.* Captains of vessels : 1. *Moon ;* 2. *Palsgrave ;* 3. *Elizabeth ;* 4. *Bull ;* 5 to 8. Cāpe Merchants of the above ships.

[1] E. I. Mss. *Japon Series.*

It is to be remarked, that as far as Japon was concerned, the maritime service at this period was in a state of fearful disorganization: the English, however, better by some degrees than the Dutch. Drunkenness and debauchery were rampant. Insubordination a-land and mutiny a-float prevailed. Robbery, rape, and murder, occurred incessantly. In his Diary, *Captain Cock* records numerous instances of the above offences, and complains repeatedly and bitterly, not only of the disgraceful proceedings on the part of the crews, but of the dissolute conduct of the officers, together with the want of judgment shewn in selecting them. So early as the 17th January, 16$\frac{16}{17}$, after detailing one or two heinous cases, he observes: "There are others in these shipps of the best sort (next to the masters), that are extreme drunkards, and, to say the truth, give occation to other yongsters to do worse. I will not name them: they will shew thewselves to the world. And it were better to geue duble wages to well quallified men, then to set such a work for nothing. And it is to be supposed that they are well knowne to be such before they came out of England, and that their frends being glad to be rid of them, send them out, hoping these long voyages may make an end of them. I might say as much of some yongsters of good parentage; but I loue not to be a blab of my tong, lest I should haue no thank for my labor: as it may be, I shall haue but littell for this which now I doe."

The following account of a Dutch execution affords a strong contrast to that of the Englishman, described in the first of the preceding extracts. On the 6th of August, 1621, *Captain Cock* observes: "This day before nowne, the Hollanders did behead *Jno. Johnson von Homberg*, for killing *M. Avery* [Purser's mate of the Elizabeth], five or six Englishmen standing by at the doing thereof (they having first made the man so drunk, that he could scarce stand

vpon his leggs), and cut affe his head within their own
howse."[1]

## NOTE A A.

### Fate of the English Factory at Firando.

As some interest may be felt in the matter, the result of
the English adventure to Japon will be given, preceded by a
brief review of the state of commerce at the time of the
arrival of the Clove.

As far as can be ascertained, the *Spaniards* imported
broad-cloths from *Nova Spania*, and spices from other parts.
The *Portuguese* from some places imported spices, and from
*Macao*, china goods. The *Dutch*, from *Holland*, imported
broad-cloths, purchased in England, lead, steel, looking-
glasses, Dantzic flask-glasses, amber, diapers, and Holland
cloth ; from *Patania*, damasks, taffeties, velvets, satins, a red
wood used for dyeing, resembling Brazil wood, deer skins,
and spices.

The demand for various articles, and the prices they
brought in the market, were, as far as they can be gleaned,
as follow, viz. :

1°. *Broad cloth.* With this commodity the market proved
to be over-stocked. A quality which had cost £16 the
cloth, about thirty-two yards English, was selling for £8 the
matt, a native measure equal to about $2\frac{1}{4}$ yards. This was
deemed a low price ; and to prevent further depreciation, in
consequence of the additional supply brought into the mar-

---

[1] *Abhorson.* Look you, the warrant's come.

*Barnadine.* You rogue, I have been drinking all night, and I am
not fitted for 't.

. . . . . . .

*Duke.* A creature unprepar'd, unmeet for death ;
     And to transport him in the mind he is,
     Were damnable.

*Measure for Measure.*

ket by the English, Captain Saris endeavoured to effect an arrangement with the Dutch factor, calculated to proportion the sale to the demand. The Dutchman, however, excused himself, on the ground of his not being authorized by his superiors to enter into an arrangement of the description proposed ; and, the next morning, in order to forestall the English, that functionary shipped off a great quantity of cloth to the adjoining islands, to be disposed of at what are termed " base rates", viz. : at £4, £3 : 12, and £3 : 4, the matt. The price of broad-cloth, however, was low, through other causes than the quantity in the market. The demand was limited, because the Japonese " as yet were so addicted to silks, that they did not enter into the consideration of the benefit of wearing cloth."[1] This distaste of the natives of Japon for cloth, is corroborated by Captain Saris, but he attributes the circumstance to a different cause. He observes, the Japonese were backward in purchasing that commodity, on account of the little use made of it by the English. When pressed to buy, he represents them to have argued thus : " You commend your cloth vnto vs, but you yourselues weare least thereof, the better sort of you wearing silken garments ; the meaner, fustians, etc." And little contemplating the change which, in process of time, would be effected in the material of our national costume, he adds : " Wherefore, hoping that good counsell (though late) come to some good·purpose, I will that our nation would be more forward to vse and spend this naturall commodity of our owne countrey. Soe shall we better incourage and allure others to the intertainment and expenses thereof."[2]

2°. *Steel* was in little request, and averaged from £3 : 15,

---

[1] *Richard Cock to the Gouernour of the Company*, dated 30 November, 1613. E. I. Mss.

[2] All the broad-cloth purchased by the Japonese, appears to have been expended in horse coverings, and in cases for arms.

to twenty crowns the pecul, equivalent to one hundred and twenty-five pounds English.

3°. *Ordnance* was barely saleable at 30s. the pecul.

4°. *Calicos,* and *fine Cambaia goods,* in little demand, on account of the quantity of cotton produced in Japon, and its cheapness, viz.: ten mas (5s.) the pecul.

5°. *Pepper* and *cloves,* likewise, were not used extensively, and the market was, moreover, over-stocked. The former was selling at 5d. per lb., sometimes for less, but never exceeding 6d. per lb. The latter entailed loss.

The list of exportable commodities is exceedingly meagre. In the year 1612, it appears the Dutch vessels sailed from Japon " deeplie laden with fishe, biskit, monicions [? *munitions of war*], marreners, sojores [*soldiers*], and the like." But circumstances must be peculiar to render an investment of this description advantageous to the exporters, and such was the case at the period in question. The Dutch were engaged in active warfare with the Spaniards in the Molluccas, and the exports above specified were of essential importance to them in a political and a military point of view, though, perhaps, not commercially beneficial.

To the above-named articles, Captain Saris specifies some others of little importance ; but his expectations were either hastily formed, or founded on imperfect information, and proved in effect fallacious. Certain it is, that although the Clove remained at Japon a period sufficient to have taken in a full cargo, the vessel sailed " unladen".

The interchange of commodities was not, however, the principal inducement to the adventure. The fact was notorious, that the Spaniards and Portuguese had obtained enormous quantities of the precious metals in return for merchandize.[1] The resources of Japon, in respect to gold and

[1] The exact amount of treasure conveyed out of Japon by the European traders, will perhaps never be ascertained ; but some idea may be formed from the following items culled from *Kæmpfer;* and it must be

silver, were believed to be nearly inexhaustible; and strong hopes seem to have been entertained, that from the Empire, ample supplies of specie might be drawn in aid of the newly established trade with the East Indies, by which England, from whence the supplies in question had hitherto been drawn, would be relieved from an inconvenient drain.

Unfortunately, however, neither that nor any other anticipation was realized. The Japonese proved exceedingly fickle in their tastes, rejecting at one time what they had on a previous occasion eagerly sought after; so that no little difficulty was experienced in the selection of articles suitable for importation. Experience shewed, moreover, that they esteemed most highly goods which the English were not in a position to supply to any extent: while their indisposition to purchase what the English could supply plentifully, continued without abatement. Sales of the English staples

borne in mind, these transactions have reference to a period when the export of specie had been restricted by the Government, and when the trade of the Portuguese and Dutch was on the decline.

| | £. Stg. |
|---|---|
| PORTUGUESE.—In one year, date not ascertained, there were exported 100 *Tuns of Gold* - - - | 875,000 |
| 1636: Exported 2350 *Chests of Silver* - - | 587,500 |
| 1637: - - - - | 535,591 |
| 1638: - - - | 314,756 |
| | 2,312,847 |

| | £. Stg. |
|---|---|
| DUTCH.—One year, date not ascertained, 80 *Tuns of Gold* = £. *Stg.* 700,000 ; and 1400 *Chests of Silver* = £. *Stg.* 450,000 - - - - | 1,150,000 |
| From 1611 to 1641, or thirty years, average rate of export per annum, 60 *Tuns of Gold* = £. *Stg.* 500,000 - - - - - | 15,000,000 |
| Also, 1400 *Chests of Silver* = £. *Stg.* 450,000 - | 13,500,000 |
| And 6000 *Chests of Copper*, value not given - | ... ... |
| | 29,650,000 |

TOTAL, £. STG. 31,962,847.

were consequently limited, and the profit on the portion
actually sold, was reduced to a *minimum*, by the system of
underselling, originally resorted to by the Dutch on the
arrival of the English, and persisted in by them to the last.
Officers of influence in the state also proved venal. The
Dutch lavishly disbursed the ample means at their command
in bribes, greatly to their own benefit and to the proportionate disadvantage of the English, whose limited means
prevented them from competing with their rivals in expenditure. But the Dutch found a method of indemnifying
themselves for the loss entailed on them by underselling, and
by the heavy sums they disbursed in bribes. They had recourse
to a system by which the English were further depressed.
They unscrupulously attacked and plundered both English
and Chinese vessels, whenever opportunities occurred; and the
produce of their piratical proceedings they unblushingly
brought into market, and sold as openly as if it had been
obtained by legitimate purchase, at exceedingly low, but
very profitable rates. Further, the great distance of Japon
from England : the want of a commanding intermediate
station : the imperfect state of navigation ; and the reckless
interference with the trade by a competitor, not less an
enemy because wearing the mask of friendship, rendered
intercourse with the factory uncertain. Ships were delayed,
wrecked, captured, and plundered. Supplies were, consequently, irregular : sometimes superabundant : sometimes,
when most needed, looked for in vain. Then unsuitable
consignments would arrive : or suitable consignments were
received in so bad a condition as to be unsaleable. As if
these obstacles to success were not sufficient, the Privileges
originally granted to the Company by Ogosho Sama, were
curtailed by Shongo Sama, his successor, to a serious extent.
Moreover, being apprehensive of evil on account of the
quantity of specie drawn from Japon, the new Emperor took
measures to prevent the unlimited exportation of the pre-

cious metals from the country. And, finally, the native traders becoming jealous of the favour shewn to the foreign merchants, sought and obtained immunities for themselves: by which they were empowered to buy whatever they chose, at such times, and at such prices, as suited their convenience.

Under this accumulation of adverse circumstances, it cannot be considered extraordinary that the Adventure to Japon proved a total failure. Such was the case, after upwards of £40,000 had been uselessly expended. But though commercially unsuccessful, the English preserved their character in the Empire without impeachment. Worthy Captain Cock, with his associates, retired from Japon in 1623, honoured by the esteem of the higher classes: blessed and regretted by the humble in condition.

## NOTE B B.

### Slavery in Japon.

Slavery in the Empire of Japon is different from that prevailing in the Western-hemisphere. The person of a party, male or female, may be sold under certain circumstances, or a party may sell his, or her, service for a stipulated period, for a sum of money which may be agreed on, and which must be paid down at once in the gross. On the expiration of the stipulated period, the party is free to dispose of his, or her, person again. Masters have power over the lives of their slaves, if they commit offences which by the law are punishable with death; but if a man should kill his slave for any cause that the law does not deem worthy of death, the offender is adjudged guilty of murder, and subjected to the penalty of the crime.

# MEMORIALS OF JAPON.

---

## APPENDIX.

---

SUMMARY OF A NARRATIVE BY HIS EXCELLENCY DON RODRIGO DE
VIVERO Y VELASCO, GOVERNOR GENERAL OF THE PHILIPPINE
ISLANDS, OF HIS RESIDENCE IN THE EMPIRE:
A.D. 1608-1610.

# SUMMARY, ETC.[1]

In the year 1608, Don Rodrigo de Vivero y Velasco,[2] the Governor General of the Philippines, was shipwrecked on his return to Spain, and cast upon the coast of Japan.

Don Rodrigo's vessel struck upon a reef off the coast of Niphon, in about latitude 35½° : the crew, with himself, reached the shore on parts of the wreck totally destitute, and not knowing where they were cast, whether on a continent or an island. They soon found the country to be Japan; and as Don Rodrigo had shown much kindness to two hundred natives of that country, in confinement in the Philippine islands when he became governor, whom he liberated and conveyed home, he concluded that, as the event proved, the emperor would avail himself of the opportunity to requite the obligation.

Amongst the crew of the Spanish vessel was a Japanese Christian, who soon discovered that they were near a small village called Yu Banda, whither they proceeded. It contained about 1,500 inhabitants, and was dependent upon one of the inferior nobles, who, nevertheless, had many vassals, several towns and villages, and lived in a strong fortress. The people of the village, when they learned the disaster of the

---

[1] This summary is reprinted, with permission, from the *Asiatic Journal* of July 1830 ; the endeavours made to trace the original work referred to, having proved fruitless. The interest of many of the details will probably be accepted as an apology for the form in which they are communicated.—Ⅽ. Ⓚ.

[2] This personage was a favourite of Anne, the wife of Philip II. He filled several important posts, in which he distinguished himself; and on the death of Don Pedro d'Acuna, he obtained the place of governor and captain-general of the Philippines.—Ed. A. J.

party, evinced much compassion, and the females shed tears. They gave them clothing and food (consisting of rice, pulse, and a little fish), and sent word to the *tono*, or lord, who desired that the party might be well treated, but not suffered to remove.

In the course of a few days, the tono paid a visit to Don Rodrigo, in great pomp, preceded by three hundred men, bearing banners, most of them armed with lances, harque-busses, and halberds. The ceremony of visiting was con-ducted with great form; an officer, announcing the tono's arrival at the village, and another his nearer approach, etc. The tono saluted Don Rodrigo with great politeness, by a motion of his head and hand, much in our own manner, and placed him on his left, the sword-side, and therefore the post of honour and confidence. He made Don Rodrigo a variety of presents, took upon himself the expense of the subsistence of the whole party, and allowed two Spanish officers to pro-ceed to court, to communicate to the emperor and the prince royal the details of the case.

JEDDO [*Edo*], where the prince royal resided, was forty leagues from the village; and ZURUNGA [*Sorongo*], the residence of the emperor, was about forty leagues further. The envoys returned in twenty-four days with an agent of the prince, who brought compliments of condolence from the emperor, and permission for Don Rodrigo to visit the courts of his majesty and the prince. All the property that could be saved from the wreck belonged to the crown, but it was given up to the Spaniards.

The first place on their route to Jeddo was a town named HONDAK, containing from 10,000 to 12,000 souls. Don Rodrigo entered an inn, but the tono insisted upon his residing with him. He dwelt in a fortress situated on a height, and surrounded by a ditch fifty feet deep, passed by a draw-bridge. The gates were of iron, the walls of solid masonry, eighteen feet high, and the same in thickness.

Near the first gate, one hundred musketeers stood under arms, and between that and the second gate, which opened through a second wall, were houses, gardens, orchards, and rice-fields, for the subsistence of the garrison. The dwelling-rooms of the castle were of wood (owing to the number of earthquakes), exquisitely finished, and elegantly adorned with a profusion of gold, silver, varnish, etc. At dinner, the tono carried to his guest the first dish, agreeably to Japanese etiquette towards a person whom it is desired to honour : the repast consisted of flesh, fish, and various kinds of excellent fruit.

Nothing worthy of notice was observed during the rest of the journey, except the immensity of the population, which kept the strangers in perpetual wonder. They were everywhere well received, lodged, and treated.

Previous to entering Jeddo, several gentlemen of the city met Don Rodrigo, requesting him to accept their hospitality ; but he had been advertised that the prince had prepared a house for his reception. He entered the city amidst a crowd so dense, that the officers of police were obliged to force a way for the Spaniards : notwithstanding, Don Rodrigo remarks, the prodigious width of the streets in comparison with ours. The report of their arrival attracted such multitudes, that for the eight days of his first residence at Jeddo the party had no rest. A guard was at length placed in the house, and a placard, posted by the magistrate, prohibited the populace from molesting the travellers. He thus describes the city :

" JEDDO contains 700,000 inhabitants, and is traversed by a considerable river, which is navigable by vessels of moderate size. By this river, which is divided in the interior into several branches, the inhabitants are supplied with provisions and necessaries, which are so cheap, that a man may live comfortably for three-pence a day. The Japanese do not make much wheaten bread, though what they do make is excellent. The streets and open places of Jeddo are very handsome, and so clean and well kept, that it might be imagined no person walked in them. The houses are of wood, and mostly of two stories. The exterior of them is less imposing than of ours, but they are infinitely handsomer and more comfortable within. All the streets have covered galleries, and are occupied each by persons of the same trade ; thus, the carpenters have one street, the tailors another, the jewellers another, etc., including many trades not known in Europe. The merchants are classed together in the same way. Provisions are also sold in places appropriated for each sort. I remarked the market where game is sold : there was a vast quantity of rabbits, hares, wild boars, deer, goats, and other animals, which I never saw before. The Japanese rarely eat any flesh but that of game, which they hunt. The fish-market is immense, and extremely neat and clean. I observed more than a thousand different kinds of fish, sea and river, fresh and salt. Large tubs contained besides a vast quantity of live fish. The inns are in the same streets, adjoining those where they let and sell horses, which are in such number, that the traveller who changes horses, according to the custom of the country, every league, is only embarrassed where to choose. The nobles and great men inhabit a distinct part of the city. This quarter is distinguished by the armorial ornaments, sculptured, painted, or gilt, placed over the doors of the houses. The Japanese nobles attach much value to this privilege. The political authority is vested in a governor, who is chief of the magistracy, civil and military. In each street resides a magistrate, who takes cognizance, in the first instance, of all cases, civil and criminal, and submits the most difficult to the governor. The streets are closed at each end by a gate, which is shut at nightfall. At each gate is placed a guard of soldiers, with sentinels at intervals ; so that if a crime is committed, notice is conveyed instantly to each end of the street, the gates are closed, and it rarely happens that the offender escapes. This description is very applicable to all the other cities in the kingdom."

Two days after arrival of Don Rodrigo, the prince sent his secretary, whose name (or rather title) was Conseconduno, to invite Governor General to visit him. He accordingly proceeded to the prince's residence, which he represents as an astonishing place. He says: "I should think myself fortunate if I could succeed in affording an exact idea of all the wonders I saw there, as well in respect to the material of the edifices at this royal residence, as to the pomp and splendour of the court. I think I may affirm, that from the entrance to the prince's apartment, there were more than 20,000 persons, not assembled for the occasion, but constantly employed and paid for the daily service of the court."

The principal wall which encloses the palace, he says, is composed of immense blocks of free-stone, put together without cement, with embrasures, at equal distances, for artillery, of which there is no small quantity. At the foot of this wall is a very deep wet ditch; the entrance is by a drawbridge of a peculiar and extremely ingenious construction. The gates were very strong. Don Rodrigo passed through two ranks of musketeers, about one thousand strong, to the second gate in the second wall, about three hundred paces from the other. Here was stationed a body of four hundred lancers and pikemen. A third wall, about twelve feet high, was guarded by about three hundred halberdiers. At a short distance from this wall was the palace, with the royal stables, containing three hundred saddle horses, on one side, and the arsenal, filled with armour and arms for 100,000 men, on the other.

The first apartment of the palace was entirely covered with rich ornaments, carpets, stuffs, velvet, and gold. The walls were hung with pictures representing hunting subjects. Each apartment excelled the preceding in splendour, till he reached that in which the prince was seated on a superb carpet of crimson velvet, embroidered with gold, placed upon a kind of alcove, raised two steps, in the centre of the apartment. He wore a green and yellow surtout over two of the vests called *quimones*, and a girdle, in which were stuck his dagger and sword. His hair was tied up with ribbons of different colours, without any other ornament on his head. He was about thirty-five years of age, of a brown complexion, a pleasing figure, and good height. Don Rodrigo was conducted to a seat on the left hand of the prince, who desired him to be covered, and conversed with him upon indifferent subjects.

Four days after, our traveller set off to Zurunga, on a visit to the emperor. The population was immense; several towns below the rank of cities, contain upwards of 100,000 inhabitants, and in the one hundred leagues from Meaco to Zurunga, a village occurs every quarter of a league. " On whichever side the traveller turns his eye, he perceives a concourse of people passing to and fro, as in the most populous cities of Europe; the roads are lined on both sides with superb pine-trees, which keep off the sun; the distances are marked by little eminences planted with two trees." Our traveller declares he was so pleased with Japan, that " if he could have prevailed upon himself to renounce his God and his king, he should have preferred that country to his own."

ZURUNGA contains from 500,000 to 600,000 inhabitants. The climate is more agreeable than that of Jeddo, but the city is not so handsome. A residence, with every convenience, was provided for Don Rodrigo here as at Jeddo, and the mob was equally troublesome. The emperor sent a secretary to compliment him on his arrival, with a present of rich dresses, which he desired him to wear. In about a week, our traveller was presented to the emperor. The intimation came from his majesty, for Don Rodrigo had been advised not to express any wish to this effect. He was conveyed in an elegant litter to the palace, which was in a fortress like that at Jeddo. He was conducted in a similar manner through the various apartments, his eyes being dazzled with the splendour of the furniture; but in some particulars there seemed rather more pomp at the prince's court. There was more power at the residence of the emperor, but, at the same time, more indications of fear. In the ante-chamber of the emperor's apartment, a crowd of ministers attended our traveller, among whom was a *conseconduno*, who felicitated him upon his being permitted to look upon the august face of the sovereign, adding, however, that although a rich noble would regard it as an eminent favour to regard the emperor at one hundred paces' distance, prone on the earth, without a word being addressed to him by his Majesty, yet he (Don Rodrigo) might, according to his own notions, fancy that his reception was cold and formal. Don Rodrigo perceived the drift of this speech, and replied with much address, that his own monarch, King Philip, was the greatest and most potent sovereign in the universe; that though kings were not expected to relax their dignity before their own subjects, there was good state reason why they should be affable towards those of other princes; that, as the servant of a powerful sovereign, what was conceded or withheld would be to his king, not to himself; that, as a private individual, he had already much to be grateful for to the emperor, but as the representative of King Philip, no distinction conferred upon him could be too great.

This took Conseconduno by surprise. He slapped his forehead with the palm of his hand, and begged the traveller would remain till he had communicated with the emperor. In half an hour he returned, and stated that his highness intended to honour him in a manner hitherto unparalleled, and which would excite universal astonishment throughout the empire.

" I followed the minister, who conducted me into the presence of the sovereign, whom I saluted. He was in a kind of square box, not very large, but astonishingly rich. It was placed two steps above the floor, and surrounded, at four paces' distance, by a gold lattice-work, six feet high, in which were small doors by which the emperor's attendants went in and out, as they were called from the crowd, on their hands and knees around the golden lattice. The monarch was encircled by nearly twenty grandees, ministers, or principal courtiers, in long silk mantles, and trowsers of the same material, so long that they entirely concealed the feet. The emperor was seated upon a kind of stool, of blue satin, worked with stars and half-moons of silver. In his girdle he wore a sword, and had his hair tied up with ribbons of different colours, but had no other head-dress. His age appeared to be about sixty; he was of the middle stature, and of a very full person. His countenance was venerable and gracious; his complexion not near so brown as that of the prince."

The emperor, after receiving the traveller's salutation, inclined his head a little, and desired him to be seated and covered. After some conversation, in the course of which the prince said he intended to bestow upon Don Rodrigo more favour than he could expect from his own sovereign, our traveller prepared to retire; but the emperor desired him to retain his seat, telling him he could not permit his visit to be so short, and that he should be present at the presentation of some nobles to whom he was about to deign to be visible. Accordingly a tono of high rank, who brought presents in gold, silver, and silk, worth more than 20,000 ducats, was introduced; at a hundred paces from the throne, he prostrated himself with his face to the ground, and remained in this posture for several minutes in perfect silence, neither the emperor nor either of the ministers vouchsafing a word : he then retired with his suite, amounting to 3,000 persons. Other introductions took place, and Don Rodrigo was permitted to retire on a promise that he would make any requests he chose to the emperor, two ministers attending him to the third apartment, where other great officers escorted him with great ceremony out of the palace.

At a visit he paid to the consecónduno, or prime minister, where he was treated with a magnificent collation and exquisite wine (the host drinking his health by placing the glass upon his head), Don Rodrigo gave him a note, translated into Japanese, of his requests. They were three in number; first, that the royal protection might be granted to the Christian priests of different orders who then resided in the empire, that they might have the free disposal of their houses and churches, and not be molested; secondly, that amity might continue between the Emperor and the King of Spain; and lastly, that, as an evidence of that friendship, the emperor would not permit the Dutch (who had, about this time, introduced themselves here) to reside in his territories, but would drive them out : adding that, besides their being enemies to Spain, their malpractices on the sea, and piracy, ought to be sufficient to induce the emperor to refuse them a retreat and shelter in the Japanese dominions. The minister communicated the note to the emperor, and on the following day reported his answer, after the usual ceremonies, and a collation, which always precedes business in Japan. The minister stated that his majesty was highly pleased with the note, desiring his courtiers to remark that Don Rodrigo had asked nothing for himself, but, though destitute, had limited his requests to the service of religion and his king. He granted them all except the expulsion of the Hollanders. "That," said his majesty, "will be difficult this year, as they have my royal word for permission to sojourn in Japan; but I thank him for letting me know what characters they are!" His majesty offered the Spaniard a vessel furnished with all necessaries for his return; and begged him to request King Philip to send to Japan fifty miners, men he understood were very skilful in extracting silver in New Spain, because, those in Japan did not procure half the silver the mines were capable of yielding.

Don Rodrigo soon after set out, on his return, to take ship in the province of Bungo. From Zurunga to Meaco, nearly 100 leagues, the country was mostly level, and very fertile. Several considerable rivers were crossed in ferry-boats, which were capable of containing a great number of men and horses, and which cross by means of a strong cable stretched from from one bank to the other. The cities and towns were numerous, large, well built, and prodigiously populous. Abundance reigned everywhere, and provisions were so cheap, that the poorest could purchase them. In the whole of the journey, he says, he " never passed a town or village of less population than 150,000 souls." That of Meaco he fixes, from various data, at 1,500,000 : he considers it the largest city in the world.

MEACO is situated upon a plain highly cultivated. Its walls are ten leagues in circuit, which our traveller certifies from actual observation, having rode round them on horseback ; he set out at seven in the morning, and did not reach the point of departure till night. At this city resides the Daïri.

Meaco is governed by a viceroy appointed by the emperor ; his jurisdiction does not extend beyond the canals which surround the city ; he has no authority in the cities of Faxima, Sacay, and Osaka, which are very considerable, and situated at a short distance from Meaco. The court of the governor of Meaco is almost as sumptuous as that of the emperor; he has six vice-governors under his orders. His excellency was very communicative to Don Rodrigo, and told him that the city contained 5,000 temples, and more than 50,000 public women. He showed him the tomb of Taïcosama, in a magnificent temple, the daïbu [*Daibod*], an idol of bronze, and a superb building which contains the statues of all the gods of Japan. These sights consumed three days, owing to the distance of the different objects from each other. The daïbu, he says, is worthy of being classed among the wonders of the world. Its dimensions rendered him mute with astonishment. "I ordered", he says, "one of my people to measure the thumb of the right hand of the idol, and I perceived that, although he was a man of large size, he could not embrace it with his two arms by two palms. But the size of this statue is not its only merit: the feet, hands, mouth, eyes, forehead, and other features, are as perfect and as expressive as the most accomplished painter could make a portrait.[1] When I visited this temple it was unfinished; more than 100,000 workmen were daily employed upon it. The devil could not suggest to the emperor a surer expedient to get rid of his immense wealth." The tomb of Taïcosama is magnificent. The author, like a good Catholic, deplores the dedication of such an edifice to the remains of one "whose soul is in hell for all eternity." The entrance is by an avenue paved with jasper, 400 feet by 300. On each side, at equal distances, were posts of jasper, on which are placed lamps, lighted at night. At the end of the passage is the peristyle of the temple, ascended by several steps. On the right hand is a monastery of priests. The principal gate is encrusted with jasper, and overlaid with gold and silver ornaments skilfully wrought. The nave of the temple is supported by lofty columns and pilasters. There is a choir, as in our cathedrals, with seats and a grating all round. Male and female choristers chant the prayers, much in the same manner as in our churches; and the costume of the former put our traveller in mind of that of the prebends of Toledo, except that the train of their robe was excessively long, and their caps were much wider at top than at bottom. Four of these priests accosted him, and gave him

[1] This representation is confirmed by the details given in the Diary of Captain Cock; and by the statements made by Kæmpfer. The dimensions will also be found in the "*Nipon o Daï*," translated by Titsingh, edited by Klaproth; and published by the Asiatic Society of London, 1834.—T. R.

much uneasiness, apparently, by conducting him to the *altar* of their "infamous reliques", surrounded with an infinite number of lamps. The number of persons, their silence and devotion, surprised him. After raising five or six curtains, covering as many gratings of iron or silver, and the last of gold, a kind of chest was exposed, in which were contained the ashes of Taïcosama : within this sacred enclosure none but the chief priest could enter. All the Japanese present prostrated themselves; but our traveller quitted this "accursed spot", and proceeded, accompanied by the priests, to see their gardens, which were more tastefully laid out, he says, than those of Aranjuez. "The Japanese", he continues, " use, like us, holy or rather unholy water, and chaplets consecrated to their false gods, Jaca and Nido, which, moreover, are not the only ones they worship ; for there are no less than thirty-five different sects or religions in Japan. Some deny the immortality of the soul, others acknowledge divers gods, and others adore the elements. All are tolerated. The bonzes of all the sects having concurred in a request to the emperor that he would expel our monks from Japan, the prince, troubled with their importunities, inquired how many different religions there were in Japan ? 'Thirty-five', was the reply. ' Well,' said he, ' where thirty-five sects can be tolerated, we can easily bear with thirty-six: leave the strangers in peace.'"

The pantheon was the largest building he had yet seen in Japan ; it contained 2,600 gilt bronze statues of gold, each in his own tabernacle decorated with emblems. The revenues of this temple are immense, and the expenditure for the priests proportionate.

From Meaco our traveller proceeded to Faxima [*Fushima*], at a very short distance, where the sovereigns of Japan resided prior to the reigning monarch, who removed to Zurunga. The streets of Faxima are narrower than those of other cities in Japan, but this ancient capital is equal to any in magnificence. Here he embarked for OSAKA, ten leagues lower down the river, which is as large as the Guadalquivir at Seville, and was full of vessels. Osaka contains near a million of inhabitants; the houses are commonly of two stories. It is built close to the sea, which washes it walls.

At Osaka he embarked on a junk for BUNGO, the route to NANGASAKI, where there was then a Portuguese establishment.

Finding the vessel he had intended to take a passage in not in proper repair, Don Rodrigo accepted an invitation from the emperor to return to Zurunga, where he renewed his endeavours to persuade the prince to expel the Dutch; but without effect. After procuring sundry concessions from the emperor, and receiving presents and dispatches for the King of Spain, he set sail (from what port is not mentioned) on the 1st August, 1610, after a stay of nearly two years in Japan.

Don Rodrigo has appended to his narrative some remarks upon the character and customs of the Japanese. He says the men are addicted to drunkenness and incontinence; the number of public women is very great. Japanese wives, he says, are exemplary; scarcely an instance is known of their infidelity. They live rigorously secluded even from their fathers, brothers, and sons; and when they go out to pay visits, or to the temples, they are carried by servants in a sort of cage.[1]

The Japanese are very industrious, ingenious, and expert: they are clever at invention and imitation.

The municipal government is excellent. The internal police is admirably regulated: the chiefs and the subalterns are animated with the same zeal and intelligence. The streets

[1] The women, as well as the men, are conveyed frequently in *cangos*, or *norrimons*, a species of *palanken*. The seclusion of the women is not only not corroborated, but is contradicted, by the statements of other writers.—C. R.

are kept very neat; it is the same with the interior of every house, even of the meanest artizan.

Rice is the ordinary food of the people; but wheat grows well in the country. Cotton is cultivated abundantly in the province of Bogu; they manufacture it into fabrics for the dress of the people. The grandees are clothed in stuffs of silk, which is obtained entirely from China, it being of better quality than their own. Their weapons are of extraordinary strength and temper, and they are much prized among them. A Japanese could cleave a man in two with one of their swords. They ridicule the extraordinary value we attach to diamonds and rubies, considering the worth of a thing to consist in its utility.

The nobles of Japan are fond of pomp and a retinue; they never go out unattended by a vast suite, and exact from their inferiors the same respect they themselves pay to the emperor.

Pride, arrogance, and a resolution which is almost carried to ferocity, are the distinctive traits of the Japanese of all classes.

THE END.

RICHARDS, PRINTER, 100, ST. MARTIN'S LANE.

# DIRECTIONS FOR THE BINDER.

## ERRATA.

Page 177, line 4 from top of page, between *after* and *arrival*, insert *the*.

——— line 6 from top of page, between *invite* and *Governor*, insert *the*.

For EU product safety concerns, contact us at Calle de José Abascal, 56–1°, 28003 Madrid, Spain or eugpsr@cambridge.org.